Healthy Young Children
A Manual for Programs

2002 Edition

Editors

1st and 2nd edition: Abby Shapiro Kendrick, Roxane Kaufmann, and Katherine P. Messenger

3rd edition: Karen Sokal-Gutierrez, MD, MPH

4th edition: Susan S. Aronson, MD, FAAP

National Association for the Education of Young Children, Washington, D.C.

Primary reference

American Academy of Pediatrics, American Public Health Association, & National Resource Center for Health and Safety in Child Care. 2002. *Caring for Our Children: National Health and Safety Performance Standards: Guidelines for Out-of-Home Child Care Programs,* 2d ed. Elk Grove Village, IL: American Academy of Pediatrics. Specific references to scientific evidence appear at the conclusion of each chapter of *Caring for Our Children.*

Photographs

Nancy P. Alexander, 75, 90, 96, 126
BmPorter/Don Franklin, 18
Jim Bradshaw, 32, 83
William K. Geiger, 8
Robert Koenig, 62
Jean-Claude LeJeune, 15, 48, 52, 74
Lois Main, 77
Jonathan A. Meyers, cover (top left & center), 106
Wendy Press, 25
Rick Reinhard, 143
Paul M. Schrock, 43
Ellen B. Senisi, cover (bottom left)
Kathy Sible, cover (bottom right)
Steve & Mary Skjold, 2
Subjects & Predicates, cover (top right), 71, 162

Illustrations

Dilworth Design

Some of the information in this manual applies to specific conditions of individual children. It is not a substitute for the advice of a child's clinician or a program's health consultant. The manual reflects current research and standards in the fields of health and early childhood education. However, in such rapidly changing fields, new information constantly emerges. Be alert to such changes and check with your local department of public health for the most current recommendations.

Copyright © 1988, 1991, 1995, 2002 by the National Association for the Education of Young Children

Published by the National Association for the
    Education of Young Children
1509 16th Street, NW
Washington, DC 20036-1426
202-232-8777 or 800-424-2460
www.naeyc.org

Library of Congress Control Number: 2002112198
ISBN 1-928896-06-5
NAEYC #704

Printed in the United States of America

Preface

Here, in one convenient manual, you will find answers to questions about keeping young children healthy when they participate in group programs.

- What are the most effective methods of preventing the spread of disease?
- How do we create a safe and healthy environment to prevent injuries?
- Why is preventive health care so important?
- How do we help children develop healthy eating habits?
- What do we do in emergencies?
- How do we inform families about possible exposure to contagious diseases?
- How do we foster inclusion of children with special needs?
- When should ill children or staff be excluded? When can they return?
- How do we promote good adult health for staff?
- How do we prevent and handle suspected child abuse?
- How do we integrate the health component with all the other tasks involved in operating a quality child care program?

Healthy Young Children is a manual for caregivers and directors, health professionals who work with child care programs, and other individuals who give technical assistance to child care professionals. The manual is a tool for those working in child care settings and a textbook for those who are preparing to enter the field. Using the manual will help implement national standards and guidelines for the health component of group care programs for children. For those working on accreditation of an early childhood program or family child care home, the manual provides details related to compliance with health and safety criteria.

Healthy Young Children: A Manual for Programs was first published by NAEYC in 1988 and has been extensively reviewed and updated. This, the fourth edition of *Healthy Young Children,* reflects the most current recommendations from health professionals for keeping children healthy and safe in early childhood programs available at the time this edition was written. Easy access to referenced information via the Internet provides companion documents to which the reader can refer for more detail and, in some cases, more frequently updated information.

Healthy Young Children is one of a set of resources that child care providers will find helpful in integrating health and safety effectively with the child development, administrative, and other components of the program. The manual is compatible with and is an implementation tool for the second edition (2002) of *Caring for Our Children: National Health and Safety Performance Standards: Guidelines for Out-of-Home Child Care Programs.* Known by its short title, *Caring for Our Children* is more than a compendium of detailed requirements for providing child care in group and home-based settings. The standards document includes clear statements about what to do to protect health and safety, as well as the scientific rationale that justifies each requirement and the authoritative references to the scientific literature. *Caring for Our Children* is published collaboratively by the American Academy of Pediatrics, the American Public Health Association, and the Maternal and Child Health Bureau of the Health Resources and Services Administration of the U.S. Department of Health and Human Services—in hard copy by the authoring organizations and on the Internet at www.uchsc.edu. The second edition of *Caring for Our Children* and the fourth edition of *Healthy Young Children* are being published around the same time so readers can use these two publications together.

Note that *Healthy Young Children* contains some information copied directly from the standards. Readers of the manual should look for literature citations (references) and additional documentation in *Caring for Our Children*.

There are other tools that will help meet the standards in *Caring for Our Children*:

• NAEYC and the American Academy of Pediatrics jointly publish a set of six videotapes also called *Caring for Our Children*. Videotaped in center- and home-based child care programs across the United States, these videos show what child care looks like when it meets the national standards. A few items illustrated in the videos have changed—for example, children in diapers who develop diarrhea that is contained by their diapers must now be excluded until the diarrhea resolves; a new universally recommended vaccine (pneumococcal conjugate vaccine) has been added to the routine schedule; and putting infants down to sleep on their backs is now required. Although some new standards are not illustrated in the videos, most of the content shown in the 1995 video series is still useful and appropriate.

• To help programs implement the standards for written health and safety policies, the American Academy of Pediatrics and NAEYC jointly publish *Model Child Care Health Policies (MCCHP)*. These fill-in-the-blank policy statements provide an easy starting point for programs to customize policy statements to appropriately serve their needs. At this time, the fourth edition, published in 2002, is available. This material also is periodically updated to include new information—for example, handling threats of terrorism and improved forms based on feedback from previous users. The model policies give child care providers an easy start in drafting the written document that every program needs—to orient new staff and parents as well as to identify and decide on the practices that fit their facility's operations.

• Since illness among children and their caregivers is inevitable, and medical jargon can be confusing to those not in the medical field, NAEYC and the American Academy of Pediatrics publish a booklet on when to exclude children for illness and how to know when they can return. Based on the international reference book on infectious disease in children—called *The Red Book*—that is also published by the American Academy of Pediatrics, this booklet is called *Preparing for Illness*. The booklet translates the pediatric standards on infectious disease into parent- and provider-friendly language. It includes suggestions for parents to plan for illness, a symptom record for parents and providers to document a child's illness, and tables of commonly recognized conditions and medical diagnoses as well as when to exclude and when to readmit children with these problems. Periodically this booklet is updated to match the current recommendations. The fourth edition was published in 1999.

• Assessing immunizations of children is a tedious and complex task. The child's record of immunization dates must be matched against the recommended schedule by age. To help identify children who are overdue for vaccines, the American Academy of Pediatrics distributes the *Immunization Dose Counter*, a device that allows the user to line up a dot that matches the child's age and then to read the numbers of doses of each type of vaccine that the child should have received by that age. The current recommended schedule of vaccines is on the front of the device so families can be reminded about what vaccines might be due now, even if none are overdue. This device is distributed at the cost of mailing only. To receive an updated one, send a self-addressed, first-class-stamped business-size envelope to the American Academy of Pediatrics, 141 Northwest Point Boulevard, Elk Grove Village, IL 60009.

All child care programs, child care licensing staff, and child care health consultants should have and use these publications as their references for the health component of child care: *Healthy Young Children, Caring for Our Children, Caring for Our Children* (the video series), *Model Child Care Health Policies, Preparing for Illness,* and *The Immunization Dose Counter*. These publications should help all those who work with children in group care settings to improve quality of care—whether full day or part day, full year or part year, in child care centers, nursery schools, family child care homes, Head Start programs or any of the many other types of less than 24-hour group care arrangements where families share the responsibility for their young children.

Acknowledgments

This manual was originally funded through an intra-agency agreement between the Administration for Children, Youth and Families; the Division of Maternal and Child Health, U.S. Department of Health and Human Services; and the Massachusetts Department of Public Health, through federal Maternal and Child Health Block Grant funds to the Commonwealth of Massachusetts and to Georgetown University Child Development Center, 3307 M Street NW, Suite 401, Washington, DC 20007.

Background

The origin of this manual was a handbook called *Health Power,* written by Hannah Nelson and Susan Aronson for Head Start. Subsequently the Preschool Health Program, Division of Family Health Services, Massachusetts Department of Public Health, tackled the enormous task of pulling together additional material and completely rewriting the text for distribution to child care providers in that state. Soon after, Georgetown University Child Development Center and the National Association for the Education of Young Children decided to publish material on child care health. A grant from the Administration for Children, Youth and Families and the Division of

For your convenience

You may copy any part of this manual for staff, families, your health consultant, or community agencies, but be sure to acknowledge the source of the material each time you use it.

Any undertaking of this magnitude necessarily involves many people with expertise in different areas. NAEYC acknowledges the hundreds of people who have been involved in the preparation of previous editions of *Healthy Young Children.* The Association gratefully acknowledges the American Academy of Pediatrics for its cooperative efforts and permission to quote Academy documents extensively in each of the revisions of this publication—with special thanks to the Academy's Committee on Early Childhood, Adoption, and Dependent Care.

Maternal and Child Health of the U.S. Department of Health and Human Services was awarded to Georgetown to develop and publish such material.

Georgetown and NAEYC were fortunate to learn of the work of Abby Shapiro Kendrick from Massachusetts and collaborated to adapt the manual, written especially for Massachusetts, for a national audience. A national version was made available through Georgetown University Child Development Center. Since those volumes were released, the material has been revised further and updated by the National Association for the Education of Young Children, with special assistance from Karen Sokal-Gutierrez, M.D., M.P.H., and Susan Aronson, M.D., FAAP, who reviewed the 1995 and 2002 editions respectively. These revisions corresponded with the publication of the first and second editions of *Caring for Our Children: National Health and Safety Performance Standards: Guidelines for Out-of-Home Child Care Programs* by the American Academy of Pediatrics and the American Public Health Association in 1992 and 2002.

Contents

List of Figures

Chapter 1

This Manual and the Child Care Health Component

Major Concepts

- Young children need warm, positive, continuous relationships for healthy brain development—the core of service in quality child care.
- The role of early childhood educators working in group care programs (center- and home-based) includes prevention of harm to children from known risks as well as promotion of children's health through medical, nutrition, oral health, and mental health practices.
- The highest risks of physical harm to children in group care settings are from injury and infectious disease.
- The health component of a child care program must be carefully planned and carried out through comprehensive health policies and procedures developed from up-to-date information supplemented by use of community resources.
- All staff and families must understand and work on implementing the child care program's health policies.
- The experiences of children and families in a child care program can lay the foundation for future personal health practices.

As program directors, teachers, students learning to be teachers, or other professionals working with child care facilities, you must be able to protect and promote the health and well-being of the young children, staff, and families in child care. You can achieve major health gains by taking simple steps. Washing hands, for example, is the single best defense against the spread of infectious disease. Including toothbrushing in the daily routine teaches children a good habit for life. Frequent site safety checks can prevent an injury. Careful, regular observations of children may reveal health problems that can respond to early treatment. Specific information, procedures, and recommendations on each of these topics, as well as on many others, are provided in this manual.

About This Manual

This manual, based on national standards, has been reviewed by both health and early childhood professionals. Child care providers and health professionals who work together can use this manual as a guide to implement currently accepted standards for health policies and practices. The standards are practices for which good evidence exists that failure to perform

the practice poses an unacceptable risk of harm to the health of children and staff. If you find it impossible to meet some of the standards in your program, implement as many as possible. Assess your priorities for avoiding significant risks; don't expect to change everything overnight. Plan carefully and thoroughly before making any changes.

Some recommendations in *Healthy Young Children* may differ from materials from other credible sources. Materials are published and updated in different time periods, drawing on a changing base of information. Also, within the medical and scientific community, experts differ on specific approaches. When there is a conflict, seek the *rationale* for the

recommendations. Sometimes the different approaches are equally acceptable alternatives. Other times, you will have to make the best decision you can after exploring the basis for the differing points of view. If the issue involves technical information, you may want to consult a trusted local expert with the appropriate scientific background. Your state or local department of public health can usually provide guidance or suggest where to get the help you need.

Healthy Young Children can be used as a textbook and a guide. When other publications would be particularly helpful on a topic, they are mentioned. To use *Healthy Young Children* effectively, read it through at least one time so you become familiar with the contents and grasp the scope of what you need to do to ensure a safe and healthy child care program. If you are using the manual as a textbook, address the chapters in convenient units, noting that each chapter ends with a list of suggested activities that may help adult learners apply the concepts to real world experience.

The Purpose of the Child Care Health Component

Research shows that development of the social and the intellectual parts of the brain depends on the quality of early experiences. In addressing health and safety, the critical nature of children's experiences to the development of the brain is mental health. Children need protection from injury and infection, both of which can lead to discomfort, disability, or death. They also need activities that promote healthy growth and development. Childhood is a unique period of life with physical, intellectual, emotional, and social growth all occurring simulta-

neously and interactively. Children's bodies and minds are learning how to meet challenges of the environment all the time.

The health component of child care should be planned to respond to the predictable developmental patterns of young children as they progress from young infants to toddlers to preschool children to school-age children and then to self-sufficient older children. The needs of each developmental stage differ. At each developmental level, early childhood professionals must simultaneously function as protectors, role models, and teachers for the children in their care.

Health and safety are not external patches or optional aspects of programs. Regardless of the limits imposed by funding, staffing, physical, or curricular constraints, the health component should be an integrated part of daily program activity. The health component involves risk management and anticipatory learning for the group. Compromises are necessary since a completely risk-free and infection-proof program is not possible. Actually, a risk-free environment is undesirable because it would not meet the child development need of children to experience challenge. Risk management involves making choices and finding acceptable alternative approaches so children can experience challenges without major adverse consequences.

Suggested Activities

- Do a self-assessment of your own health behavior. When you are in a hurry or distracted, do you take risks that you would not consider acceptable if you gave more thought to them? What are those risks? What practices would you change?

- Look at the table of contents for this manual. What aspects of a child care health component have you given most attention? Which could you give more consideration? Are there areas that you avoid or emphasize because you find some more or less appealing? Which are these and why are they more or less appealing to you?

- What references and resources inform your work on health and safety in child care settings? How current are they? How can you determine whether they are authoritative and up-to-date? Who in your community can you consult as an expert on medical, nutrition, oral health, and mental health issues?

Chapter 2

Preventing Infections

Infectious diseases are illnesses caused by infection with viruses or bacteria or by fungi or parasites. *Contagious* or *communicable* diseases are infectious diseases that can spread from one person to another.

Concern about infectious disease in child care is an everyday worry for child care providers, parents, and health professionals. When children become ill in child care, they may require more attention from caregivers and pass their illnesses on to other children, to caregivers, and to caregiver's families. Caring for infected children in group care settings is costly and burdensome to families. They may miss work days to care for sick children and to bring them to clinicians for diagnosis and treatment. Many doctors and nurses are aware of studies that show infants and toddlers have more frequent infections when they are in group care. While not every infection is attributable to participation in child care, families often hear and are troubled by comments about this increased risk, not realizing that while the number of infections is increased for children in child care, children who receive care only at home also get many infections.

Much can be done to reduce the risk of transmission of infectious disease in group care settings. Child care providers, families, and clinicians need to

Major Concepts

- Child care programs must establish detailed policies to prevent and manage infectious illness.

- Always treat body fluids from children, adults, and animals and surfaces that may have been in contact with body fluids as possibly infectious. You must handle body fluids carefully and clean them up carefully, even when the process requires a lot of work.

- Despite your best efforts, children and adults will get sick; infectious illness is an expected part of life. Your role is to prevent unnecessary consequences of exposure to infections in group settings.

- Take active steps to educate staff, families, and children about infectious illnesses, techniques to prevent their spread, and proper care of ill children.

- Good handwashing and cleaning of the materials and facility help prevent the spread of disease.

- Some sanitation procedures in diapering and toileting differ in child care from what parents do at home.

- To keep everyone mindful of health practices on sanitation and hygiene, someone in the program should be responsible for regular checks of opportunities to improve infection control routines.

work together to help children avoid preventable illnesses. Occasionally, outbreaks of serious diseases may occur. If precautions are not taken, these serious diseases can spread quickly.

The germs that cause infections and contagious diseases are spread in four main ways:

- through the respiratory tract (via fluids from the eyes, nose, mouth, and lungs)
- through the intestinal tract (via the stool)
- through direct contact or touching
- through blood contact

1. Prevent Infections from Spreading

The viruses and bacteria that cause infectious illnesses thrive in warm, wet, and stuffy environments. Conversely, these infectious agents have difficulty growing in clean, dry environments with lots of fresh air. To prevent the spread of illness, take these steps:

• Require correct handwashing procedures for adults and children (see Figure 2.1).

• Air out all the rooms in the facility daily, and take the children outside often.

• Allow sufficient space for the group.

• Clean and sanitize areas for diapering, toileting, and eating, as well as toys and furniture.

• Reduce germs by cleaning the environment with detergent and water and then sanitizing with a bleach solution (see Figure 2.2) or an EPA-registered sanitizer or disinfectant.

• Remember, an ounce of prevention is worth a ton of cure.

People who do not look or feel sick can spread infectious illnesses. Body fluids get into the air, food, or onto surfaces where they are inhaled, eaten, or touched by others. To control the spread of illness,

• teach children and staff how to keep a sneeze/ cough from spreading germs and how to dispose of tissues. Tissues are rarely in hand when a sneeze or cough occurs. Teach children and adults to sneeze and cough away from other people and toward the floor—or if someone is crawling on the floor, "give germs a cold shoulder" by sneezing or coughing on your own shoulder. If it is likely that your shoulder will come in contact with other surfaces or children afterward, drape a cloth over the shoulder you used. Covering or sanitizing the surface you contaminated by coughing or sneezing will help prevent

transmission of your germs. If you sneeze or cough into your hands or into a tissue, be sure you wash your hands before you touch anything or anyone!

• use running water, liquid soap, and individual paper towels for handwashing.

• do not allow sharing of personal items.

2. Require Certain Immunizations

All children in your program must be immunized against vaccine-preventable diseases. Each January, a new schedule of recommended vaccines is published jointly by the Centers for Disease Control and Prevention, the American Academy of Pediatrics, and the Academy of Family Practice. This schedule is available online at Websites of the Centers for Disease Control (**www.cdc.gov**) and the American Academy of Pediatrics (**www.aap.org**). At the time of publication of this edition of *Healthy Young Children*, the universally recommended vaccines include those that protect against diphtheria, tetanus, pertussis, poliomyelitis, measles, mumps, rubella, Haemophilus influenzae (Hib), varicella (chicken pox), pneumococcus, and influenza at appropriate ages. All children should have these vaccines unless they are exempted by state law for religious or medical reasons.

If you do not exclude children who are not properly immunized, you may have legal liability if a child in your program develops a vaccine-preventable disease. Check with an attorney before you accept this risk.

Most children complete their basic series of immunizations before the age of 18 months and get boosters as they get older. However, appointments for checkups do get missed and immunization schedules are disrupted. *Partial immunizations may not provide protection against disease.* For this reason, children with delayed or disrupted vaccine schedules must receive makeup immunizations. Those who start immunization after 12 months of age must follow a special schedule. Remember, underimmunized children increase the risk of exposure of children who are too young to have completed their own immunization series. Consider the risk of exposure to the other children in the group when you accept a child who is not immunized.

To assess a child's immunized status, use the current national immunization schedule. As mentioned in chapter 1, since the schedule is complex, with many details, the American Academy of Pediatrics provides a free tool (available for the cost of a first-class-letter postage stamp). This Immunization Dose Counter identifies children who are overdue for vaccines and carries a copy of the immunization schedule that was current at the time that edition of the device was published. Be sure to check immunizations to determine if a child is protected and monitor the intervals when the child is due for next doses of vaccine. Checking immunizations is a tedious task, but it must be done to ensure the safety of children in group care.

Before enrollment, ask the families to obtain a completed Certificate of Immunization or record the immunization information on the child's Child Health Assessment form. Remind parents to obtain an updated Child Health Assessment form that includes updated immunizations and other helpful health information from each checkup visit to keep the child care program informed about the child's health status. (See Figure 2.3.) If you have questions about whether a child is up-to-date with immunizations, check with your program's child care health consultant or the public health department.

In *Caring for Our Children*, the national standards state that children must have documentation of their immunized status and a current checkup visit within 6 weeks of enrollment. Children who are up-to-date do not need a special visit to the clinician and their families only need documentation of the up-to-date status from the clinician. (Some clinicians charge for the work of filling out forms.) For those children who need services, it may take some weeks to get an appointment. In the meantime, the child care provider can offer enrollment as long as the family has an appointment within the next 6 weeks to obtain the necessary documentation and whatever vaccines the child can receive at that time. If catch-up vaccines are needed, the process may take a matter of months while the child continues to be enrolled in the program. Child care providers must be supportive and persistent to be sure families follow through with these plans as expeditiously as possible. It may be difficult to exclude noncompliant families who have been allowed this conditional enrollment.

Every child should have a source of medical care where preventive and treatment services, including vaccines, are given. A comprehensive, continuous source of care that is compassionate, family-centered, and competent is called a *medical home*. If you find a family lacking such a resource, make a referral to local physicians or the health department to obtain the necessary services. If financial problems

Fig. 2.1. Handwashing—The First Line of Defense Against Infectious Disease

Everyone should wash hands at the following times:

- **Upon arrival for the day or when moving from one child care group to another**
- **Before and after**

—eating, handling food, or feeding a child;

—giving medication;

—playing in water that is used by more than one person.

- **After**

—diapering;

—using the toilet or helping a child use a toilet;

—handling bodily fluid (mucus, blood, vomit), from sneezing, wiping and blowing noses, from mouths, or from sores;

—handling uncooked food, especially raw meat and poultry;

—handling pets and other animals;

—playing in sandboxes;

—cleaning or handling the garbage.

Source: Standard 3.020, Situations that Require Handwashing, from *Caring for Our Children*.

and lack of insurance are a factor, refer the family to state-run child health insurance and public vaccine programs. Additional information on vaccine-preventable diseases is provided later in this chapter.

In addition to the universally recommended vaccines, some children should receive special vaccines. In communities where hepatitis A is a big problem, universal hepatitis A vaccination is recommended. As of 2002, annual flu vaccine is recommended for all children between the ages of 6 and 23 months. For older children with serious respiratory disease like asthma, or those with other chronic illnesses that might cause them to have serious complications of influenza, a flu vaccine in the fall of each year is a must. Actually, anyone who wants to reduce the risks of serious illness from influenza is a candidate for the flu vaccine. Since child care has been identified as a reservoir for influenza in the community, when vaccine supplies are sufficient, immunization of all people in child care should be considered.

Figure 2.2. Bleach Solution for Disinfecting Surfaces

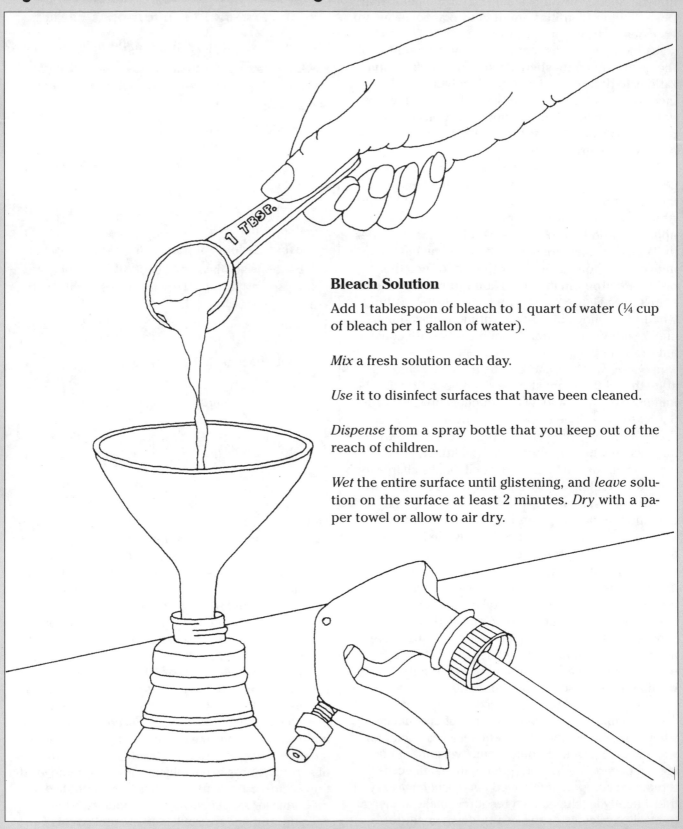

Bleach Solution

Add 1 tablespoon of bleach to 1 quart of water (¼ cup of bleach per 1 gallon of water).

Mix a fresh solution each day.

Use it to disinfect surfaces that have been cleaned.

Dispense from a spray bottle that you keep out of the reach of children.

Wet the entire surface until glistening, and *leave* solution on the surface at least 2 minutes. *Dry* with a paper towel or allow to air dry.

3. Report Some Illnesses

Every state has laws requiring early childhood programs to report the occurrence of certain infectious diseases to the state department of public health. Reportable diseases vary from state to state, so contact your local health department for the current list. *Be sure to include this list and a reporting procedure in your facility's health policy.* The purpose of reporting is to enable public health officials to conduct investigations and take appropriate measures to prevent further spread of contagious diseases.

For some diseases (for example, hepatitis and meningitis), any occurrence must be reported. Other diseases must be reported when an *outbreak* occurs—that is, when two or more children or staff become ill. Generally, an *epidemic*—a large number of cases in a short period—should be reported, even if the disease is not listed as reportable (for example, flu, mononucleosis, conjunctivitis, or pneumonia).

Special reporting requirements usually exist for illnesses caused by consumption of contaminated food. Suspect food contamination if a number of your staff and children experience stomach cramps, vomiting, diarrhea, and/or dizziness, and report the situation to your local board of health.

Finally, a number of diseases, such as Acquired Immune Deficiency Syndrome (AIDS) and sexually transmitted diseases (STDs) must be reported to the state public health department. Physicians, health care providers, and laboratories that diagnose these diseases are generally the mandated reporters.

4. Exclude Some Children

Contrary to popular belief and practice, only a *few* illnesses require exclusion of sick children to ensure protection of other children and staff. *Children who have fever and are behaving normally do not need to be excluded. Neither do children with colds who are behaving normally.*

For exclusion guidelines that comply with the national standards, use the booklet *Preparing for Illness* (NAEYC). It contains the most recent recommendations on infectious disease in child care settings. With many illnesses, children either have already exposed others before becoming obviously ill (with colds) or are not contagious at some point after beginning treatment (with strep throat, conjunctivitis, impetigo, ringworm, parasites, head lice, and scabies). The waiting period after the onset of treatment varies with the disease (see *Preparing for Illness*).

In chapters 3 and 6 of *Caring for Our Children*, the standards on exclusion define the general reasons why children should be sent home or refused admission for temporary conditions, and offer detailed criteria on specific excludable conditions. In general, there are only *three reasons to exclude an ill child from a child care setting:*

1. The illness prevents the child from participating comfortably in the program's activities, as determined by the child care provider.

2. The illness makes the child have a greater need for care than the caregivers can manage without compromise to the care of other children in the group.

3. The child has a specific condition that is likely to expose others to a communicable disease.

The first two criteria are determined by the child care program and always override any other consideration. With the exception of lice, for which exclusion is not required until the end of the day, the specific conditions listed under the third criterion for exclusion in the *Caring for Our Children* standards require that parents be asked to remove the child from care as soon as possible. In the meantime, the ill child should receive appropriate care, in an area where the child will not increase the risks of contagion.

The detailed list of specific conditions in the standards and in *Preparing for Illness* not only make it clear when to exclude but also when the child can return based on symptoms, treatment, or evidence that the child is no longer contagious. In general, most conditions do not require a doctor's note to return since the basis of the doctor's determination of when the child is able to return is whether the parent thinks the child is acting normally. A doctor's note is useful when the child needs continued special care while in child care or has a type of bacterial diarrhea for which a report of negative cultures must be obtained from a clinician before the child returns.

The specific conditions that meet the third criterion for exclusion are applicable unless a physician determines the child can attend the program with symptoms or until after the child receives treatment. Consult chapters 3 and 6 of *Caring for Our Children* or use *Preparing for Illness* for details about each condition. The standards are clear: Children with common respiratory infections do not need to be excluded unless they are unable to participate comfortably or they require care that compromises the care of other children. The specific conditions that require exclusion are as follows:

- both fever and behavior change (note again that a child with a fever who is acting normally does not need to be excluded)
- symptoms of severe illness such as lethargy, uncontrolled coughing, inexplicable irritability or crying, difficulty breathing, wheezing, or other unusual signs (until medical evaluation determines the child can remain in care)
- diarrhea, defined as more watery, less formed, more frequent stools not associated with a diet change or medication—a stool not contained by the child's ability to use the toilet. (Children in diapers who develop diarrhea must be excluded, and children who have learned to use the toilet, but can't make it to the toilet in time, must also be excluded.)
- blood in the stools not explained by diet change, medication, or hard stools
- vomiting two or more times in 24 hours
- persistent abdominal pain
- mouth sores with drooling
- rash with fever or behavior change
- purulent conjunctivitis (pink or red eye lining or whites of the eyes with white or yellow pus coming from the eyes)
- lice (exclude at end of the day)
- scabies
- tuberculosis
- impetigo
- strep throat
- chickenpox or shingles (varicella)
- whooping cough (pertussis)

- mumps
- hepatitis A
- measles
- rubella
- herpes simplex

Children who are carriers of viral illnesses such as cytomegalovirus (CMV), hepatitis B, or HIV infection should not be excluded. These diseases can be present without symptoms, so the precautions for handling body fluids to prevent spread of these diseases must be used for everyone.

See chapter 10 for how to handle situations when your program allows mildly ill children to attend.

5. Prepare—Don't Wait until an Outbreak Occurs!

Do some advance planning and take these steps:

- Insist that staff learn and follow handwashing, cleaning, and ventilation guidelines all the time, but especially during spring, fall, and winter, when illness seems more common.
- Choose a health consultant who knows about infectious disease in early childhood settings.
- Prominently post telephone numbers of local and state departments of public health.
- Make sure children's immunizations are up-to-date before you admit them. Keep track of when children are due for their next immunization and remind families to get these important protections. If an outbreak of a vaccine-preventable disease does occur, you will need the immediate ability to identify which children are fully immunized and which are not protected—either because they are not old enough to have received all their doses or because their families have not obtained the recommended vaccines.
- Staff also should be up-to-date on their immunizations to protect themselves and the children. Keep track of staff protection from vaccine-preventable disease just as you do for the children.
- Make sure families recognize their responsibility for taking their sick child to their usual source of health care and for reporting a contagious illness to you. Do not assume that parents will read all the material you give them. Review health procedures orally at enrollment in addition to sending an annual letter to all families. Describe each of your health policies and ask parents to
  —call or e-mail your program when a child is ill

Figure 2.3. CHILD HEALTH ASSESSMENT

Parents & Child Care Providers fill-in this part.

CHILD'S NAME: (LAST)	(FIRST)	PARENT/GUARDIAN
DATE OF BIRTH:	HOME PHONE:	ADDRESS:
CHILD CARE FACILITY NAME:		
FACILITY PHONE:	COUNTY:	WORK PHONE:

To Parents: Submission of this form to the child care provider implies consent for the child care provider to discuss the child's health with the child's clinician.

PA child care providers must document that enrolled children have received age appropriate health services and immunizations that meet the current schedule of the American Academy of Pediatrics 141 Northwest Point Blvd., Elk Grove Village, IL 60007. The schedule is available at <www.aap.org> or Faxback 847/758-0391 (document #9535 and #9807). Print copies provided by DPW have the schedule on the back of the form.

Health history and medical information pertinent to routine child care and emergencies (describe, if any):	Date of most recent well-child exam:
☐NONE	
Allergies to food or medicine (describe, if any):	Do not omit any information. This form may be updated by health professional. (Initial and date new data.) Child care facility needs 2 copies.
☐NONE	

Parents may write immunization dates, health professionals should verify and complete all data.

LENGTH/HEIGHT	WEIGHT	HEAD CIRCUMFERENCE	BLOOD PRESSURE (BEGINNING AT AGE 3)
_____ IN/CM %ILE	_____ LB/KG %ILE	_____ IN/CM %ILE	_____ / _____

PHYSICAL EXAMINATION	✓ = NORMAL	IF ABNORMAL - COMMENTS
HEAD/EARS/EYES/NOSE/THROAT		
TEETH		
CARDIORESPIRATORY		
ABDOMEN/GI		
GENITALIA/BREASTS		
EXTREMITIES/JOINTS/BACK/CHEST		
SKIN/LYMPH NODES		
NEUROLOGIC & DEVELOPMENTAL		

IMMUNIZATIONS	DATE	DATE	DATE	DATE	DATE	COMMENTS
DTaP/DTP/Td						
POLIO						
HIB						
HEP B						
MMR						
VARICELLA						
PNEUMOCOCCAL						
OTHER						

SCREENING TESTS	DATE TEST DONE	NOTE HERE IF RESULTS ARE PENDING OR ABNORMAL
LEAD		
ANEMIA (HGB/HCT)		
URINALYSIS (UA) (at age 5)		
HEARING (subjective until age 4)		
VISION (subjective until age 3)		
PROFESSIONAL DENTAL EXAM		

HEALTH PROBLEMS OR SPECIAL NEEDS, RECOMMENDED TREATMENT/MEDICATIONS/SPECIAL CARE (ATTACH ADDITIONAL SHEETS IF NECESSARY)

☐NONE NEXT APPOINTMENT - MONTH/YEAR:

MEDICAL CARE PROVIDER: SIGNATURE OF PHYSICIAN OR CPNP:	SIGNATURE OF PHYSICIAN OR CPNP:
ADDRESS:	
	PHONE	LICENSE NUMBER:	DATE FORM SIGNED:

Source: Appendix Z, *Caring for Our Children,* reprinted with permission from the Pennsylvania Department of Public Welfare.

—call or e-mail if a clinician makes a specific diagnosis (such as strep throat) or provides a specific treatment

—tell you *immediately* if the child is hospitalized or treated for a serious infection such as Hib or meningococcal disease

—keep the child home if he or she has an excludable illness

—call and discuss whether or not their children should attend when they have mild illness

—inform the program of any changes in emergency numbers where parents can be reached promptly at any time during the day.

- *Be watchful!* Learn to look for signs of infectious disease. Call or send a note home if you suspect a problem.

- Inform staff and parents of any contagious disease that occurs in the child care program so families can watch for symptoms and alert their child's clinician to the exposure in child care.

Diseases Spread through the Respiratory Tract

Respiratory tract diseases spread through microscopic infectious droplets of the nose, eye, or throat. Most droplets are shared via hand contact of infected individuals who get their inflected fluids on their hands and then touch surfaces that uninfected people subsequently touch to pick up the germs. Some germs spread by airborne droplets from infected people's sneezes and coughs. These droplets infect a healthy person through contact with mucus membranes of the eyes, nose, and mouth.

People touch their hands to their mouths, noses and eyes all day long—usually without washing first. Each time they touch their mucus membranes with contaminated hands, they inoculate their bodies with the germs they have picked up from surfaces they have touched. Respiratory tract diseases range from mild (viral colds and strep throat) to life threatening (bacterial meningitis). Some are more common in children than in adults. For example, while the common cold affects people of all ages, infants and toddlers usually have six to eight of these viral infections per year.

Young children are more susceptible to infection because they have little experience with infectious agents in the environment, and they are less likely than adults to wash their hands before and after touching their noses, eyes, or mouths. This lack of personal hygiene combines with their constant

physical/oral contact with objects around them to maximize opportunities for the spread of disease. As a result, respiratory tract diseases spread easily in a child care group setting.

Stop-spread methods for respiratory tract diseases

- Handwashing and cleanliness are essential to stop the spread of all respiratory tract diseases.

- Do not allow food to be shared.

- Wash and sanitize any mouthed toys and frequently used surfaces (such as tables) according to the recommended schedule in Figure 9.2.

- Wash eating utensils carefully in hot soapy water; then sanitize and air dry. Use a dishwasher whenever possible.

- Use disposable cups whenever possible. When reusable cups must be used, wash them in a sanitizing solution after each use and allow them to air dry. Label each child's cup.

- Air out the rooms daily, even in winter. Open windows whenever possible to maximize ventilation.

- Allow children to play outdoors as often as possible.

- Since coughs and sneezes come too quickly to allow use of a tissue to cover the mouth and nose, teach children and staff to cough or sneeze toward the floor or to their shoulder. If someone sneezes or coughs into a tissue or hand, properly dispose of the tissue and wash hands.

- Wipe runny noses and eyes promptly, and wash hands afterward.

- Use disposable towels and tissues.

- Dispose of towels or tissues contaminated with nose, throat, or eye fluids in a stepcan with a plastic liner. Keep cans away from food and classroom materials. Teach children to drop tissues into waste cans and to not poke around in waste cans.

Diseases Spread through the Intestinal Tract

These diseases are caused by viruses, bacteria, or parasites that multiply in the intestines and pass out of the body in the stool. Anyone can catch these diseases, sometimes repeatedly (except for hepatitis A). Programs that care for children in diapers are especially at risk because staff and children frequently get feces on their hands. When infectious stool gets on hands or objects, people who fail to wash before touching their mouths or food swallow the germs. Swallowing as few as 10 shigella or giardia germs can cause intestinal tract illness; salmonella and campylobacter germs must be swallowed in larger quantities to cause illness.

Children or staff with disease-causing germs in their stool may not act or feel sick or have diarrhea. Laboratory tests are the only way to tell if a particular stool has these germs. Tests are sometimes done as part of an effort to control an outbreak of disease, but not routinely when a child is ill.

In cases of infectious diarrhea, pinworms, or hepatitis A, notify parents, staff, and the program's health consultant. Also report infectious diarrhea from reportable types of germs and hepatitis A to your local health department. (Refer to local reporting requirements.)

How to stop spread of intestinal tract diseases

Because children and staff who have intestinal tract diseases don't always feel sick or have diarrhea, the best method for preventing spread of disease is to have a constant prevention program in place. Take these precautions:

- *Insist on frequent, thorough handwashing for both staff and children* (see Figures 2.1 and 2.4).
- *Insist on general cleanliness and sanitizing.* (See detailed information on cleaning, sanitizing, and diapering in chapter 3 of *Caring for Our Children*.)
- *Separate children into three groups whenever possible*—infants, older diapered children, and children who use the toilet reliably. Try to have a staff member work with only one group to avoid carrying germs from group to group. (Note: Because this type of grouping may not meet administrative or child development needs of a particular program, directors often consider a variety of factors when grouping children and assigning staff. If mixing staff and child groups is necessary, minimize the number of people involved and emphasize careful handwashing when moving from group to group and within mixed groups.)

Infectious diarrhea—giardia, shigella, salmonella, campylobacter, and viruses and parasites

People have diarrhea when they have more frequent stools than normal for them and their stools are loose, watery, and unformed. (Babies may have unformed and frequent stools, but until they eat solids this is normal and not diarrhea.)

Infectious diarrhea is caused by viruses, parasites, or bacteria and can spread quickly from person to person. Noninfectious diarrhea can be caused by food allergies, food intolerances (such as milk/lactose), toxins (certain types of food poisoning), chronic diseases (like cystic fibrosis), or antibiotics (such as amoxicillin) or other medication. Noninfectious diarrhea does not spread from person to person. The only sure way to tell whether diarrhea is infectious is by a stool culture. Routine stool cultures identify bacterial causes. Cultures for viruses are generally done only in the investigation of outbreaks or special studies. In general, stool cultures are done when diarrhea is *bloody* or *persistent* (more than four or five days). If a child has diarrhea that is bloody or persistent, or more than one child in a group develops diarrhea at the same time, the clinicians who routinely care for the involved children, or the public health department, should be asked to investigate the cause and advise the child care program about whether or not the diarrhea is infectious.

Special precautions

- *Strictly enforce* all handwashing, diapering, toileting, and cleaning procedures
- *Exclude* children with diarrhea not explained by a change of diet or use of medication *and* whose stool is not contained by use of the toilet. All children in diapers who have diarrhea that may be infectious must be excluded from their usual child care group because of the high risk of contamination involved in failing to strictly follow correct diaper changing routines. If you allow children with diarrhea to remain in the facility, set up a separate room or area to provide extra attention and to ensure staff involved in caring for children with diarrhea do not come in contact with children who are well.

Return guidelines

Excluded children and staff may come back when diarrhea is gone or they are well except if they have assumed a new stool pattern for a week or so that seems to be their new normal pattern. Some bacterial diarrhea requires a specific number of negative cultures before the infected person can return. These details are in *Caring for Our Children* and in *Preparing for Illness*.

Continue to take special precautions after diarrhea has been a problem. Laxity of precautions can easily lead to a new outbreak.

Figure 2.4. Handwashing Poster

Wash your hands properly and frequently.

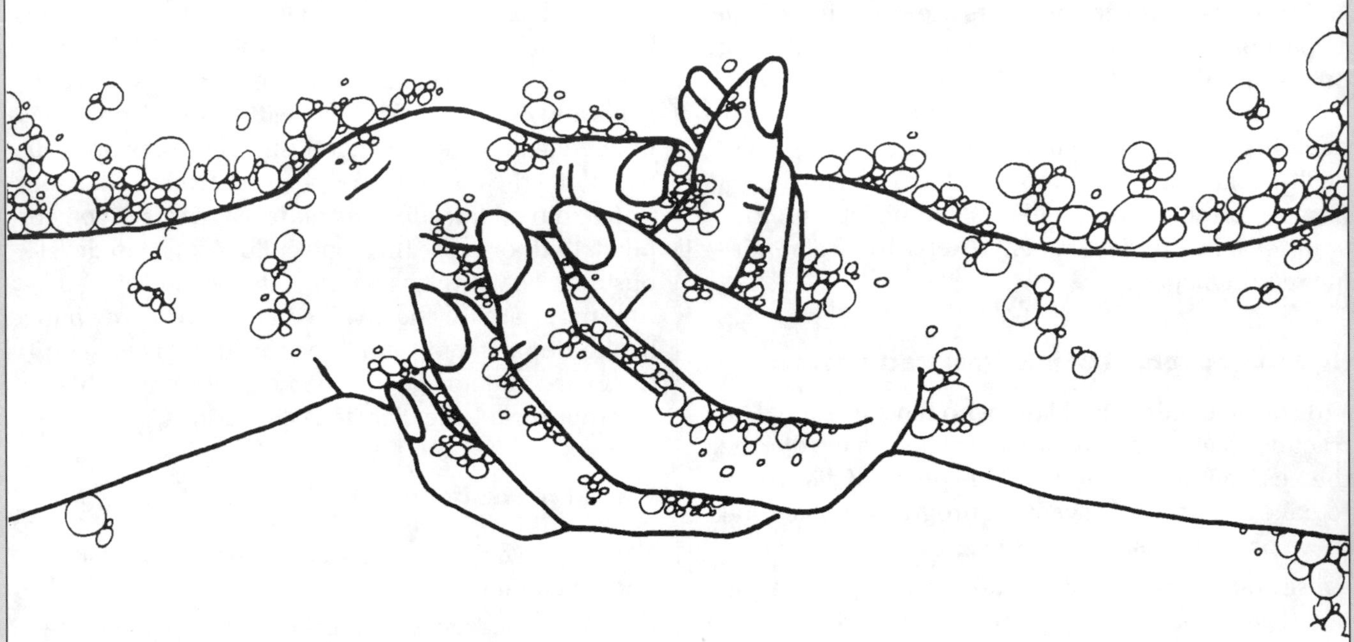

Use liquid soap and running water.

Rub your hands vigorously for at least 10 seconds.

Wash everywhere:

• backs of hands

• wrists

• between fingers

• under fingernails

Rinse well.

Dry hands with a paper towel.

Turn off water using a paper towel, not your clean hands.

Help children learn the proper way to wash their hands too.

How to stop spread of infectious diarrhea

• Follow handwashing and cleanliness procedures.
• Keep track of the number of cases of diarrhea and, when *two or more* people have diarrhea, ask the health department or the your health consultant to determine what steps are necessary.

Diseases Spread by Direct Contact

Superficial infections and skin infections—impetigo, ringworm, conjunctivitis, scabies, and head lice—are caused by superficial bacterial or viral infections or parasitic infestation. They are common and are not serious. They are spread by direct contact with infected secretions, infected skin areas, or infested articles. Because young children constantly touch their surroundings and their caregivers, these infections can spread easily among children and their caregivers. The direct contact method of disease spread is illustrated in these examples:

• A child with oozy sores on her arm brushes against a playmate. A small amount of ooze gets on his arm and then into a cut or scratch on his skin.
• A louse on the hood of a child's jacket crawls onto another jacket on the adjacent clothes hook. The second child puts on the jacket and the louse crawls onto his head.
• A child with an eye discharge rubs her eyes and then handles a toy. Another child later plays with the toy, then rubs his eyes, and puts eye discharge from the first child into his own eyes.

How to stop spread of superficial/skin infections

1. Follow these handwashing and cleanliness guidelines:
   • Make sure staff and children thoroughly wash their hands after contact with any possible infectious material and at all the times listed as appropriate for handwashing in Figure 2.1.
   • Use free-flowing clean water for handwashing.
   • Use liquid soap.
   • Always use disposable tissues or towels for wiping and washing.
   • Never use the same tissue or towel for more than one child.
   • Dispose of used tissues and paper towels in a lined, covered stepcan away from food and materials. Be sure children don't go into the can to retrieve objects.

   • Wash and sanitize toys and all other surfaces/objects (tables, counters, floors, linens, etc.) following the guidelines in Figure 9.2.
2. Each child should have his own crib or mat and never switch unless all surfaces are first cleaned and sanitized. Sheets and mats should be kept clean and stored so that sleeping surfaces do not touch each other.
3. Do not allow children to share personal items such as combs, brushes, blankets, pillows, hats, or clothing. Do not allow children's stored clothing or bedding to touch. If clothes hooks are too close, use a large laundry bag to store each child's articles separately.
4. Store each child's dirty clothing separately in plastic bags and send it home for laundering.
5. Promptly wash and cover sores, cuts, and scrapes and exclude children whose eyes are discharging pus.
6. Report rashes, sores, running eyes, and severe itching to the family so they can consult their child's usual source of health care.

Cytomegalovirus (CMV), herpes simplex virus (HSV), and sexually transmitted diseases (STDs)

These infections are caused by direct contact. CMV is transmitted by contact with saliva and urine. HSV and STDs most commonly spread through skin and mucus membrane. CMV, HSV, and STDs are more serious than the skin infections previously described. People with these infections may experience no symptoms, mild illness (such as cold sores), or a total body illness. Some infections (such as syphilis) are treatable, but others (like cytomegalovirus) are not. Anyone can get these infections and can carry the germs in their body secretions for months or years and not experience symptoms. Transfer occurs when germs get on skin that is broken, cut, or scraped, or on mucus surfaces such as the inside linings of the mouth, eyes, nose, rectum, or sex organs. A mother can pass on infection to her newborn infant.

How to stop spread of these infectious diseases

Assume that every body secretion is potentially contagious and take these preventive actions:
• Insist that staff and children wash their hands well, especially after any contact with blood, saliva, urine, stool, skin sores, or genital secretions.

- Make sure that staff and children place disposable items that are contaminated with body secretions (diapers, tissues, bandages, paper towels) in a covered stepcan lined with a disposable plastic bag and kept away from food and other materials. Children should not retrieve objects from or touch the inside of the container.
- Store clothing and other personal items contaminated with body secretions separately in plastic bags, and send them home for laundering.
- Wash and sanitize all surfaces and toys, especially those contaminated with body secretions or blood. Clean and sanitize or dispose of cleaning items (mops, rags, and towels) properly.
- Stop aggressive behavior (biting, scratching) that can draw blood.
- Do not allow sharing of personal items (toothbrushes, washcloths, teething rings).

Infectious Diseases Spread through Blood

Hepatitis B and HIV/AIDS are two serious viral infections that can be spread when infected blood comes in contact with a broken surface of a mucus membrane (such as the inside lining of the mouth, eyes, nose, rectum, or sex organs). This can also happen when the skin is accidentally or intentionally punctured by a contaminated needle. An infected mother can pass on a virus to her newborn infant during pregnancy or childbirth or by breast-feeding. Once these viruses enter a body, they may stay for months or years. An infected person may appear to be healthy but can spread the virus.

How to stop spread of infectious diseases transmitted through blood contact

The diseases spread through blood contact are more difficult to catch or spread to another person than other diseases described in this chapter, yet you *should treat all blood and body fluids as if they are contagious.* Wear disposable latex or vinyl gloves whenever contact with blood may occur—for example, during first aid and for cleanup. Immediately clean up all blood spills with detergent and water and then sanitize every blood-contaminated surface with the bleach solution (Figure 2.2) or other approved sanitizing solution (check the label). Thoroughly wash hands and exposed skin with soap and water.

Vaccine-Preventable Diseases

Before specific immunization programs, measles, mumps, rubella, polio, pertussis, diphtheria, tetanus, Haemophilus influenzae type b, chicken pox, and pneumococcus were major causes of severe illness, sometimes with permanent medical complications, even death. The diseases were a problem particularly for children, although adults were also affected. Prior to the development of the specific vaccines, many people thought getting some of these diseases was a necessary part of growing up. While it is true that many people caught and got over measles, mumps, chicken pox, and rubella with some discomfort, many others died from complications. Young children died or were brain-damaged from meningitis and other deep tissue infections caused by Haemophilus influenzae type b and pneumococcus.

Some people believe that these diseases are no longer a problem in the United States and that children can't get them anymore. *However, cases of these diseases still occur, particularly in non-immunized or inadequately immunized children and adults.* When skeptical parents withhold vaccines from their children, the incidence of these diseases predictably increases. Group programs are especially at risk because the children may be too young to be fully immunized and because the close contact occurring in the group allows easy spread of any infectious disease. Programs that have a relatively young staff (born after the late 1950s) are at particular risk because this age group does not have the natural immunity from having caught some of the diseases in childhood.

How to stop spread of vaccine-preventable diseases

- Make sure all children are immunized as completely as possible for their age.
- Check to ensure that all adults in child care (including volunteers) have immunity to diphtheria, tetanus, measles, mumps, rubella, polio, and varicella (chicken pox) and consider getting influenza vaccine too. Remember, adults should have boosters for diphtheria and tetanus every 10 years. (Adult vaccination against pertussis is not recommended at this time, but efforts are under way to develop a safe vaccine for adult use. Pertussis not only causes whooping cough in young children but also can cause bronchitis in adults.)

Noncontagious Infectious Diseases

Some infectious diseases caused by bacteria, viruses, fungi, or parasites are not easily spread from person to person. Two of these noncontagious infections—otitis media (middle ear infection) and candida (yeast infection)—occur frequently in young children. Tick-borne infections also can occur.

Otitis media (middle ear infection)

Otitis media is an infection of the part of the ear behind the eardrum. There is a small passageway (the eustachian tube) from inside the throat to this middle ear. Bacteria and/or viruses can travel from the throat area through the eustachian tube to the middle ear and cause an infection. When infection occurs, pus develops, pushes on the eardrum, and causes pain and often fever. Sometimes the pressure is so great that the eardrum bursts, and the pus drains out into the ear canal. Although this can frighten a parent, the child feels better when the ear drains, and the hole in the eardrum usually will heal.

Rarely, untreated ear infections can spread to the mastoid bone just behind the middle ear and cause mastoiditis. In the past, mastoiditis was a serious problem. Today, children usually recover from ear infections, even without antibiotics. For children at least 3 years of age, some clinicians initially will give pain medicine and then look at the ear the next day to see if antibiotics are truly needed. Overuse of antibiotics has led to antibiotic-resistant infections—sometimes life-threatening ones. The majority of ear infections are caused by viruses that are not affected by antibiotics at all. Infants and toddlers usually get antibiotics when a clinician diagnoses an ear infection. Even though most of these infections are caused by viruses, when the cause is bacteria, young children are less able to fight bacterial infections than older children.

Middle ear infections are common in children between the age of 1 month and 6 years and most common before age 3. Some children develop ear infections a few days after a cold starts. Some have one infection after another, whereas others never have any. The tendency to have ear infections runs in families. The bacteria and viruses that cause otitis media start out in the throat. It is impossible to tell which germ is causing the infection without inserting a sterile needle through the eardrum, pulling out some of the pus or fluid, and culturing it. This is somewhat difficult and done only for special reasons.

The biggest problem from otitis media is the potential for hearing loss. Fluid may remain in an ear for as long as six months after an infection is gone. This is called serous otitis media. Recent studies suggest that children who have short-term hearing loss related to ear infections do not suffer long-term cognitive delays. Nevertheless, being unable to hear well is socially and intellectually challenging for children.

Because ear infections themselves are not contagious, there is no reason to exclude a child with one unless he cannot comfortably participate in the program or requires more care than the staff can offer without compromising the care of the other children.

Special care notes to prevent ear troubles

- Never use cotton swabs or put anything smaller than your finger into a child's ear. Do not allow the child to do so either.
- Do not feed solids or bottle-feed infants lying on their backs. In that position, it is easier for the food or milk (with mouth germs) to come in contact with the opening of the eustachian tube.
- Be especially alert for any sign of hearing or speech problem. If one is suspected, refer the child to the family's usual source of health care or to the local early intervention program. (Contact the local school district for information on how to make such a referral.)

Special care notes for children who have ear tubes

- An ear tube creates a hole in the eardrum so fluid and pus may drain out and not build up. The tube usually stays in for 3 to 6 months.
- Since pus can drain out, water from the outside (that has germs in it) can also run into the middle ear. Therefore, be very careful that children with tubes do not get water in their ears. This usually means no swimming unless there are special earplugs and a doctor's permission.
- Watch for any sign of hearing or speech problems.

Notification of Exposure to Communicable Diseases

Inform staff and families abut exposure to communicable diseases. Figure 2.5 provides a sample letter to families. Use it with fact sheets on specific types of infectious diseases as needed. Make this information available to staff as well. An Internet source for up-to-date fact sheets is **www.paaap.org** (ECELS); Appendix 2 provides a listing of fact sheets currently available on that Website. Become a regular visitor to the Website to check for the most current information and any newly added topics.

Controlling the Spread of Infection through Sanitation and Hygiene

Many programs for young children cannot totally control their environments. Some spaces are rented and were not designed to meet children's needs. Even so, there are ways to improve the space. As you work toward ideal conditions, establish policies to control the spread of infectious diseases and maintain a healthier environment.

Keeping clean

This manual repeatedly emphasizes the importance of cleaning with detergent and water *and* sanitizing surfaces and objects with a recommended bleach solution or EPA-registered sanitizer or disinfectant (see Figure 2.2).

The national standard for sanitizing with bleach in child care programs is to use a bleach solution applied with a spray bottle. The solution, a ¼ cup of household bleach to 1 gallon of water (1 tablespoon per quart), must be made fresh daily. This 1:64 dilution of household bleach delivers 500–800 parts of hypochlorite per million parts of water, sufficient for sanitizing if left in contact with surfaces for at least 2 minutes. After a day, the solution becomes too diluted by evaporation and breakdown of the chlorine, so it is no longer strong enough to kill germs on surfaces in typical child care facilities. More dilute solutions are acceptable for sanitizing dishes (see chapter 5 for details). Bleach solutions for dipping mops or sponges are more concentrated.

More concentrated bleach solutions are fine, but they decolorize and damage surfaces and are irritating to body tissue. Household bleach is a safe chemical to store in facilities that serve children. Even though full-strength household bleach is quite irritating, it will not cause lethal poisoning. Other EPA-registered sanitizers or disinfectants can be used if the manufacturer's instructions are followed, but be cautious about using any toxic chemical around children.

Use the sanitizing solution to sanitize items and surfaces (diaper changing surfaces, table tops, toys, eating utensils) after cleaning with detergent and rinsing with water. If bleach is used, spray the clean, rinsed surface until it glistens. Leave the bleach solution on the surface for at least two minutes before drying with a paper towel or allowing the surface to air dry. It takes that long for the bleach to kill the germs. If you use a soaking method to sanitize toys, use a more concentrated solution because each object can introduce germs into the solution. The recommended solution of household bleach for soaking toys is ¾ cup of bleach to 1 gallon of water. Put toys into a net bag, soak them for 5 minutes, rinse with clean water, and hang the bag to air dry.

Figure 2.5. Sample Letter to Families about Exposure to Communicable Disease

Name of Child Care Program:_____

Address of Child Care Program:_____

Telephone Number of Child Care Program:_____

Date:_____

Dear Parent or Legal Guardian:

A child in our program has or is suspected of having:_____

Information about this disease:

The disease is spread by:_____
_____

The symptoms are:_____
_____
_____

The disease can be prevented by:_____
_____
_____
_____

What the program is doing:_____
_____
_____
_____

What you can do at home:_____
_____
_____
_____

If your child has any symptoms of this disease, call your doctor to find out what to do. Be sure to tell your doctor about this notice. If you do not have a regular doctor to care for your child, contact your local health department for instructions on how to find a doctor, or ask other parents for names of their children's doctors. If you have any questions, please contact:

_____   at (_____)_____

(Caregiver's name)   (Telephone number)

Source: Appendix K, *Model Child Care Health Policies*, 2002.

Handwashing

Handwashing is the first line of defense against infectious disease. Numerous studies show that unwashed or improperly washed hands are the primary carriers of infections. When you wash and how often you wash are more important than what you wash with. Ensure that staff and children thoroughly wash their hands at the times described in Figure 2.1.

There are five important handwashing components:

- Use running water that drains—not a stoppered sink or container. A common container of water spreads germs!
- Use liquid soap for children, preferably for adults too.
- Rub your hands together for at least 10 seconds. (To count off the seconds, children can chant "Bubble one, bubble two, bubble three, bubble four … bubble ten" or sing to the tune of Row, Row, Row Your Boat "Wash, wash, wash your hands; wash the germs away. Rub a dub, backs and fronts. Germs go right away." Friction helps remove soil that holds germs. Rinse hands, fingertips down, from wrists to nails, under running water until all soil and soap are gone.
- Turn off the faucet with a paper towel. Because dirty hands turn on a faucet, consider a faucet to be dirty at all times. Don't contaminate clean hands. Ideally, throw the paper towel into a lined, covered trash container with a foot pedal.
- Have hand lotion available for staff to apply. Lotion prevents dry or cracked skin. Dry skin traps germs, so using lotion is not only for comfort but also for germ control.

Post the handwashing instructions or poster (Figure 2.4) above every sink. Review all the procedures for handwashing with everyone—and check to see that the procedures are followed.

Ideally, sinks should be located near all diapering, toileting, and food areas. If you are renovating or building new space, consider installing a sink with a hands-free faucet (electric eye or knee or elbow faucet handle) to avoid recontamination. Electric-eye faucets are more sanitary and are not much more expensive than conventional faucets. Even where new plumbing is not possible, you might develop some creative alternatives. Portable sinks with a water tank for fresh water and another to receive soiled water are available from portable toilet companies. One with an electric water pump and a

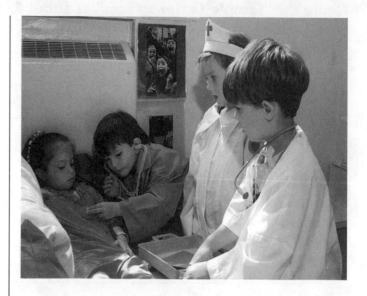

stainless steel sink is being marketed by a California-based company. Camp sinks also work and, in a pinch, a dispenser of water mounted over a screened water-collecting basin can be used.

The critical features are *running* water and a place to collect the soiled water that the children cannot get into. Warm water is more comfortable than cold water for handwashing, but the temperature is not critical as long as complete rinsing occurs. The essentials are

- *running* water—not a common basin
- water temperature between 60 and 120 degrees F
- container of contaminated water out of the children's reach
- a system safe for children
- liquid soap and paper towels readily available.

When handwashing with running water is impossible, such as on a field trip, use disposable wet wipes with an alcohol base or wipes that contain a sanitizing solution (better than nothing but not as effective as washing with running water). Disposable items such as paper towels, diaper table covers, and wet wipes are expensive. Consider buying in bulk from medical or paper supply companies. Use centralized buying whenever possible. If the program is not part of a system or large agency, ask other programs to join in bulk purchases. It is worth it!

Disposable gloves

Gloves can provide a protective barrier against germs that cause infections. Use disposable latex (vinyl for those allergic to latex) ones and remove

Figure 2.6. Prevention of Exposure to Blood and Other Body Fluids

1. Surfaces that may come in contact with potentially infectious body fluids must be disposable or of a material that can be sanitized. Use of materials that can be sterilized is not required.

2. The staff shall use barriers and techniques that
   • minimize potential contact of mucous membranes or openings in skin to blood or other potentially infectious body fluids and tissue discharges an
   • reduce the spread of infectious material within the child care facility. Such techniques include avoiding touching surfaces with potentially contaminated materials unless those surfaces are sanitized before further contact occurs with them by other objects or individuals.

3. When spills of body fluids—urine, feces, blood, saliva, nasal discharge, eye discharge, injury or tissue discharges, and human milk—occur, these spills shall be cleaned up immediately, and further managed as follows:
   • For spills of vomit, urine, human milk, and feces, all floors, walls, bathrooms, tabletops, toys, kitchen counter tops, and diaper-changing tables in contact shall be cleaned and sanitized as for the procedure for diaper changing tables in Standard 3.014, Step 7 (use the spray technique allowing 2 minutes of contact with a bleach solution of ¼ cup household liquid chlorine bleach in one gallon of tap water, mixed fresh daily).
   • For spills of blood or other potentially infectious body fluids, including injury and tissue discharges, the area shall be cleaned and sanitized. Care shall be taken to avoid splashing any contaminated materials onto any mucus membrane (eyes, nose, mouth).
   • Blood–contaminated material and diapers shall be disposed of in a plastic bag with a secure tie.
   • Floors, rugs, and carpeting that have been contaminated by body fluids shall be cleaned by blotting to remove the fluid as quickly as possible, then sanitized by spot-cleaning with a detergent-disinfectant, and shampooing, or steam–cleaning the contaminated surface as soon as possible.

Source: Standard 3.02, *Caring for Our Children.*

and dispose of them properly after contact with each child. *Gloves should never be used as a substitute for handwashing.* Hands and other skin surfaces should be washed immediately and thoroughly if contaminated with blood and/or other body fluids. Also, immediately after gloves are removed, hands should be washed.

Disposable gloves should always be worn

• when contact with blood or blood-containing fluids is likely, particularly if the caregiver's hands have open cuts or sores (when providing first aid or changing a diaper with bloody diarrhea)

• when cleaning surfaces contaminated with blood or body fluids (such as large amounts of vomit or feces)

For added protection, wear gloves when changing the diaper of a child with diarrhea or a diagnosed gastrointestinal disease. Wearing gloves for routine diaper changing is optional.

Handling Contaminated Items and Surfaces

Contact with heavily contaminated materials such as tissues, toilet paper, soiled diapers, bandages, soiled clothing, and vomit encourages the spread of disease. Be sure that as few people as possible handle contaminated items and that cleanup areas are completely separate from food-handling areas. Use Standard Precautions (see Figure 2.6) as defined in *Caring for Our Children* when handling body fluids. Child care providers are subject to the regulations of the Occupational Safety and Health Administration (OSHA) for handling anything that might involve contamination with blood. Using Standard Precautions meets the Universal Precautions, OSHA's containment and contamination requirements for blood.

In addition, those who come in contact with blood must have hepatitis B immunization offered to them by their employer either prior to exposure or immediately upon exposure. OSHA also requires staff training on management of blood-borne pathogens, a written plan and documentation of all these activities.

Do *not* rinse or wash soiled cloth diapers or clothing at the child care facility. Place the soiled items in a plastic bag, close it tight, label with the child's name, keep it out of the reach of children, and ask the family to launder at home. Keep changes of clothing handy. Place soiled disposable diapers in a tightly covered, foot-pedal-operated container lined with a disposable plastic bag.

Wash, rinse, and sanitize all mouthed toys before they pass from one child to another. Also wash and sanitize all toys frequently so they do not gather dirt and grow germs. One easy way to manage mouthed toys is to put a soiled toy into a dishpan labeled SOILED on a counter when the child is no longer using it. Use a diluted solution of dishwashing detergent and water for soaking. These toys should be thoroughly cleaned and sanitized by the end of the day. If toys are dishwasher safe, use a dishwasher with hot water that reaches 170 degrees F and heat-dries the objects. Other toys can be washed by hand, rinsed, and sanitized by spraying them with or soaking them in a bleach solution. (See previous instructions for concentration of bleach for different applications.)

A program should not own anything not washable in a dishwasher, by hand, or in a laundry machine. Allow such an item only if it is a child's personal belonging that will not be shared. Adequate numbers of toys should be available to correspond with the washing frequency.

- Wash and sanitize all surfaces, as indicated in Figure 9.2, page 128.
- Label all toothbrushes and personal items. Make sure they are used *only by their owners and that the bristles do not touch any other surface than the child's mouth.*
- Vacuum carpeted areas on a daily basis, and shampoo at least every 6 months or when soiled.

The Role of Ventilation, Temperature, and Humidity in Resistance to Infectious Disease

Exchanging indoor air with outdoor air is key to reducing the density of infectious particles in the air. Wherever people gather in groups, they put their germs into the communally breathed air. Even in winter, some form of ventilation is necessary to assure sufficient air exchange. The easiest and least expensive approach is to open the windows at least once a day. *Caring for Our Children* specifies a requirement for 15 cubic meters of air exchange with outdoor air per minute, based on the professional guidelines used by the American Society of Refrigeration, Air Conditioning and Heating Engineers. Most certified heating and cooling contractors can measure air exchange and give advice on how to achieve desired levels with mechanical ventilation.

In winter

Low indoor humidity occurs in cold weather because cold outdoor air holds very little water. When the dry air is brought inside and warmed, it can hold much more water. Unless some method is used to put an appropriate amount of moisture into the air, the dry air will pull moisture from anything that has available water—people, plants, rugs, clothing.

When air is excessively dry, it draws water from mucus membranes. The loss of fluid from the membranes interferes with the protective functions of the mucus barrier. Keeping rooms too warm when outdoor temperatures are low makes it more difficult to maintain humidity at the comfort level of 30 to 50%. When you get static shocks from a walk across the floor, you have too little moisture in the air.

Winter indoor temperatures between 65 and 75 degrees F are fine. During naptime, put a sleeper garment over infants' clothing and a warm blanket over older children to keep them comfortable.

In summer

Humidity can be excessive in summer. High humidity can lead to growth of mold and dust mites in fabrics—a problem for many children with allergies. Children with allergic irritation of their respiratory tract are more likely to pick up infectious diseases.

Dehumidification and cooling of air in summer may be necessary. The room temperatures should be 68 to 82 degrees F at a humidity of 30 to 50% during the warmer months.

Staff/Child Turnover and Infectious Disease

Aside from the obvious emotional benefits of having low turnover of staff and children, there are also health benefits. High turnover constantly introduces new infections. New staff need orientation and training to reliably practice the hygiene and sanitation routines required in child care.

Of course, turnover is a persistent problem. It is mentioned here so you will be aware of the health risks involved. Because of the number of comings and goings, large programs (with 50 or more children) open more than 10 hours a day appear to be at greater risk for spreading infectious diseases. Such centers should be particularly careful about preventive health routines.

Do not enroll new children during an outbreak of a serious infectious disease (for example, hepatitis A). Consult with local health authorities and your health consultant about an appropriate waiting period for each infectious disease. While delaying enrollment can be a costly business decision, having an epidemic is a public relations disaster from which a child care program may never recover.

Try to limit the mixing of children in diapers with older children when possible. Although keeping children in developmentally similar peer groups may inhibit developmental learning opportunities, mixing them is a special challenge for sanitation and hygiene. If you decide to serve mixed age groups, pay special attention to handwashing and surface sanitation. If you can, avoid having staff care for different groups of children during the same day. Remember that handwashing is the best tool for daily prevention of infectious disease.

Suggested Activities

- Observe handwashing behaviors in a child care program. How many people wash their hands at the proper times? How many follow the correct procedure?

- Observe diaper changing in a child care program. Use Standards 3.012–3.019 in *Caring for Our Children* to check for the required technique and equipment. What common problems in technique for preventing spread of infection do you see? What would make keeping the routines easier?

- Check the immunization records of a group of children in child care against the current recommended schedule. Are the children up-to-date? How hard is it to work with the schedule? How hard is it for families to make sure their children are current? How hard is it for child care providers to share responsibility for tracking immunizations of children and staff?

- What are the points of view involved in implementing an exclusion policy? Whose interests are in conflict? How can these conflicts be lessened?

Chapter 3

Preventing Injuries

During certain situations and times of day, children are more likely to be injured. Injuries are more likely when

- another child becomes ill or injured and the routine is disrupted (other children become more at risk)
- staff are absent or busy
- children are not engaged in a planned activity and they are tired or hungry (for example, immediately before lunch)
- hazards are too attractive to children
- staff are not aware of what children's abilities allow them to do or do not anticipate what children are likely to do
- there are new places to explore and safety rules may be forgotten (for example, on field trips)
- late morning and late afternoon, especially in the spring and fall—times of day when children are more likely to be involved in gross motor activity trying to do new or unpracticed activities.

Program Planning for Safety inside the Facility

To be licensed, child care programs must follow certain safety standards and practices. Local building, sanitary, and fire safety codes must be observed. Create a safe environment by carefully following these additional basic guidelines:

- Be alert to hazards both indoors and outdoors and eliminate or avoid them.
- Look at the world through the eyes of a young child—it is colorful, mysterious, and has new places and objects to experiment with and explore.

Major Concepts

- Early childhood is when people are most likely to be injured.
- Most injuries can be prevented.
- Regular safety checks of the indoor and outdoor environment are necessary, and hazards should be corrected immediately.
- Specific types of equipment and practices are known to cause injury to children.
- Infants and toddlers require special safety precautions.
- Child care operators should provide safety education of staff, children, and families.
- Safety rules stated as *do's* help children and staff make safe choices that lessen risk-taking.

Get down on your hands and knees to see what a child sees. You may be surprised at what you find!

- Conduct regular safety checks. Each room and the outdoor play area should be checked at least once a month. Use the Health and Safety Checklist (in Appendix 3) from *Model Child Care Health Policies* for checking the facility and surrounding areas.

Of course, no checklist can include *all* potential hazards to children or identify *every* health and safety factor specific to a particular site. The items included on the MCCHP checklists are the ones most commonly associated with injury. These should be checked on a regularly scheduled basis to promote the health and safety of children and staff of a child care program.

Whenever a hazard is found, fix it immediately if you can. If you cannot fix it, make a note of it, put the hazard off-limits with easy-to-see barriers, and follow up with plans to get it fixed. Some features need to be checked daily, others weekly or monthly. Encourage all staff to participate in conducting the checks and planning ways to deal with hazards.

Families and older children can help too. The more people are involved in watching for hazards, the more they will help prevent and fix hazards. Safety is everyone's business!

- Know what you're buying or what is being donated to the child care program. Do not accept materials for which you cannot obtain manufacturer's instructions. Read labels and instructions carefully. If you have any questions or complaints about the safety of a product, call the Consumer Product Safety Commission (CPSC) toll-free at 800-638-2772.

Traffic and play areas

- Make sure there is enough space for all furniture and equipment and for traffic around them.
- Bolt top-heavy furniture (cubbies, for example) to the wall or floor.
- Experiment with different equipment and furnishing arrangements until you find one that best suits the needs of the children and your program.
- Place chairs and other furniture away from windows, cabinets, and shelves to prevent children from climbing or reaching hazards.
- Keep aisles free of toys, furniture, and other tripping hazards such as spilled water. Break up long aisles to discourage children from running.
- If you have indoor equipment intended to be used for climbing or sliding or anything from which a child could fall, provide an impact-absorbing surface that meets the standards of the American Society for Testing and Materials (ASTM) for play surfacing. Cover the entire fall zone—as if the equipment was mounted on a playground.
- For both indoor and outdoor equipment that could be used for large-muscle active play, use the CPSC Playground Safety Standards. Watch out for the "dirty dozen," the 12 most common playground hazards identified by the National Playground Safety Institute/National Recreation and Parks Association (see Appendix 1 for contact information).
- Involve the children in setting rules to limit running, pushing, and other such behaviors. Enforce these rules consistently.

Doors

Young children need to be in safe spaces secured by doors or barriers. As they develop mobility, their options should be limited by adults to safe alternatives. Since young children lack experience to judge danger, they can get into trouble quickly. They are likely to use an open door to go exploring unnoticed.

- Simple devices that fit over doorknobs are available in hardware stores to keep children from opening doors, yet adults can easily open them.
- Finger-pinch injuries and bumps from doors being opened onto children are common problems in child care. To avoid these problems,
  —use doors with full vision panels so you can see at child height on both sides of the door.
  —install finger-pinch protection devices that are available commercially. For the hinge gap area on the door, use a strip of durable and flexible material like indoor-outdoor carpeting held by molding strips screwed onto the door and door jamb.
  —install devices that slow the door closing, giving extra time for a person to enter or exit without body parts getting caught in the door.

Kitchen and cooking facilities

- The kitchen should not be accessible to children, unless you can provide constant adult supervision. Be sure cleansers, sanitizing agents, and other chemicals are not accessible to children and that they are stored in a way that prevents contamination of food.
- Place other cooking facilities or equipment (for example, hot plates, toaster ovens) out of reach of children.
- Do not let electrical cords and extension cords dangle within children's reach.
- Turn handles of pots and pans toward the back of the stove.
- Do not carry hot foods or liquids when children are near you.
- Do not place hot items at the edge of a counter or table, or on a tablecloth that could be pulled down by a child.
- Prevent scalds by keeping tap water temperature no higher than 120 degrees F.

Electrical wiring

- Cover unused outlets with covers that have spring-loaded cover plates or similar safety mechanisms. Cover outlets in use with appropriate screw-in plug covers, especially near sinks and where young children can reach them. Many types of child-resistive shock guards and outlet covers are available in hardware and baby equipment stores.

Do not use removable plastic plugs; they attract some children and are choke hazards.

- Use extension cords only when absolutely necessary and be sure they are labeled UL approved. Place extension cords so they run along the wall, behind furniture, to reduce the chance of tripping. Never run an extension cord underneath a carpet or rug; it may become worn or frayed and cause a fire. Never run cords through doorways or walls. Do not nail extension cords to the wall. Extension cord guards are commercially available to reduce tripping hazards and keep cords out of the reach of infants and toddlers. Young children may bite on cords, getting electric shock and mouth burns.

Choking hazards

Choking receives considerable attention in *Caring for Our Children* (see Chapters 3, 4, and 5). Nearly all (90%) fatal choking episodes occur in children under 4, and at least one study reported that 16% of first aid situations in child care involved a choking episode. Young children may choke during meals or during playtime as they use their mouths to explore and experiment with unfamiliar objects.

Children should not be allowed to eat or drink while walking, running, playing, lying down, or riding in vehicles. When eating, they should be closely observed by an adult who sits with them, not only to have social interaction and promote a pleasant mealtime but also to watch for squirreling of food and slumping posture that promotes choking. Having a foot rest for children whose feet cannot reach the floor helps them adjust their body position and avoid choking.

- Objects smaller than 1¼ inch in diameter and shorter than 2¼ inch in length should not be accessible to children who mouth items. No object should be small enough to completely fit into a child's mouth (for example, Lego pieces, beads, coins, small wads of paper, paper clips, safety pins, loose buttons).

- Check toys and equipment regularly for small parts that may break off, such as eyes and noses on stuffed animals, buttons on doll clothes, plastic hats or shoes on miniature people, or Styrofoam parts. Remove or securely attach these items.

- Foods that are round, hard, small, thick and sticky, smooth, or slippery should not be offered to children younger than 4. Such foods include hot dogs (unsliced or cut into rounds), whole grapes, hard candy, nuts, seeds, raw peas, dried fruit other

than soft raisins, pretzels, chips, peanuts, popcorn, marshmallows, spoonfuls of peanut butter, and raw carrot rounds.

- Solids should not be fed to infants in bottles or feeding syringes. Bottles should not be propped. Foods for babies should be cut in small pieces no larger than ¼ inch cubes. For toddlers, food pieces should be no larger than ½ inch cubes.

- Soft bedding and other soft objects should not be allowed where infants sleep.

- Learn proper first aid techniques for a choking infant or child. Learning how to manage a blocked airway and perform rescue breathing should be part of a pediatric first aid course for every adult who works in child care. (*Note:* CPR training is not needed for child care unless you have wading and swimming activities or have a child with a special cardiac problem. See chapter 1 of *Caring for Our Children* for the content of an appropriate pediatric first aid course and explanation of when CPR training is required.)

- Do not allow latex balloons. Deflated or broken balloons are a choking hazard. Mylar balloons are acceptable.

- Plastic bags and Styrofoam objects should not be accessible to children younger than 4.

Toys

If you are careful in choosing toys that are appropriate for the age and developmental level of the children who will use them, and that can be easily cleaned, most toys will pose a danger only if they are misused. Balls are for throwing and kicking, blocks are not. Pick hard surface toys that can be washed in a dishwasher many times without damage. Select cloth toys that can go through the laundry without falling apart. Have some safe disposable toys for children to use when they are ill. When selecting toys, or when children bring toys from home, follow the age recommendations of the manufacturers. If, for example, a toy is labeled "Not for children under 3 years of age," do not allow a younger child to play with it.

Here are some other precautions you can take:

- Carefully examine toys for sharp, splintered, or jagged edges and small pieces that can be easily broken off. Tug at different parts to test for strength. Pull on the heads and limbs of dolls to make sure they won't come off and expose sharp wires. Reject any with such hazards.
- Check toys frequently and do minor repairs whenever necessary.
- Cover hinges and joints of toys to prevent fingers from being pinched or caught.
- Destroy projectile toys, such as darts, because they are not appropriate for children.
- Cut off or shorten toy pull strings that are long enough to wrap around a child's neck.
- Bend plastic toys to test for brittleness. Cheap, hard plastic breaks easily, leaving sharp edges.
- Look for the nontoxic label on all painted toys and play equipment.
- Keep wooden toys smooth and free of splinters.
- Look for the flame retardant label on cloth toys. Check seams regularly for tearing and weak threads.
- Remove toys hung across cribs as soon as the child can either sit up or get to hands and knees.
- Be extra vigilant when using toys for water play. Only plastic or metal toys are suitable. Do not allow water toys on the walking surface; they can trip a child or make the surface slippery.
- Teach children how to play safely and to put toys away immediately after playing.
- Comment positively on children's safe play behavior. Tell those who are using a toy in a way that could lead to injury how to play with it, rather than how not to use it.

Gross-motor equipment

- Be sure that riding toys, such as tricycles, are stable and well balanced. Helmets must be worn for riding any wheeled toy that has a wheel more than 20 inches in diameter, but children should remove their helmets when getting off so that the helmet does not pose a hanging hazard by catching on other objects.
- Provide an impact-absorbing surface under indoor climbers and for outdoor climbers. The surfacing material should be warranted by the manufacturer to meet the American Society for Testing and Materials (ASTM) play surface safety standards to cushion a fall from the highest point on the equipment to which children could climb. Tumbling mats *do not* provide a safe surface *unless* their manufacturer warrants that they pass the ASTM playground surfacing test. Few do. Indoor surfaces need to be just as safe as outdoor surfaces. A tile, carpeted, concrete, or wood floor is not suitable for any type of climbing.
- Do not use trampolines. They can cause very serious injuries.
- Teach children how to use equipment correctly and safely.
- Compliment children on safe play behavior.

Toy chests

Toy chests are not appropriate for groups of children. Use open shelves instead to limit toy breakage and increase children's ease of selection. Toy boxes tend to be cluttered. Instead of a toy chest, use a sturdy, open laundry basket. The Consumer Product Safety Commission offers the following advice about toy chests when they *are* used:

- When considering a chest with a hinged lid, be sure the lid is lightweight, has a flat inner surface, and has a device to hold it open in a raised position so that it will not slam shut from its own weight. The device to hold the lid open should not pinch. You may want to remove the lid to avoid possible danger.
- Check for rough or sharp edges on all metal components and for splinters and other rough areas on wooden boxes.
- Try to buy toy chests with rounded and padded edges and corners.
- Be sure the toy box or chest is well ventilated with holes or with a lid that cannot close completely should a child decide to climb into it.
- Do not buy a toy chest with a lid that locks.

Poisons

You probably think first of cleansers and medicines, but your program has many other things that could be harmful if eaten or sucked. You must always be prepared to call a Regional Poison Control Center in poison emergencies. A country-wide number—800-222-1222—will automatically connect you to the regional poison control center nearest you. These centers can also advise about risks for materials you are considering bringing into the program.

Fig.3.1. How to Choose Art Supplies

AVOID powdered clay, which contains silica that is easily inhaled and harmful to the lungs.
USE wet clay that cannot be inhaled.

AVOID glazes, paints, or finishes that contain lead.
USE poster paints/water-based products.

AVOID paints that require solvents, such as turpentine, to clean brushes, and materials with fumes.
USE water-based paints, glues, etc.

AVOID cold-water or commercial dyes that contain chemical additives.
USE natural dyes such as vegetables or onion skins.

AVOID permanent markers that may contain toxic solvents.
USE water-based markers.

AVOID instant papier-mache that may contain lead or asbestos, and **AVOID** use of color-print newspaper or magazines with water.
USE newspaper (printed with black ink only) and library paste or liquid starch for papier-mache.

AVOID epoxy, instant glues, or other solvent-based glues.
USE water-based white glue or library paste.

AVOID aerosol sprays.
USE water-based materials/pump sprays.

AVOID powdered tempera paints.
USE liquid tempera paint or any nontoxic paint.

For additional information, see Art and Creative Materials Institute (ACMI) online at **www.acminet.org**.

Art materials. Always read labels on art materials and select products that are appropriate for the ages of the children who will use them. Watch children closely during art projects for mouthing of paint-brushes, fingers, crayons, or other objects and materials. Some children are attracted to fruit-scented markers and may try to eat them. *(Home-made dough clay has large amounts of salt, which can be a problem if much is eaten.)* Do not allow children to eat or drink while using art materials, and be mindful of proper handwashing after using art and craft materials. Avoid transferring art materials to other containers, as you will lose the valuable safety information on the original package.

The Labeling of Hazardous Art Materials Act (1988) requires that all art materials be reviewed to determine the potential for causing a chronic hazard and that appropriate warning labels be put on those found by the American Society for Testing and Materials (ASTM) Standards to pose such chronic hazards. Families and others buying art materials (for example, crayons, chalk, paint sets, clay, and pencils) for the program should be alerted to only purchase products that are accompanied by the statement "Conforms to ASTM D-4236" or similar indication by the Art and Creative Materials Institute (ACMI Non-Toxic Seals—the AP [Approved Product] label identifies art materials certified in a toxicological evaluation by a medical expert; it replaces the previous non-toxic seals of CP [Certified Product] and HL [Health Label]).

Additional tips on purchasing art supplies are given in Figure 3.1. If you have any questions, call ACMI or CPSC, as listed in Appendix 1.

Plants. Plants are a leading cause of poisoning of young children. If eaten, some plants can cause a skin rash or stomach upset—others can even cause death. *Many common household plants are poisonous.* Assume that a plant is poisonous unless you specifically know it to be nontoxic.

Here are some indoor plants that are safe for growing around young children: African violet, aluminum plant, anthurium (taliflower), aphelandra, baby tears, begonia, blood leaf, Boston fern, Christmas cactus, coleus, corn plant, draceaena, hen-and-chickens, hoya, impatiens, jade plant, parlor palm, peperomia, prayer plant, rubber plant, schefflera, sensitive plant, snake plant, spider plant, Swedish ivy, velvet (purple passion), wandering jew, wax plant, weeping fig, and yellow day lily.

Most plant poisonings can be prevented with some simple measures:

- *Assume* all plants are poisonous unless you know otherwise. Check library books, garden and floral shops, arboretums, or ask your local cooperative extension service to identify plants in your play area, and then find out from your Regional Poison Control Center if any parts of the plant are poisonous.

- *Remove* poisonous plants.

- *Supervise* young children closely around plants. Eating too much of any plant may make a child sick. Label plants in every area accessible to children, including around the perimeter of the building and in the play yard, so if ingestion occurs, accurate information can be given to the poison control center. It is best to locate all plants out of children's reach if they are not being used in a specific activity.

- *Teach* children not to put plants, fruits, or berries in their mouth without first asking a grownup.

Batteries. The small button batteries in some toys, cameras, and calculators present a choking hazard and can be extremely poisonous if swallowed. When replacing a button battery, be sure that you discard the old one immediately, away from children's areas.

Cooking and kitchen utensils

Cooking and preparing foods are key learning activities for young children. During these activities, make sure that children do not have access to sharp or hot cooking utensils without one-on-one adult supervision. Use only cookware and utensils intended for food preparation. Some decorative bowls, pots, and utensils are for display only and may have toxic materials on them.

Microwave ovens should be inaccessible to young children. Food heats unevenly in microwaves and can easily reach scalding temperature. Microwave ovens *should not* be used to warm infant bottles or infant food. Other foods prepared in a microwave should be removed carefully to prevent spilling and stirred thoroughly before serving.

Hazards in the diaper-changing area

Staff should be careful about giving potentially hazardous items to children to "keep them occupied" during diaper changing. Instead, have laminated pictures or other easily washed toys, mirrors, or

interesting objects hanging out of reach and talk with the child at this special one-on-one time.

For sanitation reasons, only the supplies that will be used up in the course of a diaper change should be brought to the changing table. (Containers of lotion, cream, wipes, or any other materials used in diaper changing will become contaminated and can spread the contamination around the child care area.) Powder can be dangerous if swallowed or inhaled; lotions and creams can be toxic. A child mouthing a container might ingest some of the contents. Talcum powder should not be used on babies at all because some inevitably gets into the air and can be inhaled and damage the lungs. Also, keep the sanitizing solution well out of reach of children. The recommended dilution of bleach and water is not toxic but it can be irritating if sprayed into eyes or mouth. Many commercial sanitizers are toxic.

Safety Beyond the Classroom

Playgrounds

A well-designed and well-managed play environment provides a wide range of opportunities for children's development, including motor development, decisionmaking, social development, and learning opportunities enhanced by seeing the world from new perspectives. Playgrounds provide the space in which children can challenge themselves physically. While it is important for children to take risks and experiment, they can also get hurt. Some common playground equipment is not appropriate for younger children; in fact, some have design flaws that make them unsafe and even deadly.

Use the Health and Safety Checklist on p. 188, the U.S. Consumer Product Safety Commission guidelines, and the "dirty dozen" list of the 12 most common playground safety hazards available through the National Recreation and Park Association (see contact information in Appendix 1) to check the safety of your equipment. Even better, arrange for a Certified Playground Safety Inspector (CPSI) to evaluate your playground. The issues involved in playground safety are fairly technical. Special testing devices can check for head entrapment and protrusion. While you can study these issues and obtain the safety testing tools, the cost of an inspection by a CPSI is usually reasonable and the results very helpful. To find a CPSI near you, follow the online instructions at the National Recreation and Park Association's **www.nrpa.org**, or send your request by fax to 703-858-0794.

Recognize the range of developmental differences in children when planning the type, size, accessibility, and layout of playground equipment. Playgrounds with equipment designed for school-age children are not safe for preschool age children; equipment for preschool age children is not suitable for toddlers. For suggestions on how to improve children's outdoor play spaces, see *The Great Outdoors: Restoring Children's Right to Play Outdoors* (NAEYC 1995); *Playgrounds: Safe and Sound* (NAEYC 1999); and *Caring for Our Children,* chapter 5. The National Program for Playground Safety (**www.uni.edu/playground**) recommends that schools and child care centers have risk-management policies regarding playgrounds.

Minimally, these include a system for reporting playground injuries and playground maintenance/repair problems, and a detailed supervision plan.

Whether your playground is on your property or down the street, you can reduce the chance that a child will be injured by teaching children the basic playground safety rules in Figure 3.2. Many injuries are due to misuse of equipment. The safest equipment is designed to prevent misuse, but there is no substitute for good supervision.

- Supervise children closely at all times to prevent misuse of equipment, such as swinging too high, running close to moving swings, or playing with equipment that is too advanced. Assign extra staff to be positioned in areas of high risk.

- Daily check play equipment and the whole playground area before use. Programs should develop a plan for systematic inspection and maintenance. A

Fig. 3.2. Basic Playground Safety Rules

SWINGS

- Sit in the center of the swing. Never stand or kneel.
- Hold on with *both* hands.
- *Stop* the swing before getting off.
- Stay *far away* from moving swings.
- Be sure only *one* person is on a swing at a time.
- Don't swing empty swings or twist unoccupied rings.
- Keep head and feet out of the exercise rings.

SLIDES

- Wait your turn. Give the person ahead lots of room.
- Hold on with *both* hands climbing up.
- Before sliding down, make sure no one is in front.
- Slide down feet first, sitting up, one at a time unless the slide is double or triple width.
- After sliding down, *get away* from the front of the slide.
- Check whether metal slides that have been in the sun are too hot to use.

CLIMBING APPARATUS

- Only __ people at a time (fill in your limit).
- Use *both* hands, and use the lock grip (fingers and thumbs).

- Stay away from other climbers.
- Don't use when wet.

HORIZONTAL LADDERS AND BARS

- Only __ people at a time (fill in your limit).
- Everybody starts at the same end and goes in the same direction.
- Use the lock grip (fingers and thumbs).
- Keep a *big space* between you and the person in front.
- Don't use when wet.
- Drop down with knees bent. Try to land on both feet.

SEESAWS (older children only)

Seesaws are not recommended in general but, if used, the seesaw should be a spring-type, counter-balanced model, or it should be used only by older children.

- Sit up straight and face each other.
- Hold on tight with *both* hands.
- Keep feet out from underneath the board.
- *Tell your partner* when you want to get off. Get off carefully, and *hold your end* so it rises slowly until your partner's feet touch the ground.

Source: Adapted from U.S. Consumer Products Safety Commission, *Play Happy, Play Safely*, Washington, DC: U.S. Government Printing Office, 1992.

Suggested General Maintenance Checklist is included in the *Handbook for Public Playground Safety* available from the Consumer Product Safety Commission.

- Look for sharp edges, rough surfaces, and loose or broken parts. Remove them or repair equipment immediately.

- Since most playground injuries are due to *falls,* the most important safety feature is an impact-absorbent surface in accordance with the standards of ASTM (American Society for Testing and Materials). The standards specify the size of the area under and around equipment (the fall zone) that should be covered with the recommended amount of specific types of impact-absorbing material. The CPSC has conducted tests on the shock-absorbing properties of commonly used loose-fill surfacing materials to develop recommendations of appropriate depths for specific fall heights (see Figure 3.3).

  Commonly used loose-fill materials include wood chips, shredded bark mulch, sand, pea gravel, and shredded rubber tires. Each has drawbacks that must be addressed. Wood and bark chips scatter, harbor insects, and in wet climates deteriorate in less than a year. Sand packs down when wet and freezes into a concrete-hard surface. Pea gravel has pieces small enough to fit into noses and ears. Shredded rubber burns if a lit match is dropped onto it.

  Commercially manufactured playground surfacing materials (often described as unitary materials) are a good option. These materials may be expensive to install but save money in three or four years because they require less maintenance and less frequent replacement. If a manufactured surface is used, it should be one that the manufacturer warrants to meet ASTM standards.

  Cement, asphalt, grass, and hard-packed or frozen sand/soil are dangerous surfaces underneath or around equipment such as swings, climbers, and slides, even when children are supervised. Frequently rake sand and other loose materials to keep them soft and of sufficient depth.

- Keep play areas clean and free from glass, litter, and large rocks.

- Teach children how to play safely. Involve them in making rules for playground behavior, and enforce these rules consistently. Praise children when they use the playground appropriately.

- Remove misbehaving children from play and explain how their actions could hurt someone.

- Protect all play areas from streets, traffic, and access by people with inappropriate intentions. Locate play areas and install barriers to minimize the chance of a child darting into the street, vehicles crashing into the play area, or intruders interacting with the children.

- If water is nearby (stream, pond, drainage ditch, etc.) be sure there is adequate fencing to prevent drowning.

- Check the outdoor environment for poisonous plants and remove them.

- Avoid poisonous wood preservatives. Use pressure-treated wood instead. However, do not use pressure-treated wood that has creosote or PCP. For all types of treated wood, use a double coat of nontoxic, nonslippery wood sealer every 2 years.

Riding toys

Have several sizes of tricycles or other riding toys available for the older toddlers and preschoolers. A riding toy too large for a child is unstable. If the child is too small, the toy may be difficult to control properly.

- Be sure that children who ride wheeled vehicles with wheels greater than 20 inches in diameter—even those with training wheels—wear properly sized bicycle helmets and that they remove the helmets when they get off the vehicle.

- Use low-slung riding toys with seats close to the ground and a wide wheelbase; they are more stable.

- Avoid vehicles with sharp edges, particularly fenders.

- Look for pedals and handgrips with nonskid surfaces to prevent hands and feet from slipping.

- Teach children safe riding habits and monitor their performance frequently.

- Do not allow wheeled vehicles on sidewalks near streets; low toys cannot be seen by cars or trucks.

- Do not allow children to ride double; carrying a passenger makes the vehicle unstable unless the vehicle is designed for two.

- Teach children that riding down hills is dangerous; a wheeled toy can pick up so much speed that it is almost impossible to stop.

- Teach children to avoid sharp turns, to take all turns at low speed, and not to ride down steps or over curbs.

- Advise children to keep hands and feet away from moving spokes.

Figure 3.3. Depth Required for Tested Shock-Absorbing Materials for Use under Play Equipment

These data report tested drop heights for specific materials. All materials were not tested at all drop heights. Choose a surfacing material that tested well for drop heights that are equal to or greater than the drop height of your equipment.

Height of Playground Equipment (feet)	Shock-absorbing Substance	Minimum Depth Required Uncompressed (inches)	Minimum Depth Required Compressed (inches)
4	Coarse Sand	--	9
5	Fine Sand	6	9
	Coarse Sand	6	--
	Medium Gravel	6	9
6	Double Shredded Bark Mulch	6	--
	Engineered Wood Fibers	6	9
	Coarse Sand	12	--
	Fine Gravel	6	9
	Medium Gravel	12	--
7	Wood Chips	6	--
	Double Shredded Bark Mulch	--	9
	Engineered Wood Fibers	9	--
	Fine Gravel	9	--
9	Fine Sand	12	--
10	Wood Chips	9	9
	Double Shredded Bark Mulch	9	--
	Fine Gravel	12	--
10-12	Shredded Tires (see note 4 below)	6	--
11	Wood Chips—Double Shredded	12	--
	Double Shredded Bark Mulch	12	--
>12	Engineered Wood Fibers	12	--

Notes:
1. The testing of loose-fill materials was done by the CPSC in accordance with the voluntary standard for playground surfacing systems, ASTM F1292. CPSC reported these data as critical heights for varying depths of material. Since most users of the standard want to know what surfacing is required for a given piece of equipment that has a known fall height, the authors of *Caring for Our Children* converted the CPSC table to start from the known drop height, rather than a specific depth and type of surfacing material. Where CPSC offers no data, the table shows a dash (--). These playground surfacing requirements apply to play equipment whether it is located indoors or outdoors.
2. Fall height is the maximum height of the structure or any part of the structure for all stationary and mobile equipment except swings. For swings, the fall height is the height above the surface of the pivot point where the swing's suspending elements connect to the supporting structure.
3. Protective surfacing recommendations do not apply to equipment that the child uses standing or sitting at ground level like sand boxes or play houses that children do not use as a climber.
4. For shredded tires, the CPSC recommends that users request test data from the supplier showing the critical height of the material when it was tested in accordance with ASTM F1292.
5. Surfacing materials are available as two types, unitary or loose-fill. These recommendations for depth of materials apply to the loose-fill type. For unitary surfacing materials, the manufacturer should provide the test data that show a match between the critical height shock-absorbing characteristics and the fall height of the equipment where the surfacing is used.
6. Since the depth of any loose fill material could be reduced during use, provide a margin of safety when selecting a type and depth of material for a specific use. Also, provide a means of containment around the perimeter of the use zone to keep the material from moving out into surrounding areas, thereby decreasing the depth in the fall zone. Depending on location, weather conditions, and frequency of use, provide maintenance to insure needed depth and loosening of material that has become packed. By placing markers on the support posts of equipment that indicates the correct level of loose-fill surfacing material, users can identify the need for maintenance work.

Reference: United States Consumer Product Safety Commission. *Handbook for Public Playground Safety.* Washington, D.C: U.S. Consumer Product Safety Commission; 1997. Publication 325.

Source: Appendix V, *Caring for Our Children.*

- Keep the vehicles in good condition; check regularly for missing or damaged pedals and handgrips, loose handlebars and seats, broken parts, and other defects.
- Cover any sharp edges and protrusions with heavy waterproof tape.
- Don't leave riding toys outdoors overnight; moisture can cause rust and weaken metal parts.

Pedestrian safety

Children learn by imitation and experience. Walks to the nearby playground are teachable moments that can be used to introduce and practice safe pedestrian behavior. Both children and adults should cross the streets only at crosswalks. Most pedestrian/motor vehicle accidents happen when children dart out in the middle of the block. Basic rules of preschool pedestrian safety should be practiced. Teach the first five of the following rules to toddlers and preschool age children; all eight rules should be taught to school-age children.

1. Sidewalks are for people—streets are for cars, trucks, and buses.
2. Cars and trucks are bigger than you are and can hurt you.
   - To be safe, you must be seen.
   - Walk with a grownup where cars go—driveways, streets, parking lots—until you're at least 8. When you're old and big enough to go where cars and trucks ride, you must be responsible for observing all the safety rules yourself.
3. Stop at the curb or the edge of the road. Never go into the street or across a driveway without an adult.
4. Keep away from cars in driveways. Do not play in driveways.
5. When crossing a street or driveway, look left-right, then left again, to be sure it is safe to cross. Scan for cars; use your eyes like a flashlight. Stop, look, listen. Practice this method at every street and every driveway.
6. Cross only at crosswalks or corners, not between cars or in the middle of a block.
7. Use a flashlight and wear clothing that reflects light if you go out when it is dim.
8. If there is no sidewalk, walk so the drivers on your side of the road can see your face.

Use a travel rope to keep younger children together. Children can hold onto spaced knots in the rope. Make the walk fun, not confining, by playing Follow the Leader or singing songs. Explain safety rules for crossing the streets and enforce the rules consistently, even with adults. By talking about safety often, you encourage children to think and talk about the reason behind the actions in the rules. During walks, ask children to point out traffic warning signs (stoplights, signs, and crosswalks) and to explain how they help pedestrians and traffic.

See chapter 9 of *Caring for Our Children* for more about transportation, including pedestrian safety.

Field trips

Pay extra attention to safety during field trips because children tend to get excited about new and unfamiliar surroundings. You may want to add special rules to your general rules for each field trip. Increase the safety of field trips by taking these steps:

- Recruit family members, volunteers from senior citizen centers, or students from early childhood courses to help supervise.
- Obtain a signed permission slip from families for *each* excursion, even neighborhood walks, so parents can raise any safety concerns.
- Be a positive role model—wear seat restraints when riding and cross traffic areas correctly when walking.
- Involve children in making and enforcing rules. Make sure children they understand the rules *before* you leave.
- Identify children with a label that states the program's name and telephone number. Do *not* put the child's name on the label.
- Prepare for an emergency by bringing a small first aid kit with you. Bring a mobile phone and a list of

emergency telephone numbers, a folder with copies of emergency forms, and the signed permission slips.

- If you are traveling by car, be sure in advance that there are enough vehicles so that each child and adult has a size- and age-appropriate seat restraint.
- Make sure that all safety seats and/or safety belts are properly used. See chapter 9 for more on motor vehicle transportation safety.
- If possible, check out the field trip site in advance so that staff are familiar with locations, hazards, mobile-phone signal usability, emergency procedures, water, and so on.

Summer safety

Warm, sunny weather presents additional areas of concern for outdoor play. Children can easily be burned by the hot sun or by contact with hot surfaces such as sand, asphalt, and playground equipment. Dehydration and heat-related illness can also occur. Make sure children have access to drinks before and after vigorous play and at least every 2 hours during the day. If National Weather Service says the heat index is above 89 degrees F, it is too hot to play safely outside. Find a cooler environment for children to engage in gross motor activity.

The risk of skin cancer from sun exposure is significantly increased by time spent in the sun in childhood.   If there is no natural shade on your playground, create some with tents or canopies. (They add lots of new fun and adventure too!) When the hot midday sun shines (10 A.M. to 2 P.M.) limit the amount of time children and staff spend outdoors. Ask families to authorize the use of sunscreen or sun block and use protective clothing such as long-sleeved, loose shirts and hats or visors. In addition to parent consent, you will need a standing order from a health professional to apply sunscreen or sun block since these products are considered medications. Use a sun-protective product that is at least SPF 15.

Drowning. Drowning is still one of the leading causes of death among young children. Most drownings occur in backyard pools, and the young drowning victim is generally "missing" for only a few minutes before the drowning occurs. States with warm climates have more drownings than average. Make sure that entrances to pools have secure locks and latches that are child resistant. Fencing needs to surround the pool on all four sides (that is, the building cannot serve as part of the enclosure). There must be constant adult supervision, with at least one adult certified in water safety and infant/child CPR, when children are near water (including swimming pools, wading pools, ponds, streams, or salt marshes). Children can drown in less than an inch of water.

Buckets filled with water (or other liquids)—especially the large 5-gallon size—present a drowning hazard to young children. Never leave a bucket unattended when small children are around. Even a partly filled bucket can be a drowning hazard to curious young children learning to walk, who pull themselves up and topple into a bucket.

Teach children these basic water safety rules right from the start:

- *Never* climb over a fence or go through a gate where there is a swimming pool unless you are with an adult.
- Swim or play in the water only when an adult agrees to watch you.
- Do not run, push, or dunk in or around water.
- Do not bring glass near the area.
- Do not swim with something in your mouth.
- Yell for help only when you need it.

Teach all adults and school-age children how to manage a blocked airway and give rescue breathing.

Preventing insect stings. Bugs like summer too. Stinging insects often swarm around sugary containers, trash cans, and ripe fruits. Although most insects will not sting unless provoked, during late summer and early fall it seems to take less to irritate them. To prevent stings, adults and children should learn to avoid getting excited and moving around rapidly when they see stinging insects. Such activity is more likely to result in a sting. Keep trash cans away from outside play areas. During picnics, avoid sweet foods such as fruits and fruit juices unless water is available to rinse off sticky areas after eating. Because perspiration and overheated skin also seem to attract stinging insects, sponge off, sprinkle, or spray children with water to keep them fresh and cool.

Obtain and use the first aid instructions from the American Academy of Pediatrics. These include details on how to handle insect bites and stings. (For contact information, see Appendix 1.) Staff should know if any child is allergic to insect stings and should be prepared to treat them as recommended by the family and physician.

Winter outdoor play

Children of all ages enjoy and benefit from playing outdoors in all except the most extreme weather. Although "extreme" weather varies according to what people are accustomed to, *Caring for Our Children* sets the parameters for outdoor child care activities above 15 degrees F windchill, as determined by the National Weather Service. In winter, be sure children dress warmly. If they are overdressed and play actively, they will get sweaty and then chilled.

Go outside, however briefly, if the weather conditions are above the windchill limit and it is not raining or snowing too hard to stay dry. Staff and children alike feel refreshed when fresh air is part of the daily routine.

Snow safety. Encourage children to play in and with snow. Take advantage of this wonderful natural resource for daily winter play activities. Remember these snow safety precautions:

- *Snowballs can be dangerous,* especially when the snow is packed hard or when children put rocks or other items in them. Being hit in the face or head with this type of snowball can cause serious injury.
- Be sure children do not throw snowballs into parking lots, streets, or at moving cars.
- Encourage children to play in the snow and with the snow—but don't let them eat it. Although eating snow is fun, it is *not* healthy, particularly in cities, where it can contain dirt or toxic atmospheric substances.
- Be sure scarves and hoods do not have strings or parts that can get caught on playground equipment. These can cause strangulation and other serious injuries.
- Keep children dry. Wet clothing allows rapid cooling and frostbite.

Special Safety Tips for Infants and Toddlers

Never assume that a child's motor abilities will remain the same from day to day. One day a baby cannot possibly turn over and fall off a changing table; the very next day the child can give a successful push and end up on the floor! In a safe environment, an infant or toddler's natural curiosity can be encouraged if you give special consideration to indoor and outdoor equipment.

Equipment and toys

Keep safety in mind when you buy and use furniture and equipment for children younger than 3. Injuries involving cribs, baby walkers, and high chairs are fairly common yet usually preventable. Reduce the possibility of injury by selecting appropriate equipment that meets U.S. Consumer Product Safety guidelines (see Appendix 1 for contact information and review CPSC publications by product type), properly maintaining it, and supervising its use. Walkers that infants can move across the floor should not be used because many children fall over, pull objects down on them, or go down steps in them. Stationary walkers that allow children to stand and turn around do not help teach children to stand and walk any earlier and may actually delay motor development. Using a prescribed walker for children with disabilities is appropriate. Using a stationary walker for typically developing children who cannot yet hold themselves upright is acceptable if children spend very little time in them.

Changing surfaces

Even though it may seem to be the safest place to change diapers, the floor should not be a diaper-changing surface in child care. Use a changing surface that is at least 3 feet above the floor to prevent back strain and the spread of infectious diseases. Keep diapering, food preparation, and play spaces separate. Always keep at least one hand on the baby. Do not use safety straps; they are neither sanitary nor safe. Never leave the baby for a moment. Whenever possible, use a table with guardrails or a recessed top; these offer some additional protection against infant falls.

Indoor play areas

Programs with infants and toddlers should make sure that enough free floor space is available for crawling and toddling children. These floors should be *clean, free of splinters and cracks, and not highly polished.*

Separate infant and toddler play areas from the general play area for older children. This encourages the younger children to explore without the danger of older children knocking them down. Provide an easily washed carpeted area for quiet activities and infants' beginning large motor movement. Bolt down top-heavy furniture such as shelving or cubbies to avoid toppling by children pulling up on furniture.

Toddlers must be well supervised especially near water tables and in bathrooms near toilets and deep sinks. These are naturally of great interest to young children and, with the unsteady gait of toddlers, present a potential drowning hazard.

Sleeping arrangements

Placement of cots and cribs is an important safety issue.

- Leave a clear aisle between cribs. Separations for infectious disease control require three feet between sleeping equipment unless shoulder-height partitions are used. However sleep equipment is arranged, in an emergency, staff must have quick access to each child.
- Place cribs away from open windows, window blinds, and shade cords.
- Do not use stacking cribs or bunk beds.

Outdoor play areas

Because infants and toddlers spend much more time on the ground than older children, *check the playground daily* for items that can be hazardous. Be sure to provide close adult supervision when toddlers and older children are together outdoors. Teach older children to watch out for the younger children to help keep them safe.

Supervision

Caring for children in a group setting is different from caring for your own children in your own home. More children of the same age usually are in a care program. Group care also involves a relatively high level of activity during waking hours and sharing of an environment by children whose usual rules of behavior differ from one another. Caregivers must be vigilant about keeping track of every child. Assign specific children to the supervision of a specific caregiver and have that caregiver routinely count and check the activity of those children at preset intervals to be sure of the whereabouts and activity of each.

Several methods are used for assigning accountability for individual children to a specific caregiver. One way is to use a token for each child with that child's name (and any other key information). The caregiver carries, wears, or posts the token visibly. Timed intervals to check for all the children assigned

A Special Note

Do not buy or use old infant cribs without first checking that they meet CPSC standards. Inventory all equipment so you can check with the CPSC at least annually for product recalls on all equipment used in the child care facility. Recalls of toys and children's products are posted online at **www. cpsc.gov**. Consider subscribing to the CPSC subscription list to automatically receive recall notices as they are issued and share this information with families. Many recalled articles are still in use and cause injury because users do not know the product has been recalled.

to the caregiver should not be longer than 15 minutes. A signal-giving wrist watch or some other not-too-intrusive reminder helps ensure that the caregiver does not become distracted and fail to do an actual count at short intervals. Caregivers need to keep an eye on those assigned to their care at all times. Knowing individual children and specific program sites well may suggest other steps to take to not let a child slip out of sight or become involved in something that could cause injury.

Use of high-risk equipment requires even closer supervision. Stationing adults within an arm's reach of children engaged in potentially injurious activities allows prompt intervention when a challenge becomes an unacceptable risk. The children and adults need to have clear rules about what is allowed and have those rules restated often. Posting key rules as "dos" rather than "don'ts" reminds staff to tell the children in a positive way about what they may do.

Safety Education and Hazard Checks

Injuries are the result of problems in the environment, a mismatch between a child's abilities and activities, or a lack of adult supervision. Sometimes there are hidden dangers seen only after a child or staff member is injured. Injuries can often be prevented by

- being aware of potential hazards
- taking action to eliminate or reduce these hazards
- knowing what to do in an emergency
- teaching children about safety.

Provide children with the skills to prevent injuries and to help care for themselves and others in case of emergency. Keep in mind that your own attitudes and behaviors toward safety are as important as the physical setup of the facility. Use the following ways to give safety messages to children and staff.

- Be a positive role model.
- Give clear statements when explaining the correct, safe way to do something.
- Compliment children for doing things safely.
- Involve the children in making and enforcing rules. This increases their safety awareness and helps them feel involved. As soon as children understand words, involve them in making safety checks. Even the youngest toddler can be asked to look for toys on the floor to put away after play.
- Teach children what to do in an emergency and where to get help.
- Use the "teachable moment" to discuss safety (for example, when a child gets a minor bump or bruise, talk to all the children about ways to prevent similar injuries).

Planned lessons on safety are most effective when integrated with other curricular activities. Classroom routines, math, science, language arts, creative drama, social studies, art, and music can all be taught with safety messages. Safety can be a part of a game with a serious motivation. Kids love to be hazard hunters. Have each child or a team of children search for a specific type of hazard, or inspect a part of the building, then notify an adult about any hazards found.

In addition to your own ideas, you may wish to use safety curricula from a variety of resources. *Risk Watch*™ is one excellent curriculum designed with input from the nation's leading safety and early childhood education organizations to teach children how to keep themselves safe. Available from the National Fire Protection Association, it addresses the eight most common causes of injury to children. Community-based Safe-Kids coalitions (see Safe Kids Campaign at **www.safekids.org**) and other safety promotion programs often have educational materials and people who will come to do special programs. Local fire, police, and disaster preparedness personnel may be willing to come teach children safety and their role as community helpers.

Select the age-appropriate safety curriculum that best fits the needs and philosophy of your program. Whatever you choose, remember that safety education is more than just a one-time activity. Safety concepts should be integrated into all your activities. For example,

- use story telling and classroom role-play with chairs and seat belts to review passenger safety rules and other safety lessons
- include poison prevention in nutrition education conversations at the table, at circle time, during cooking experiences, when doing routine cleanup, and when taking walks outside
- with the children, make a dollhouse from cardboard boxes or hollow blocks, then use real or paper dolls to act out home hazards such as hot surfaces, poisonous products, toys left on stairs
- weave messages about clothing into discussions on weather and appropriate dress (wearing light colors and reflective clothing at night or on dark, rainy days and dark colors on bright, snowy days).

Suggested Activities

- With a partner, conduct a safety check of a child care center or family child care home. Look for hazards independently, then compare observations. What hazards did you find? Are the observations of your colleague the same? When you note differences, do you agree? How could hazards be corrected? How can families, staff, and children be involved to make safety checks more effective?

- Contact the local licensing agency. Accompany a licensing inspector, a building/fire inspector, and a sanitarian to a child care site. See how hazard checks are done, whether they overlap, and whether the findings conflict or support each other. What is done when a problem is identified? How do child care staff view official inspectors?

- Discuss how to correct safety problems in child care when expense is involved. Discuss the role of staff, families, public authorities, and children.

- Discuss how routine safety checks should be done in a child care program. Who should do them? How often should they be done? How can follow-up on problems be ensured?

- Think about an activity that could be used to teach safety to toddlers, to preschoolers, to school-age children, to families. What would you need to do this activity? Try to find a child care program where you could try out the activity.

Chapter 4

Ready for Emergencies and Injuries

Major Concepts

- An emergency arouses fears that must be put aside temporarily so that the emergency can be managed appropriately.
- Advance planning for emergencies leads to sound decisions in a crisis.
- Practicing emergency procedures involving role playing is key to doing what is necessary in a time of stress.
- Staff, parents, children, and community emergency personnel must coordinate their response to an emergency.

A child falls from a playground climber. A child chokes during snacktime. A parent acts in a threatening fashion. Electrical power is lost during a storm. You smell gas in the kitchen. A tragic event occurs in the community that involves some families in your program. What would you do?

No matter how careful and safety conscious you are, emergencies will occur. If a facility has a comprehensive, written emergency policy, it is better prepared to handle such situations. Use *Model Child Care Health Policies* to be sure you have covered the basics.

- Who will give first aid?
- Who will grab the attendance list if the building needs to be evacuated?
- Where will everyone go if you cannot go back into the building?
- Who will respond when you call 911 or your local emergency number in medical emergencies? What will they do when they come? Where would they take a child who needs hospital care? Will they allow a caregiver to accompany the child?
- Who will respond quickly to electrical, plumbing, gas, or heating emergencies?

Figure 4.1 outlines emergency procedures that can be adapted to fit your program, according to size, location, and children's ages. A program policy should clearly state the roles and responsibilities of the children and each staff member in an emergency.

Families also need to be informed of the emergency policy and their roles in it.

Prepare for Emergencies

- Specify emergency policies and procedures, using *Model Child Care Health Policies* as a guide to avoid overlooking an area that needs to be thought out before a crisis occurs.
- Maintain a 3-day emergency supply of food (including infant formula), water, clothes, and diapers. Have a first aid kit, a flashlight, and portable radio with fresh batteries ready to take with you easily if you have to evacuate the building in a disaster situation.
- Keep up-to-date emergency information for children and staff. Appoint a specific person responsible for having this information on hand in emergencies, on trips, and in the event of evacuation. Ask parents to update emergency contact information every 6 months, and verify information periodically by telephone to be sure that parents or emergency contacts can be reached quickly.

Maintain Self-Control in an Emergency

In the event of an emergency, remember three important things:
• *Keep calm*—if you panic, the children are likely to panic too.
• Follow your emergency policy and procedures.
• Act quickly.

• Know where to go if the building has to be evacuated. Have a more remote location as a second backup in case the close-by refuge is involved in the problem that required evacuation of the child care facility. Families must know where to look for their children. Arrange for a stocked emergency shelter where you will take the children and inform parents by letter about this location and the second backup location.

• Record daily attendance of staff and children. Designate a staff member to carry the list out of the building so that complete evacuation is assured.

• Post emergency telephone numbers and a copy of emergency procedures beside every telephone. All adults using the building should be familiar with these numbers and the procedures to be used in an emergency. On field trips, take an extra list that includes each child's emergency contact numbers.

• Plan two exit routes from every area of the building. Post emergency evacuation exit instructions in every room where they can be seen easily.

• Stage unannounced evacuation drills at least once a month. Evacuation should include use of alternative exit routes in case of blockage. Vary the time of day to cover all activities (including naptime) and times when the fewest adults are with the children.

• Maintain logs of evacuation drills for on-site inspection and review by the building inspector. For most buildings, evacuation in less than 2 minutes is possible. In large buildings, fire-resistant exit routes are usually required.

• Ask the public education division of local police and fire departments to arrange on-site visits to help staff make appropriate emergency plans.

• Train all staff in pediatric first aid, including rescue breathing and techniques for choking. Select a competent pediatric health professional to give first aid training to caregivers. In chapter 1 of *Caring for Our Children* the standards on first aid training list the items that must be covered. The list

includes all common emergency situations and requires a return demonstration of management of a blocked airway and rescue breathing. Note that cardiac resuscitation instruction is not required except if the program includes swimming and wading activities or serves a child with a cardiac problem. Such cardiac conditions are rare, but in such cases, at least one person trained in pediatric CPR must be in attendance at all time and CPR

Figure 4.1. Emergency Procedures

1. Remain calm. Reassure the victim and others at the scene.

2. Stay at the scene and give help at least until the person assigned to handle emergencies arrives.

3. Send word to the person who handles emergencies for your program. This person will take charge of the emergency, assess the situation, and give any further help as needed.

4. Do not move a severely injured or ill person except to save a life.

5. If necessary, telephone for help. Give all the important information slowly and clearly. To make sure that you have given all the necessary information, *wait for the other party to hang up first.* Arrange for transportation of the injured person, if necessary by ambulance or other such vehicle. Do not drive unless accompanied by another adult. Bring your child care emergency information (Figure 4.4) with you.

6. Do not give any medication unless authorized by your local poison control center (for poisonings) or physician (for other illnesses).

7. Notify parent(s) of the emergency and agree on a course of action.

8. If parent cannot be reached, notify parent's emergency contact person and call the physician shown on the child's emergency transportation permission form.

9. Be sure that a responsible individual from the program stays with the injured child until parent(s) take charge.

10. Fill out an injury report (Figure 4.5) within 24 hours. File in the child's folder. Give the family a copy, preferably that day. Put a copy in the central injury log.

Figure 4.2. Emergency Telephone List

EMERGENCY NUMBERS (include area codes)

Emergency medical system (EMS) _____

Poison Control Center _____

Police _____

Fire _____

Health consultant _____

Hospital _____

Nearest emergency facility _____

Local health department _____

State department of health _____

Child abuse reporting _____

Rape crisis center _____

Battered women's shelter _____

Suicide prevention hotline _____

Gas company _____

Water company _____

Heating equipment service _____

Electric company _____

Plumber _____

Taxi _____

Parents Anonymous _____

Alcoholics Anonymous _____

PROGRAM INFORMATION

This telephone is located at _____

Telephone number _____

Program name _____

Description of building _____

Directions for reaching this location from a major road _____

_____

_____

ALWAYS PROVIDE THIS INFORMATION IN AN EMERGENCY:

1. Name
2. Nature of emergency
3. Telephone number
4. Address
5. Easy directions
6. Exact location of injured person(s) (e.g., backyard behind parking lot)
7. Number and age(s) of person(s) involved
8. Condition(s) of person(s) involved

Optional information:

9. Help already given
10. Ways to make it easier to find the building (e.g., a staff member standing out front, waving red flag)

DO NOT HANG UP BEFORE THE OTHER PERSON HANGS UP!

Figure 4.3. Inventory for a First Aid Kit

Every child care setting should have a first aid kit stocked with items needed to follow the current pediatric first aid instructions. Use the list below from the standard on first aid kits in *Caring for Our Children as* a guide. You can buy the supplies for the first aid kit at drugstores or at hospital or medical supply stores.

Each first aid kit should be large enough to hold all the necessary supplies for first aid in the child care setting. Use a container that will close tightly. Store it where adults can reach it easily, but out of the reach of children. Arrange the contents so you can reach items easily without emptying the kit. Be sure that the contents are wrapped tightly and are sanitary. Check the kit after each use and monthly as a routine to replace missing or outdated items. Remember that first aid is sufficient treatment for most injuries that occur in child care.

Standard 5.093 in *Caring for Our Children* requires first aid kits to contain at least the following items:

- disposable nonporous gloves
- sealed packages of anticeptic for cleaning
- scissors and tweezers
- nonglass thermometer for taking a child's temperature
- bandage tape
- sterile gauze pads
- flexible roller gauze
- triangular bandages (this could be a scarf)
- safety pins
- eye dressing
- pen/pencil and notepad
- syrup of ipecac (use only if recommended by the Poison Control Center)
- cold pack
- current American Academy of Pediatrics (AAP) standard first aid chart or equivalent first aid guide
- coins for use in a pay phone
- water
- small plastic or metal splints
- liquid soap
- adhesive strip bandages, plastic bags for cloths, gauze, and other materials used in handling blood
- any emergency medication needed for a child with special needs
- list of emergency phone numbers, families' home and work phone numbers, and the Poison Control Center number (see Figure 4.2)

training must be renewed every year.

All caregivers should renew their pediatric first aid training at least every three years. Use a current set of first aid instructions from the American Academy of Pediatrics or the National Safety Council as a guide for what to do in situations that require first aid and what must be taught to child care workers. (The American Red Cross no longer publishes nationally updated first aid instructions or curriculum specific for teaching pediatric first aid to child care workers.)

- Maintain a first aid kit. Figure 4.3 lists the contents for first aid kits specified in *Caring for Our Children*. Pack the kit in a tight-closing, clean container. Keep at least one first aid kit available at all times—including neighborhood walks and trips and near all high-risk areas such as kitchen or playground. Store your first aid kits out of the reach of children but easily accessible in case of an emergency. Make sure someone on the staff inspects the kits each month, checking supplies against a list of contents for the kits and keeping a record of the inspections.

- Have important forms on hand.

—*Parental permission forms.* Hospitals and emergency rooms have the right to refuse to give emergency treatment to any minor child, except in a life-threatening situation, without parental informed consent at the time of treatment. Remind parents that they must be reachable *at all times* to give consent for medical care. Ask parents to complete emergency transportation permission forms (Figure 4.4) before enrollment, and keep these on file. Take a copy of all permission forms with you on field trips.

—*Injury report forms.* Every program should use a standardized form for reporting all injuries or illnesses that require first aid or additional care (Figure 4.5 presents a sample). Give one copy of the report to the child's parents and keep another copy in the child's folder. Find out which incidents or injuries must be reported to state or local authorities. Maintain one central file of copies of all injury reports so patterns of injury or other incidents can be monitored and safety in your program improved.

Getting Help

Caregivers should carry a mobile phone to parks, playgrounds, and other places they visit with the children. Since mobile phones do not always have a reliable signal, know the locations of nearby pay telephones, fire alarm boxes, or places to go for help. Make sure that everyone in the building has ready access to a telephone to call for help.

Usually you can reach emergency assistance by dialing 911. If 911 is not available in your area, post specific numbers for police, fire, and ambulance. You can also call the operator, but this is a slower way to get help.

Near the phone in your facility, post your program's address, description of the building, and directions to it from a major road, since these may be hard to remember in a crisis. Find answers to these questions about your local emergency and medical services:

- Who answers the emergency telephone—police, fire, ambulance, dispatcher?
- What steps does the dispatcher have to take before sending the ambulance? Call another dispatcher? Call emergency medical technicians?
- Who provides the ambulance service—police, fire, volunteer, private company, a facility in another town?
- How far do they have to travel to get to your program? Where is the station?
- How long will it take them to get to your program?
- Where are the nearest emergency rooms?

Try to visit your local helpers *before* you need them in a crisis. Most ambulance services are happy to show groups of visitors their equipment, and some will even visit your facility if you ask. Emergency rooms are harder to tour, but you can at least visit the waiting area and become familiar with check-in procedures. These visits also will help reassure children and their families. Be sure your facility is well marked so rescue workers can find it easily.

Emergency Evacuation

Saving lives is the first priority in the event of any emergency. Saving property should be considered *only* when everybody is safe.

Planning, preparation, and practice are the essential ingredients of a successful evacuation plan. Develop a written plan for evacuating and reporting

---

Using a fire extinquisher

1. Stand back about 8 feet.
2. Aim at the base of the fire, not the flames or smoke.
3. Squeeze or press the lever while sweeping from the sides to the middle of the fire.

---

in case of fire, flood, tornado, earthquake, hurricane, blizzard, power failure, or other potential disasters. This plan should include specifics such as routes, assignments for all staff, and location of nearest alarm that alerts the fire department.

When your program has an emergency that requires evacuation, follow these steps:

- Sound an alarm—notify everyone in building.
- Evacuate. Use exit routes or alternate routes previously marked and practiced in drills.
- Eliminate drafts; close all doors and windows.
- Take a head count; make sure everyone is safely out of the building.
- Call fire department or police *after* leaving the building. Call from the nearest alarm box or telephone if a building alarm is not connected to the fire department.

Fire preparedness procedures

- Get out, then call 911 to alert the fire department.
- Post a diagram showing the main shutoff switches for electricity, gas, and water.
- Test fire and smoke alarms at least once each month.
- Post diagrams of exits and escape routes in each room. Mark exits clearly, and do not block them with furniture or other objects.
- Teach children to stop, drop, and roll and to crawl under smoke. Practice.
- Practice leaving the building with the children at least once a month so that they recognize the sound of the alarm and where to go.
- Include fire and burn prevention in children's curriculum.
- Have fire extinguishers inspected annually. Place them where they can be reached easily. Know when and when not to use a fire extinguisher. Use an extinguisher only if

—you are nearby when a fire starts or the fire is small (confined to its origin—in a wastepaper

Figure 4.4. Child Care Emergency Information

Child's Name:_____ Birthdate:_____

Legal Guardian #1 Name:_____

    Telephone Numbers: Home: _____Work:_____

Legal Guardian #2 Name:_____

    Telephone Numbers: Home:_____Work:_____

Emergency Contacts (to whom child may be released if legal guardian is unavailable)

    Name #1:_____

    Address:_____

    Telephone Numbers: Home:_____Work:_____

    Name #2: _____

    Address:_____

    Telephone Numbers: Home: _____Work:_____

Child's Usual Source of Medical Care   **Child's Usual Source of Dental Care**

    Name:_____   Name:_____

    Address:_____   Address:_____

    Telephone Number:_____   Telephone Number:_____

Child's Health Insurance

    Name of Insurance Plan:_____ID #_____

    Subscriber's Name (on insurance card):_____

Special Conditions, Disabilities, Allergies, or Medical Information for Emergency Situations

_____

_____

Transport Arrangement in an Emergency Situation

    Ambulance service:_____ Child will be taken to:_____

(Parents/guardians are responsible for all emergency transportation charges)

Parent/Legal Guardian Consent and Agreement for Emergencies

    As parent/legal guardian, I give consent to have my child receive first aid by facility staff, including administration of Syrup of IPECAC if staff are so instructed by emergency medical service personnel, and if necessary, be transported to receive emergency care. I understand that I will be responsible for all charges not covered by insurance. I give consent for the emergency contact person listed above **to act on my behalf** until I am available. I agree to review and update this information whenever a change occurs and at least every 6 months.

    Date:_____ Parent/Legal Guardian's Signature #1:_____

    Date:_____Parent/Legal Guardian's Signature #2:_____

Source: Appendix C, *Model Child Care Health Policies.*

basket, cushion, or small appliance) and discovered in its early stages

—other staff get all children out of the building and call the fire department

—you can fight it with your back to an exit and you can get out fast if your efforts fail

—the extinguisher is in working order and you know how to use it (see box)

If the fire spreads beyond the spot where it started or if it could block your exit, don't try to fight it. *If you have the slightest doubt about whether to fight or not to fight—don't.* Get out and call the fire department.

Helping children during emergency or evacuation procedures

To calm a group of panicked children, remove them from the scene, and reassure them. Explain simply and carefully what has happened and what will happen. Answer their questions truthfully. Then redirect their attention with a game or quiet activity. Most important: STAY CALM. If you panic, the children will too. If you need to evacuate the building and children are frightened, have them hold each other's hands. Human touch is very reassuring in scary situations.

To get nonambulatory children out of the building, carry two or three infants or use a large wagon to transport toddlers or severely disabled children outdoors (if your building has ramps) or at least to the door where someone else can take them.

To remove a child who is too scared to leave the building, use your legs to press gently on the back of the child's knees to push him forward or hold his hands with one of your arms across his back. Having everyone join hands can also help the child feel less frightened.

Closings Due to Power Failure or Natural Catastrophe

Some power failures are short and require no action, but they can pose a serious health hazard when heat or air conditioning is lost. Nearly every part of the country has some risk of weather-related or other natural catastrophe (snow, heavy storm, flood, tornadoes, hurricanes, earthquakes, and so on). Some of these events can be predicted before the facility opens, but others may occur during the child care day.

Every facility needs a plan to alert families about situations that require unexpected closings. When a need for closing occurs, families may not be able to get to the facility quickly, so alternative care plans must be made for children. Sometimes staff will have to take children to an alternate shelter until parents can arrive. An emergency supply of food, water, clothing, blankets, flashlights, diapers, and other necessary supplies should be kept at the ready, either to support care at the facility at an alternative facility to which the children must be evacuated until families can arrive to assume their care.

Security and Handling Persons Who Pose Security Risks

Unfortunately, security breaches at child care facilities have occurred. Both strangers and relatives who have mental health or substance abuse problems have taken threatening and even fatal actions involving children and staff in child care facilities. Noncustodial parents have used pick-up as an opportunity to abduct their children.

Every child care facility needs a plan for maintaining security to prevent entry of any individual into child care areas until that person is screened by a member of the staff in direct interpersonal interaction, including visual contact through windows or a reception area. To control who has access to the facility, use buzz-in gates, cameras with an intercom system, or an actual person who closely monitors entrances. All programs should also require people to sign a visitor's log upon entry, declaring the

Figure 4.5. Injury Report Form

Fill in all blanks and boxes that apply.

Name of Program:_____ Phone:_____

Address of Facility:_____

Child's Name:_____ Sex: M F Birthdate:___ /___ /___ Injury Date:___ /___ /___

Time of Incident: _____:_____ am /pm   Witnesses:_____

Name of Legal Guardian/Parent Notified:_____ Notified by:_____ Time Notified: _____:_____ am /pm

EMS (911) or other medical professional ❏ Not notified ❏ Notified Time Notified: _____:_____ am /pm

Location where incident occurred: ❏ playground ❏ classroom ❏ bathroom ❏ hall ❏ kitchen ❏ doorway ❏ large muscle room or gym ❏ office ❏ dining room ❏ stairway ❏ vehicle ❏ on field trip ❏ unknown ❏ other (specify)_____

Equipment/product involved: ❏ climber ❏ slide ❏ swing ❏ playground surface ❏ sandbox ❏ trike/bike ❏ hand toy (specify):_____

   ❏ other equipmen(specify):_____

Cause of injury: (describe)_____

   ❏ fall to surface; estimated height of fall _____ feet; type of surface:_____
   ❏ fall from running or tripping ❏ bitten by child ❏ motor vehicle ❏ hit or pushed by child ❏ injured by object
   ❏ eating or choking ❏ insect sting/bite ❏ animal bite ❏ injury from exposure to cold ❏ other (specify):_____
   _____

Parts of body injured: ❏ eye ❏ ear ❏ nose ❏ mouth ❏ tooth ❏ other part of face ❏ other part of head ❏ neck ❏ arm/wrist/hand ❏ leg/ankle/foot ❏ chest ❏ back ❏ buttocks ❏ genitals ❏ other (specify):_____

Type of injury: ❏ cut ❏ bruise or swelling ❏ puncture ❏ scrape ❏ broken bone or dislocation ❏ sprain ❏ crushing injury ❏ burn ❏ loss of consciousness ❏ unknown ❏ other (specify):_____

First aid given at the facility (e.g., comfort, pressure, elevation, cold pack, washing, bandage):_____
_____

Treatment provided by: _____

❏ no doctor's or dentist's treatment required

❏ treated as an outpatient (e.g., office or emergency room)

❏ hospitalized (overnight) # of days:_____

Number of days of limited activity from this incident: _____Follow-up plan for care of the child:_____

Name of supervisor notified:_____ Date notified:_____

Corrective action needed to prevent reoccurrence:_____

Name of official/agency (if any) notified:_____ Date:_____

Signature of staff member completing this report:_____ Date:_____

Signature of Legal Guardian/Parent:_____ Date:_____

copies: 1) child's folder, 2) parent, 3) injury log

Source: Appendix O, *Model Child Care Health Policies*.

purpose of the visit. These precautions provide a psychological deterrent for individuals who may have an impulse to walk into a facility when they don't belong there.

If an individual can enter the premises without first going through a locked door that separates the office or lobby area from the child care area, or if a person can have direct access to the children upon entering your site, both children and staff are at risk. All staff members should be taught how to properly identify people before allowing them to enter the site. They should always obtain a reason for the person's presence in the building. Anyone who works in the program should be prepared to challenge any person who is unfamiliar, asking courteously if they need help.

If the stranger or strangely acting familiar person does not accept escort, or acts nervous or evasive, the facility needs a method to alert someone else to call the police and to activate a lock-out procedure to prevent access and to separate the children from the potentially dangerous person. A false alert is better than an adverse event. Ideally, the routine entrance process will shield the program from entry of undesired visitors, but there should be a back-up process too.

Security at entrances must be carefully planned to prevent barriers to emergency personnel. Local police may have some ideas for reasonable ways to improve security at child care facilities.

Play areas located on a street are more hazardous than those placed in a more interior and less visible location. These sites are vulnerable to accidental or intentional stranger and vehicle penetration. Sierra's Light Foundation is a non-profit organization established after such a tragic breach of security. A man rode around a child care playground smiling at the children and staff in a play area that was located near the street and protected only by a chain-link fence. He then deliberately drove his vehicle into the group, killing two children, one of them named Sierra.

Sierra's Light Foundation suggests placing play areas at the farthest side from the street. If the play area must be close to the street, install *bollards,* steel reinforced posts that are at least 4 feet tall and secured 24–36 inches into the ground to reinforce an existing fence. When placed at 4-foot intervals, bollards can stop an out-of-control car from breaking through a fence, thus saving children's lives. Although a block wall looks like a sturdy barrier, it may not stop a car without the addition of the steel-reinforced posts at 4-foot intervals. Trees make excellent natural bollards if they line the fence.

A chain-link fence does little to protect children. It is not a sufficient barrier to stop impact and it can be easily climbed—by intruders and by children. If their use is unavoidable, chain link fences should be made of wire with small enough holes to discourage climbing.

Both chain-link and wrought iron fences provide visual and potential conversation contact with strangers from the outside. There is value in having children able to see outside the child care property, but weigh this against the risk. If your program uses barriers that block an outsider's view of the children, make sure teachers and directors still have the ability to see the surrounding property from the inside out. Natural buffers such as bushes and trees provide excellent visual and physical barriers if the foliage is kept trimmed to prevent someone from hiding in them. Adjust operable windows so that, when open, children cannot exit and intruders cannot enter through them.

Lighting is another often overlooked but very important aspect of security. Darkness hides those who wish to enter the premises uninvited. As the length of day shortens during the fall and winter, you'll need to re-evaluate outside lighting, turning it on earlier in the afternoon and perhaps using it also in the early hours of the morning. And if your site is equipped with security cameras, make sure there is enough lighting to create a clear recording, particularly during dusk and hours of darkness.

Security concerns include not only the possibility of an intruder coming onto the property and entering the building, but also the possibility of children leaving the premises on their own. Sometimes children run out of a gate simply because it is opened. Sometimes gates open into a busy street or parking lot. Use self-locking gates, the kind sold for swimming pool enclosures, so that the gate automatically closes and locks when nobody holds it open. A double gate with one gate separated from the other by a small corral-like area is another good safeguard. Even if a child can open the gate latch, the double-gated "corral" space will at least slow him down.

A safe area should be designated for all staff and children. All staff members should know the layout of the facility and understand the name or label for all its areas. Make sure every staff member knows where the safe area is, but do not post or announce it beforehand to anyone who does not work in the program.

Sierra's Light Foundation recommends using codes when there is an intruder in your center. For example, one center uses a statement like "Sheri left her red earring in the front classroom." When someone says this over the intercom, telephone, or walkie-talkies carried by staff, it is a signal to other staff members to stay away from a particular area and to get the children to safety. Once an emergency arises, staff members need to have the ability to communicate room to room.

Families, children, teachers, and directors must have a safe procedure for picking up and dropping off children that is understood and practiced by all concerned. Failure to observe the procedure should be grounds for disciplinary action for families or staff who break the rules. *Parents or guardians should sign in and sign out verbally and in writing in view of the teacher who takes care of the child, not just in a notebook or with a receptionist at the entrance.*

Make sure children do not cross streets or any traffic unescorted when entering or exiting the building. Do not open any gates or doors only to stand and talk; an open door may permit a child to run out or someone who shouldn't enter to run in. Open doors and gates only when you are ready to use them.

Many child care programs suffer high rates of staff turnover and hire substitutes or other temporary workers who are less familiar with parents. That's one reason to require photo identification of authorized persons who pick up children and sign-in/sign-out matching of signatures of adults whom the staff do not know by sight. Telephone authorization of a family member who is not authorized or known to the facility should not be accepted because it is too easy for someone to pose as parent or to coerce a parent to make such a request. While thinking about such possibilities is unpleasant, it is critical to the safety of the children and their families. For more information on security, contact Sierra's Light Foundation (see Appendix 1.)

Suggested Activities

- Ask a local child care director to tell you about a time when an emergency involved an individual child or was a threat to the whole facility. From what happened, consider how prior planning was done or might have been done to handle the situation.

- Research media coverage of emergencies that have occurred in child care facilities. What happened when there was a fire? What happened when a deranged person came into a child care facility with a gun? What happened when a child care program was in a building that was targeted by terrorists?

- Obtain a chart of pediatric first aid instructions from the American Academy of Pediatrics (call the publications department 847-434-4000). Review each instruction to see which differ from what you might have thought was the correct thing to do.

- Where did you learn first aid procedures? Where in your community might you find current and appropriate pediatric first aid training? What does such training cost per person?

Chapter 5

Promoting Health with Good Nutrition

Major Concepts

- Child care programs should ensure that children are offered a variety of foods each day.
- Children need regular times for meals and snacks.
- Food portions should be appropriate to a child's age and development.
- Nourishing snacks between meals round out a well-balanced diet. Snacks should provide important nutrients because a child may prefer them to foods at a regular meal.
- Nutrition experiences in child care teach lifetime food habits to children.
- Food safety is essential whether foods are prepared in the child care facility or are brought from home.

Good nutrition is an essential ingredient of quality child care. Tasty, colorful, nutritious foods and a pleasant, relaxed eating environment contribute to a child's sense of well-being. A child develops lifelong eating habits through early eating experiences. Child care providers need to know the nutritional requirements of children and how to provide a nutritious diet. Equally important is the atmosphere at meals and snacktime in child care.

Every program, even one mostly serving food brought from home, needs input from a qualified nutritionist. If a registered dietician with experience in early childhood programs is not available, look for someone with a bachelor's degree in foods, nutrition, or dietetics and two years of experience in community programs serving young children. Develop a written nutrition, feeding, and food service plan, and have the consultant review it. The plan needs to address the following key topics:

- feeding plan for each age group in the program
- adult modeling of healthy eating
- menu planning for meals and snacks
- food procurement and preparation, including staff responsible
- meal-service practices and equipment

- eating as part of social development and learning of cultural and ethnic differences
- preparing foods at home and for special events
- assessing the adequacy of nutrition for individual children
- food intolerance, food allergies, and special diets
- nutrition education
- use of community nutrition resources

Feeding Infants

During the first year of life, infants experience more changes in diet than at any other time in life. Babies grow rapidly and develop motor skills and quickly progress from suckling liquids to feeding themselves table foods. Although feeding skills are developed in a systematic order, each child progresses through this sequence at her own pace. During this period, interaction with adults has a strong influence on the infant's development of self-feeding skills and accep-

tance of a variety of foods. (See Figure 5.1 for guidelines on feeding infants.)

Breast milk is best

Human milk is the most important recommended food for at least the first year of life because it is uniquely suited to support infant growth and protects babies against infection and even some diseases that appear later in life. The advantages are greatest with exclusive use of human milk for the first 6 months of life and no other type of milk until after 12 months of age, but any amount provides some benefit to the baby.

Many factors determine how eager mothers are to continue breastfeeding. Since feeding human milk offsets the increased risk of infection from group care of infants, child care providers should do all they can to support families to maximize their infant's use of this very special food. When infants cannot be fed human milk, they should receive iron-fortified formula. Child care programs should promote breastfeeding and support nursing mothers by following some simple guidelines.

- Provide a quiet, private place with a comfortable chair where the mother can nurse on arrival, before departure, or during her work breaks.

- Encourage use of effective breast pumps by mothers at least every 4 hours while they are away from their infants and feeding at the breast at every other feeding. When babies and mothers are together, there is no reason to maintain the workday schedule.

- Try to establish a bottle-feeding schedule that ensures that the baby is eager to nurse when the mother arrives (that is, set the last feeding time at least 2½ hours before the mother's arrival).

- Follow the guidelines for safe storage and handling of expressed human milk (see pages 65 and 68).

- Be informed about the basics of breastfeeding and support the mother. With adequate rest, nutrition, and fluids, most mothers are able to maintain their milk supply when they bottle-feed parttime. Most women do not need to use formula if they express their milk at least once every 4 hours while away from their babies and breastfeed fulltime while with the baby. Some women prefer to feed some formula.

Introducing solid foods

Experts recommend starting solid food when infants are between 4 and 6 months old. Until this time, the infant's digestive tract is not able to completely break down the food; consequently, allergic reactions or sensitivities to solid food may be more likely. Also, the neuromuscular skills needed for sitting up, self-feeding, and swallowing of solids generally do not develop until the second half of the first year of life.

The first solid food is usually a semisolid form of an iron-fortified infant cereal, such as rice cereal. Cereals should not be mixed with milk or formula in the bottle unless a doctor recommends it. Eating solid foods does not help children sleep through the night; development of the brain determines when children can sleep for longer periods.

Between 6 and 8 months, vegetables and fruits can be added to the diet. At about 8 or 9 months, offer food in ¼ inch cubes or food in lumps (table food the baby can easily chew, mash, or swallow whole). By the end of the first year, the baby should be eating most table foods.

Use these guidelines to introduce solid foods:

- Allow time for the baby to get used to the feel and taste of solid foods. Use the infant's clues to tell you when it is time to offer another spoonful. If the baby looks at the spoon with an open mouth, that is a strong signal. If she turns away and seems interested in something else, try showing the food on the spoon and talking about it to encourage her to eat. Never force feed.

- Generally, families should introduce new foods at home unless the parent specifically requests introduction in child care. *Add only one new food at a time.* Wait 3 to 5 days to see if the new food is well tolerated.

- Start feeding solids with a small spoon. Let the baby suck the food off the tip of the spoon. Unless the baby has a specific medical condition that

Figure 5.1. Child Care Infant Meal Pattern

Age	Breakfast	Lunch or Supper	Snack (midmorning or midafternoon)
Infants Birth through 3 months	4 to 6 ounces formula[1] or breast milk[2,3]*	4 to 6 fluid ounces formula[1] or breast milk[2,3]	4 to 6 fluid ounces formula[1] or breast milk[2,3]
Infants 4 months through 7 months	4 to 8 fluid ounces formula[1] or breast milk[2,3] 0 to 3 tablespoons infant cereal[1,4]	4 to 8 fluid ounces formula[1] or breast milk[2,3] 0 to 3 tablespoons infant cereal[1,4] 0 to 3 tablespoons fruit and/or vegetable	4 to 6 fluid ounces formula[1] or breast milk[2,3]
Infants 8 months through 11 months	6 to 8 fluid ounces formula[1] or breast milk[2,3] 2 to 4 tablespoons infant cereal[1] 1 to 4 tablespoons fruit and/or vegetable	6 to 8 fluid ounces formula[1] or breast milk[2,3] 2 to 4 tablespoons infant cereal[1] AND/OR 1 to 4 tablespoons meat, fish, poultry, egg yolk, or cooked dry beans or peas OR 1/2 to 2 ounces cheese OR 1 to 4 tablespoons cottage cheese, cheese food, or cheese spread OR 1 to 4 tablespoons fruit and/or vegetable	2 to 4 fluid ounces formula[1], breast milk,[2,3] or fruit juice[5] 0 to 1/2 slice bread[4,6] OR 0 to 2 crackers[4,6]

[1] Infant formula and dry infant cereal shall be iron fortified.

[2] It is recommended that breast milk be served in place of formula from birth through 11 months.

[3] For some breastfed infants who regularly consume less than the minimum amount of breast milk per feeding, a serving of less than the minimum amount of breast milk may be offered, with additional breast milk if the infant is still hungry.

[4] A serving of this component shall be optional.

[5] Fruit juice shall be full strength.

[6] Bread and bread alternatives shall be made from whole-grain or enriched meal or flour.

* breast milk is a commonly used term for human milk.

Source: Appendix P, Child and Adult Care Food Program, Child Care Infant Meal Pattern, *Caring for Our Children.*

requires it (such as reflux) do not put solids in a bottle—the baby may consume too many calories and experience delay in handling solid foods properly. After the ingredients in them have been introduced as cereals, food such as bread, crackers, and dry cereals can be offered as finger foods with vigilant adults watching for choking.

- Add more finger foods (such as meat and cheese tidbits, cooked or soft vegetable strips, and fruit sections) at 8 to 10 months to encourage self-feeding. All foods should be easy for the baby to gum and small enough to swallow whole.

- Introduce more table foods at about 9 months to supplement the protein provided by human milk or formula. An adult should always sit with the child, both for social interaction and to be alert for possible choking.

    —Strain, chop, or cut cooked turkey, chicken, lean hamburger, or fish into small pieces to make chewing easier.

    —Serve cooked, mashed dried beans or peas for additional protein.

    —Offer eggs (scrambled, hard-boiled, or in other foods) after children are 9 months old. Before then, eggs (especially the whites) may promote development of egg allergies.

    —Offer a variety of 100% fruit juices (dilute by mixing 1 part juice with 1 part water). Avoid juice drinks that are mostly water and sugar. Offer juice only from a cup and never from a bottle.

    —Offer plain water during and between meals, especially during hot weather. Children need to learn to drink unflavored beverages.

Beginning whole cow's milk

Provide human milk or formula, which are particularly nutritious and more digestible, to infants until they reach at least 12 months of age. Whole cow's milk can be introduced after 12 months. Whole milk contains the nutrients toddlers need for brain and nerve development. Do not serve low-fat or skim milk until 2 years of age because these milk products have too few calories and too much protein for babies. Infants who are fed low-fat or skim milk may not consume enough calories.

Ask parents to discuss their child's diet with their pediatrician, nurse, and/or nutritionist.

Avoiding baby-bottle tooth decay

Do not allow infants or toddlers to drink from a bottle while lying down, to go to bed with a bottle, or to walk around with a bottle or sippy cup. Formula, milk, juice, and sweetened drinks contain sugars that feed bacteria on the teeth. The bacteria release chemicals that can decay existing or erupting teeth, creating a condition known as nursing bottle mouth. This may lead to early loss of teeth, particularly the front upper and lower teeth. As a result, the child may not be able to chew food properly and crowding may occur in the adult teeth.

Children who drink their bottles lying down also are prone to ear infections and choking. If parents want an infant to take a bottle to bed, fill it with plain water and encourage the child to drink the bottle before lying down.

Weaning

Weaning is the process of replacing the bottle or breast with a cup. The *right time* to wean is whenever works best for the mother and the baby. Most toddlers are ready to be completely weaned from the bottle or breast sometime during the second year, usually by 18 months of age. Weaning can be accomplished by gradually offering more fluids in a cup at meals and between meals.

A cup can be introduced around 6 to 8 months of age. While cups with a spout top are less messy and convenient, a cup without a spout is more effective in teaching children how to drink without sucking. Gradually replace naptime and bedtime bottles and nursings with soothing and relaxing activities such as reading stories, rocking, or singing lullabies.

Feeding Toddlers

A toddler's growth rate slows down during the period from 18 months to 3 years. As a result, a toddler eats less. Toddlers are demanding and energetic by nature. As they explore and gain control over themselves and their environment, they experience success and become more independent. They begin to take more responsibility for what and how much they eat. For example, they may go on food jags, eating only a few foods or going through periods when they seem to eat almost nothing at all.

Caregivers and the families are responsible for what children are offered to eat, as well as where, when, and how food is offered. But toddlers determine whether they eat what is offered. The role of adults is to help the child establish positive attitudes toward eating and to ensure that a nutritionally adequate diet is offered. You can help toddlers

Figure 5.2. Meal Pattern Requirements for Children Age 1 through 12

AGE	Children 1-2 Years of Age	Children 3-5 Years of Age	Children 6-12 Years of Age
BREAKFAST			
Milk *	1/2 cup	3/4 cup	1 cup
Vegetable or Fruit or Juice (100%)	1/4 cup	1/2 cup	1/2 cup
Grains/Breads (enriched or whole grain)	1/2 slice* (or 1/2 serving)	1/2 slice* (or 1/2 serving)	1 slice* (or 1 serving)
- or cold dry cereal	1/4 cup (or 1/3 oz.)	1/3 cup (or 1/2 oz.)	3/4 cup (or 1 oz.)
- or cooked cereal	1/4 cup	1/4 cup	1/2 cup
SNACK (select two of the following four components)			
Milk *	1/2 cup	1/2 cup	1 cup
Vegetable or Fruit or Juice (100%)**	1/2 cup	1/2 cup	3/4 cup
Meat or meat alternative	1/2 ounce	1/2 ounce	1 ounce
- or yogurt (plain or sweetened)**	2 oz (or 1/4 cup)	2 oz (or 1/4 cup)	4 oz (or 1/2 cup)
Grains/Breads (enriched or whole grain)	1/2 slice* (or 1/2 serving)	1/2 slice* (or 1/2 serving)	1 slice* (or 1 serving)
LUNCH/SUPPER			
Milk *	1/2 cup	3/4 cup	1 cup
Meat or poultry or fish	1 ounce	1 1/2 ounce	2 ounces
- or cheese	1 ounce	1 1/2 ounces	2 ounces
- or cottage cheese, cheese food, or cheese spread	2 ounces (1/4 cup)	3 ounces (3/8 cup)	4 ounces (1/2 cup)
- or egg	1 egg	1 egg	1 egg
- or cooked dry beans or peas	1/4 cup	3/8 cup	1/2 cup
- or peanut butter, soynut butter or nut or seed butters	2 Tablespoons	3 Tablespoons	4 Tablespoons
- or peanuts, soynuts, tree nuts or seeds	1/2 ounce	3/4 ounce	1 ounce
- or yogurt	4 ounces (or 1/2 cup)	6 ounces (or 3/4 cup)	8 ounces (or 1 cup)
- or an equivalent quantity of any combination of the above meat/meat alternative			
Vegetables and/or Fruits (2 or More)	1/4 cup (total)	1/2 cup (total)	3/4 cup (total)
Grains/Breads (enriched or whole grain)	1/2 slice* (or 1/2 serving)	1/2 slice* (or 1/2 serving)	1 slice* (or 1 serving)
POINTS TO REMEMBER: • Keep menu production records. • The required amount of each food must be served. • Use full-strength (100%) juice.	* Or an equivalent serving of an acceptable grains/breads such as cornbread, biscuits, rolls, muffins, etc., made of whole grain or enriched meal or flour, or a serving of cooked enriched or whole grain rice or macaroni or other pasta products. ** For snack, juice or yogurt may not be served when milk is served as the only other component.		

* Dry/reconstituted milk is not acceptable.

Source: Appendix Q, Child and Adult Care Food Program, Meal Pattern Requirements for Children Ages 1 through 12 Years, *Caring for Our Children*. Reference: U.S. Department of Agriculture, *Building Blocks for Fun and Healthy Meals: A Menu Planner for the Child and Adult Care Food Program*.

become independent by allowing them to select from a variety of acceptable foods. Be reassured that most toddlers are well-nourished if a variety of nutritious foods is available and they are continuing to grow normally. Observe how energetic toddlers are, and how they grow, play, and eat.

How much is enough?

When too much food is on a plate, a child may feel overwhelmed and not even try to eat. A good rule to follow is to offer a portion consisting of 3 to 2 of a usual adult portion, or 1 tablespoon per year of age, whichever seems more appropriate. Give less than you think toddlers will eat and let them ask for seconds. You can use the food components guide (Figure 5.2). Note that these are usual amounts for a nutritionally adequate diet and are not intended to limit the amount toddlers eat.

Daily variation is normal in type of foods and calories consumed by toddlers. Children 1 to 3 years of age consume approximately 1000 to 1300 calories per day (some days less, some days more). If you are concerned about whether a toddler is eating a nutritionally balanced diet, ask the family to seek advice from a pediatrician.

The eating environment

A pleasant, relaxed eating environment helps toddlers develop positive attitudes about food. Establish regular mealtimes and snacktimes. Prior to a meal, try to help toddlers relax and settle down. If children are tired or overstimulated from play, they may not feel like eating. Make sure toddlers sit at a comfortable height in relation to the table top. Their feet should touch the floor or a foot rest because it is

harder to adjust body position for competent eating without feet on a firm surface.

Use plates and utensils appropriate to children's sizes and skills. Offer toddlers silverware, but don't insist that they use it. If you allow toddlers to touch, smell, and explore food, they are more likely to eat it. Toddlers can be finicky about the appearance of their food and often prefer to have different foods separated on their plate. Helping toddlers develop positive attitudes about eating is much more important than achieving fine-tuned table manners.

Encourage toddlers to try new foods, and occasionally praise them for eating well. Don't praise children for eating large quantities because this interferes with self-regulation. Serve small portions, and suggest (once or twice, but do not badger) that a child try just one bite.

Basic Nutrition Facts

Snacks

Snacks are an important part of a well-balanced diet. They are especially important for preschoolers because their stomachs are small and they usually can't eat enough in three meals to meet energy needs or satisfy appetites. Within two or three hours after a meal, most young children will be hungry. Snacktime must provide nutrients missing from the rest of the day's food. The challenge is to help preschoolers eat nutritious snacks and to do so at appropriate times during the day. Good snacks are those that provide essential nutrients. They can substitute for a meal that the child may decide to skip.

Serve nutritious snacks that contain some protein, some fat, and some carbohydrate to be satisfying and tasty. A list of nutritious snack ideas is provided in Figure 5.3. Snacktimes are good opportunities for children to try new foods. Avoid such commercial snack foods as chips, sweet cakes, candies, and fruit drinks; these have limited nutritional value for the calories they contain. Unsalted pretzels are acceptable as a bread substitute, but avoid the salted type.

Appetite

After infancy, children's appetites decrease. A small appetite may be a signal that a child is tired, excited, ill, or in strange surroundings. Many preschoolers have unstable eating habits. Children may be less hungry because they are in a slow

Figure 5.3. Ideas for Nutritious Snacks

Fruits and vegetables

- **Apple sandwich**—Slice an apple, spread peanut butter on the slices, and make a sandwich. Or put a piece of cheese between apple slices.
- **Yogurt sundae**—Let children make their own—just supply bowls, plain yogurt, cut-up fruit, and toppings of chopped nuts, sunflower seeds, wheat germ, or dry cereal.
- **Fruit kabobs**—Skewer fresh fruit and low-fat cheese cubes, pitted dates, or prunes on long straws or long toothpicks (for older children). Serve kabobs with a dip made with plain, low-fat yogurt sprinkled with cinnamon or a few drops of vanilla flavoring, or well-stirred, mixed fruit yogurt.
- **Fruit juice surprises**—Divide 1 cup of cut up fruit (apple, banana, orange, strawberries) into four glasses. Add 3 cups of unsweetened fruit juice and chill.
- **Veggie kabobs**—Skewer (see note above) cut up fresh vegetables such as cherry tomatoes, zucchini, carrots, cucumbers, green peppers, mushrooms, and low-fat cheese cubes. Serve with salad dressing or a dip made with mashed beans, yogurt, or cottage cheese and seasoned with herbs.
- **Toss a salad**—Or invite children to a homemade salad bar. Set out dishes of cut up veggies for children to create their own salads.
- **Celery stuff-its**—Fill celery with part-skim ricotta cheese mixed with unsweetened crushed pineapple. Or, fill celery with peanut butter and add a few raisins (this is called "Ants on a Log").
- **Lettuce roll**—Spread tuna or chicken salad, peanut butter, or low-fat ricotta cheese on a lettuce leaf, roll it up, and eat.

Freezer delights

- **Frozen dixies**—Freeze one of the following in a paper cup with a Popsicle stick: applesauce, crushed pineapple, fruit yogurt (mixed well or made with fruit juices).
- **Frozen strawberry yogurt pops**—Blend 1 cup of frozen strawberries until smooth. Mix the strawberries with 1 cup of plain, low-fat yogurt and 3 to 5 tablespoons of honey. Pour into paper cups with a Popsicle stick in the center and freeze 1 to 2 hours until firm. Remove cup from frozen yogurt and serve. Makes seven pops.
- **Banana pops**—Mix 2 cups of low-fat, plain yogurt with 1 cup of mashed banana, 1 teaspoon of vanilla, and ½ cup of chopped walnuts (optional). Pour into six 4-oz. paper cups, insert Popsicle sticks in the center, and freeze until firm. Remove cup from frozen pop and serve.

- **Banana rockets**—Coat peeled, ripe bananas with orange juice or orange juice concentrate (to prevent discoloration), wrap in foil or plastic wrap, and freeze. Or, roll chilled, juice-coated bananas in chopped nuts or granola, press firmly to coat, and freeze until firm.

Homemade convenience snacks

- **Trail mix**—Combine dried fruits and dry cereal together, and divide into plastic bags or paper cups.
- **Cheese popcorn**—Make popcorn and sprinkle with grated Parmesan cheese. Add melted butter or margarine if desired.
- **Going crackers**—Crackers and cheese, crackers and peanut butter (with or without jelly), crackers and dip . . . just be sure to choose your crackers carefully. Crackers that are lower in fat or sodium include Melba toast, matzo, rice cakes, Wasa, Rye Krisp, bread sticks, unsalted saltines, zwieback, and graham crackers.
- **Yummo wrap-ups**—Have children make their own using flour tortillas spread with peanut butter, dried fruit, and raisins—ideal for hikes. Or use part-skim ricotta cheese and cinnamon or jam.
- **Nachos**—Cut corn tortillas into six triangles and top with grated mozzarella cheese. Place in the oven (or toaster oven) at 350° to crisp the tortillas and melt cheese. Serve with salsa.
- **Natural soda pop**—Combine half a glass of fruit juice (orange, grape, apple, or pineapple) with half a glass of club soda or seltzer. Add ice and enjoy.

Blender snacks

- **Blender basics**—For a shake, blend 1 cup of plain yogurt, 1 cup of chopped fruit (strawberries, bananas, etc.), and ½ cup of fruit juice (orange, pineapple, or grape). The shakes will be thicker if made with frozen fruit.
- **Melon cooler**—In blender, mix 1½ cups of ice cubes, 1½ cups of cubed watermelon, honeydew, or cantaloupe, and ½ teaspoon of lemon juice until smooth. Serve immediately. Makes 2½ cups.
- **Ambrosia shake**—In blender, mix four sliced, ripe bananas, ½ cup of orange juice, ¼ teaspoon of vanilla, 4 cups of low-fat, skim, or reconstituted nonfat, dry milk. Makes six servings.
- **Fruit soup**—In blender, combine ¼ cup of orange juice, ½ of a small banana, ½ of an apple, 1 teaspoon of lemon juice, 2 tablespoons of plain, low-fat yogurt, ¼ cup of strawberries, a dash of cinnamon, and a dash of dried mint. Chill before serving. Makes three ½-cup servings.

Source: Reprinted with permission from Barbara Storper, Massachusetts Nutrition Resource Center, 150 Tremont Street, Boston, MA 02111.

growth stage or are practicing newly discovered independence. Be aware of any change in a child's appetite that lasts longer than a few days, and talk to parents or caregivers to try to find the reason.

Variety is essential

Because no one food contains all the nutrients our bodies need, caregivers should serve children a variety of foods, such as fruits, vegetables, protein foods, and unsweetened cereals. Preschoolers generally enjoy eating the same foods as adults.

Adults also can help children develop good food habits by offering both different foods and the same foods prepared in different ways (for example, cooked carrots, carrot salad). Gradually introduce foods to increase food acceptance. Pay attention to what foods children eat and encourage them to eat foods from different food groups.

Food Habits Are Learned

Food habits and the ability to eat wisely are *learned!* Children are great imitators and often mimic actions of people around them. New foods will be accepted more readily if you follow these guidelines:

• Introduce only one new food at a time.
• Serve the new food with familiar foods.
• Serve only small amounts of the new food.
• Introduce new foods only when children are hungry.
• Talk about the new food—taste, color, texture.
• Let children see you eating and enjoying the new food!
• Encourage children to taste the new food. If they reject it, accept the refusal and try again in a few weeks. As foods become more familiar, they are more readily accepted.
• Find out what is not liked about the rejected food. Often it will be accepted if prepared a different way.

Food as reward or punishment

Sometimes adults are tempted to use food as a reward, pacifier, or punishment. How many times have you heard, "No dessert until you clean your plate"? This implies that dessert is a better part of the meal. Children do need positive encouragement, but using food as a reward places undue emphasis on certain foods. Praise, smiles, or hugs serve just as well. Avoid using food for reasons other than to

satisfy hunger. Desserts should be nutritious so that if the child eats only the dessert, she will have consumed food good for her.

Food Safety

Here are some suggestions that help avoid food-related problems.

• Be aware that foods that are round, hard, small, thick and sticky, smooth, or slippery are a choking hazard and should not be given to children under 4 years of age. Such foods include nuts, hard candy, popcorn, whole grapes, raw peas, dried fruit (other than moist raisins), pretzels, marshmallows, spoonfuls of peanut butter, and chunks of meat larger than can be swallowed whole. If a child chokes while eating, these foods can easily be breathed into the lungs. (Hot dogs may be used only if sliced lengthwise and then cut into bite-size pieces. Since they are usually full of fat and chemicals, hot dogs are a poor food choice for a preschooler.)
• Do not feed honey to children younger than 1 year of age. Honey can cause botulism in infancy. Check food and formula labels to be sure that honey has not been used as a sweetener.
• Cut infant food into chunks smaller than a ¼ inch. Toddler food should be cut into chunks smaller than a ½ inch.
• Do not use Styrofoam cups and plates with children under 4 years old.
• Be sure that at least one staff member knows how to handle a choking episode (see the first aid instructions from the American Academy of Pediatrics publications department). It is common for children learning to eat finger foods to gag and cough. But immediate attention is required if the child chokes—turns blue or cannot make voice sounds.
• Be sure all staff are aware of any children's food allergies and of the emergency steps to be taken should an allergic child consume the problem food. Be especially alert at birthday parties or other occasions when parents may not be aware of the allergy problem. For the safety of some highly allergic children, the offending food may need to be banned from rooms the child ever uses or from the entire facility (see "Food allergies and intolerances" on p. 58).
• Do not allow children to eat while walking, running, playing, lying down, or riding in vehicles.

- Be sure foods brought from home are prepared, transported, stored, and served safely.

Activity and Physical Exercise

Activity has a lot to do with appetite and nutritional status. Active children need more calories than inactive ones; this means that they have a better chance of getting all required nutrients. Adequate physical exercise year-round, preferably on a daily basis, is important to a child's development because it

- stimulates healthy appetites,
- uses calories and maintains muscle tissue,
- improves coordination, and
- encourages children to express themselves and develop social skills.

Common Nutritional Concerns

Fats

There is growing concern about the role of fat in heart disease and controversy about the kind of fat and amount of cholesterol permissible in children's diets. Polyunsaturated and saturated fats are important nutrients to include in the proper ratio. *Polyunsaturated fats* are usually found in liquid vegetable oils that contain essential fatty acids the body cannot manufacture. *Saturated fats,* the solid fats found in beef, pork, lamb, chicken, and dairy products, are the ones to be limited. Some fat from both sources, however, is necessary to maintain the proper balance of fatty acids in the body. Foods such as hot dogs, luncheon meats, and potato chips are high in saturated fat and salt and should be limited in a child's diet.

Sugar

Many factors determine how foods affect children's teeth. The more often children snack on foods containing sugars and starches, the greater the chance for tooth decay. You can easily avoid serving foods high in sugar to children. There is really no reason to sweeten food.

Honey, molasses, raw sugar, and refined sugar all contain the same number of calories. Avoid adding natural or artificial sweeteners to vegetables, fruits, fruit juice, or cereal. Limit empty calorie foods such as candy, sweetened beverages, and refined, sweetened baked goods that provide mainly calories and low levels of essential nutrients.

Salt

Preference for salty foods is learned. Caregivers should not teach the unhealthy salt-craving lesson. High-salt diets may lead to the development of high blood pressure in people with a family background of hypertension (high blood pressure). Reduce salt intake by not salting food at the table, decreasing the amount of salt used in cooking, and limiting salty foods (pickles, canned soups, chips, some crackers,

Figure 5.4. Types of Vegetarian Diets

Diet	FOODS CONSUMED				
	Beef and pork	Fish and poultry	Milk and milk products	Eggs	Vegetables, fruits, breads, cereals, and nuts
Nonvegetarian	X	X	X	X	X
Semi-vegetarian		X	X	X	X
Lacto-ovo-vegetarian			X	X	X
Ovo-vegetarian				X	X
Lacto-vegetarian			X		X
Vegan (total vegetarian)					X

Source: Adapted from Ivens, B.J., & W.B. Weil, *Teddy bears and bean sprouts—The infant and vegetarian nutrition,* 1984, Fremont, MI: Gerber.

Figure 5.5. Dietary Sources of Calcium

EXCELLENT

Yogurt, low-fat or whole milk, plain or fruit flavored

Skim milk

Low-fat milk (1 or 2%)

Buttermilk

Whole milk

Swiss cheese

Sardines, canned with bones

GOOD

Cheeses: cheddar, Muenster, mozzarella, blue

American or Swiss pasteurized process cheese food

Parmesan cheese, grated

Tofu*

Dry skim milk, instant

Mackerel, canned, solid and liquid

Salmon, pink, canned with bones

Collard greens, cooked

FAIR

Blackstrap molasses

Vanilla, soft-serve, frozen dairy products

Figs, dried

Kale, cooked

Mustard greens, cooked

Ice cream, vanilla

Chickpeas, cooked

Broccoli, cooked

Cottage cheese, creamed

*Calcium content of tofu differs according to the processing method. Tofu contains calcium if it is processed with a calcium coagulant such as sulfate. Look on the nutrition label or in the ingredient list. Nigari is a popular tofu coagulant that does *not* contain calcium.

and salted nuts). Remember the hidden sources of salt found in hot dogs, bacon, sausages, condiments, and canned and some frozen foods.

Vegetarian diets

A well-planned vegetarian diet can provide all the nutrients a child needs for growth and activity. Vegetarian diets, often high in fiber and low in cholesterol and saturated fat, have many positive health benefits. However, there is also the possibility that the child who eats a vegetarian diet will not get enough calories.

Vegetarian diets vary. Figure 5.4 describes vegetarian eating patterns. Vegetarian diets that include dairy products and eggs readily provide all the needed nutrients for young children. Vegan or total vegetarian diets that omit all animal protein can be nutritionally inadequate and may not provide enough protein, calcium, iron, zinc, vitamin D, and vitamin B12. These very strict vegetarian diets also may be low in calories due to their high bulk and low fat content. Problems of short stature, low weight, and rickets have occurred in children on very restrictive vegetarian diets.

Legumes, seeds, or nuts, when combined with grains, provide a good protein source. But to get enough protein, children on vegan or strict vegetarian diets need to eat more than children who eat meat, fish, poultry, and cheese. The number of servings from each food group are different for a child eating a vegetarian diet, particularly a vegan diet. Families who wish to have their children follow a vegan diet should be referred to a dietician or nutritionist to ensure that intake of nutrients and calories is adequate for growth.

Milk

If children drink too much milk, they may spoil their appetites for other foods and may develop iron deficiency anemia. Offer water if a child is thirsty. A preschooler needs approximately 16 to 24 ounces (2 to 3 cups) of milk daily. If a child doesn't drink much milk, do not make an issue of it. Left alone, the child will probably go back to drinking milk. Other foods rich in calcium, such as hard cheese and yogurt, can be substituted for milk (see Figure 5.5).

Some children have lactose intolerance, a lack of intestinal enzymes to digest the milk sugar, lactose. This problem can be avoided with special milks, calcium supplements, or use of enzyme preparations before having a milk product. (See "Food allergies and intolerances," page 58.)

Special nutritional problems and special diets

Early childhood programs must follow the instructions of the family and the child's physician in preparing and feeding a special diet. Sometimes special diets are requested for cultural or religious reasons. Where possible, accommodate these requests as long as the child's nutritional needs are met and the preparation does not pose an undue burden for staff. For diets required due to health problems, the child care facility must address the special need just as it must accommodate any child with a disability. Consult a nutritionist for assistance in menu planning and feeding adjustments to meet the child's needs.

Obesity

Obesity is a complex problem with multiple causes. Some combination of overeating, poor food choices, inactivity, social or emotional factors, and genetics is usually responsible. Helping children learn healthy eating and exercise habits is key to preventing obesity. Although an overweight child will not always become an overweight adult, many children who become obese will remain so throughout life. Obesity can significantly affect a child psychologically and emotionally and can result in low self-esteem.

Many young children learn eating and activity patterns that lead to obesity later in life. Using food as a reward or pacifier, force-feeding, providing large portions, and requiring clean plates may contribute to obesity. Physical activity is essential to maintain a normal weight. Surprisingly, inactivity is more likely than calorie intake to result in obesity. TV watching is known to be associated with obesity, probably because of inactivity and inappropriate snacking.

The goal of weight management for children is to limit further weight gain. Children will grow slimmer as they grow into their weight. Actual weight loss may not be recommended as children need adequate nutrients and calories for growth. Nutritious meals and snacks are essential to good weight management.

Early childhood programs can manage and prevent obesity in young children by taking the following measures.

- Encourage children to be physically active.
- Have designated mealtimes, and designated eating places, with eating and social interaction during the meal as the focus. Do not let children eat while watching television or doing other activities. (Television viewing should be no more than 2 hours per day in any case.)
- Limit high-calorie foods (high in fat, sugar, or both).
- Limit excessive drinking of sweetened beverages such as fruit drinks, powdered or syrup-based drink mixes, and chocolate-flavored milk that add many extra calories. Commercial chocolate milk often is made with skim milk so that the calories come from the fat in the chocolate, and not from the milk, and chocolate is a stimulant like caffeine.

Frequent use of chocolate teaches children to look for it as a regular part of their diets. A child's thirst should be satisfied with water after the proper amount of milk is consumed.

- Use low-fat or skim milk with children older than 2.
- Put food on small plates.
- Provide high-fiber, filling, crunchy foods.
- Limit eating to small meals at designated eating times (three meals plus two snacks, preplanned for portion control and nutrient balance).
- Provide lots of nonfood rewards. Plan activities as the centerpiece for birthday parties, holidays, and other celebrations, rather than special foods.
- Help children learn to deal with emotions or stress without turning to food.
- Remember, *your* food habits and attitudes influence those of the children. Be a good role model.

Iron deficiency

Anemia occurs when too little blood is produced or too much blood is lost. Barring blood loss, the usual reason for anemia is an inadequate intake of iron. This problem occurs most commonly during periods of rapid growth, such as early infancy and adolescence. With iron fortification of bread, cereal, and pasta, anemia from nutritional deficiency is unusual after infancy. Here are some things child care providers can do to prevent iron-deficiency anemia:

- Encourage children to consume a varied, well-balanced diet that includes iron-rich foods.
- Provide iron-rich foods at meals and snacks. Good sources of iron include liver, dried beans and peas, lentils, beef, pork, lamb, whole wheat and enriched breads, and cereal products. Raisins and peanut butter also contain a small amount of iron. Iron from animal sources is absorbed better than iron from plant sources.
- Serve iron-rich foods with a source of vitamin C. Vitamin C increases the body's ability to use iron. The amount of iron absorbed from plant sources increases significantly when these foods are combined with food high in vitamin C. For example, with chili serve spinach, broccoli, or tomato slices; with split-pea soup serve half an orange, cantaloupe cubes, or strawberries. These fruits and vegetables also provide fiber.
- Limit milk consumption to 24 ounces per day and assure adequate intake of other foods, particularly iron-containing foods.

Failure-to-thrive

Some children do not grow properly. They are small or thin for their age; their height may be short for their age, or their weight may be low for their height. They may tire easily, be inattentive, disinterested in eating, and undernourished. This complex syndrome, known as failure-to-thrive (FTT), may be due to medical, nutritional, or psychosocial factors.

When you suspect FTT, immediately refer the child for a complete medical, nutritional, and social evaluation. Consult a nutritionist who can plan a nutritionally appropriate diet and support the family, child, and your program during the critical period of growth. Be available to assist the family with carrying out the recommended treatment plan. If you have a child who has been diagnosed in the past as having FTT, watch for signs of poor growth closely, even when the crisis is past.

Sometimes FTT can signal child abuse or neglect. In these cases, the child care provider should be alert to other possible signs of child abuse/neglect (see Chapter 11) that would require immediate reporting to child protective services.

Food allergies and intolerances

Infants and young children sometimes have food allergies or are intolerant of certain foods. An allergic reaction occurs when a child is sensitive to a particular food and the immune system produces increased amounts of antibodies. The allergic reaction can be avoided only by avoiding the food.

The most common food to cause allergic reactions is peanuts, but other common causes are tree nuts, eggs, cow's milk protein, wheat, fish, shellfish, citrus fruits, and berries. Some of these products are present in very small quantities in ordinary foods where you might not suspect them to be present. For example, peanut oil is used in some spaghetti sauces. When a child has a food allergy, scrutinize every food and read every food label very carefully.

A food intolerance is present when a person has some metabolic factors (for example, lack of an enzyme or chemical) that make it difficult or impossible to digest or use certain food. Sometimes foods can be modified so that the child can tolerate them. Intolerance to the sugar in cow's milk (lactose) is a common problem in infants and children. Soy formulas are an alternative to cow's milk or regular formula for children with milk allergies or lactose intolerance. Sometimes the intolerance is relative, affected by the amount of the food the child takes. Some children can have a small amount of the food to which they are intolerant without difficulty.

When allergic children eat or even touch a surface that has a small amount of a food to which they are sensitive, they may develop symptoms such as diarrhea, vomiting, abdominal pain, rash, irritability, breathing problems—and even death. Reactions may be immediate or delayed, and symptoms may be mild to severe.

When a child in child care has a food allergy or intolerance,

- confirm the nature of the food problem with the child's clinician and obtain a clear set of instructions to follow routinely and in the event of inadvertent exposure of the child to the problem food
- post the child's food allergies prominently in the areas the child will use
- read labels to identify hidden sources of the problem foods or substances
- work with families to find acceptable substitutes for problem foods
- carefully plan menus with a nutritionist to ensure adequate nutrition, particularly if a child has multiple food allergies or is allergic to other major food groups
- plan with staff and families as necessary to protect the allergic child from exposure to the problem food.

Hyperactivity

Hyperactivity is not caused by food allergies or food intolerance. However, if a child is hyperactive *and* has food allergies or food intolerance, inappropriate behavior may be exacerbated. Additive-free diets have not been found to be of value in the treatment of hyperactivity. Eliminating artificial food colorings and salicylates (aspirin-like compounds) does not harm children and may improve a diet's nutritional value, but does not affect the hyperactivity itself. Any diet should be carefully planned along with appropriate medical and psychological treatment. Consult a nutritionist to ensure nutritional adequacy.

Feeding children who have other special needs

Children with special needs have the same care and feeding needs as all children. Often these basic needs are overlooked in the concern for the disability. Children may have nutritional problems (such as poor food intake, inability to chew or swallow normally, inadequate weight gain, short stature,

Figure 5.6. Food Guide Pyramid for Young Children

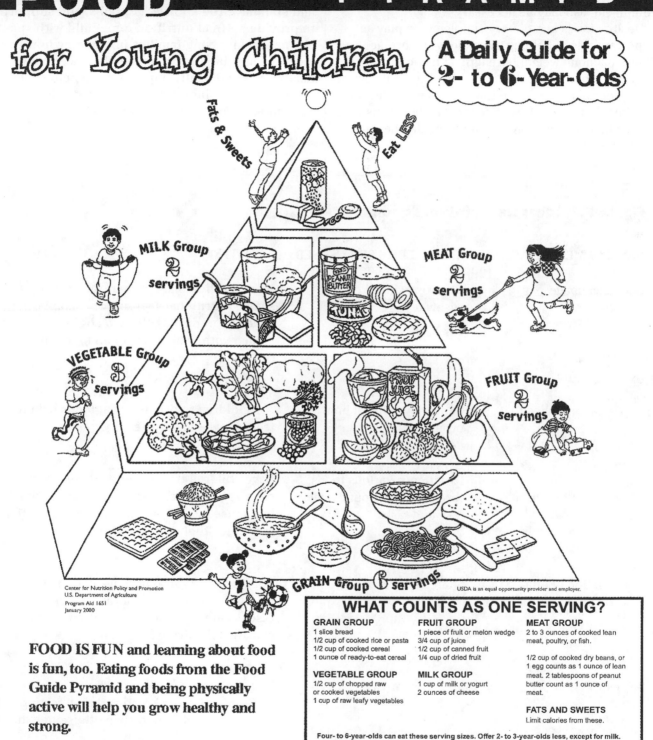

FOOD Guide PYRAMID
for Young Children

A Daily Guide for 2- to 6-Year-Olds

Fats & Sweets — **Eat LESS**

MILK Group 2 servings

MEAT Group 2 servings

VEGETABLE Group 3 servings

FRUIT Group 2 servings

GRAIN Group 6 servings

Center for Nutrition Policy and Promotion
U.S. Department of Agriculture
Program Aid 1651
January 2000

USDA is an equal opportunity provider and employer.

FOOD IS FUN and learning about food is fun, too. Eating foods from the Food Guide Pyramid and being physically active will help you grow healthy and strong.

WHAT COUNTS AS ONE SERVING?

GRAIN GROUP
1 slice bread
1/2 cup of cooked rice or pasta
1/2 cup of cooked cereal
1 ounce of ready-to-eat cereal

VEGETABLE GROUP
1/2 cup of chopped raw or cooked vegetables
1 cup of raw leafy vegetables

FRUIT GROUP
1 piece of fruit or melon wedge
3/4 cup of juice
1/2 cup of canned fruit
1/4 cup of dried fruit

MILK GROUP
1 cup of milk or yogurt
2 ounces of cheese

MEAT GROUP
2 to 3 ounces of cooked lean meat, poultry, or fish.

1/2 cup of cooked dry beans, or 1 egg counts as 1 ounce of lean meat. 2 tablespoons of peanut butter count as 1 ounce of meat.

FATS AND SWEETS
Limit calories from these.

Four- to 6-year-olds can eat these serving sizes. Offer 2- to 3-year-olds less, except for milk.
Two- to 6-year-old children need a total of 2 servings from the milk group each day.

Source: U.S. Department of Agriculture Center for Nutrition Policy and Promotion; Appendix O, *Caring for Our Children.*

obesity, or iron deficiency anemia) *and* behavioral problems associated with eating, placing them at nutritional risk. Infants or children with special needs may have feeding needs that require more patience, time, and understanding than usual. Special adaptive equipment also may be necessary.

Healthy foods and dietary supplements play an important role in helping the child with chronic illness maintain weight, strength, and energy and fight infections. Some children with chronic illness or other special needs can follow a normal diet most of the time. During bouts with fever, diarrhea, nausea, or weight loss, they may require a special diet and food supplements.

Whatever the disease, disorder, or disability, good nutrition always contributes to optimal growth and development and can decrease or prevent some debilitating effects. Use the services of a nutritionist or dietician to ensure that families and staff have the knowledge, skills, and support to provide optimal nutrition for a child with special needs. Involving families in planning how to meet the special nutritional needs of a child with a disability is especially important. To help solve any complex problems, involve pediatricians, occupational and physical therapists, social workers, or other health professionals.

Figure 5.7. Ideas for Nutrition Education

DEVELOPMENTAL AREAS	KNOWLEDGE/SKILLS USED	ACTIVITY
Good self-image	Develop skills to choose wisely	Have children plan, prepare, and serve simple nutritional snacks. For example, have children prepare "Ants on a Log"—celery stuffed with peanut butter and topped with raisins.
Appreciation of health	Gain knowledge of how food promotes growth and development	Ask children to discuss what foods help their teeth grow and stay healthy.
Enjoyment of food through all the senses	Experience various foods through sight, sound, smell, feel, and taste	Have children try to identify different fruits such as a banana, orange, and apple using one sense (sound, smell, feel, taste) at a time and check their answers through sight.
Appreciation of ethnic/ cultural background	Share cultural background	Choose the cultural heritage of one or more children for a day's meals and snacks. Discuss at mealtimes how factors such as climate help shape food habits.
Self-expression	Foster creativity	Have children try various whole grain breads by first baking the bread and then tasting it. Encourage children to shape the dough in different ways.

Source: Wanamaker, N., K. Hearn, & S. Richarz, *More than graham crackers: Nutrition education and food preparation with young children,* NAEYC, 1979 (out of print).

Dietary Guidelines for Young Children

The U.S. Department of Agriculture (USDA) and the Department of Health and Human Services (DHHS) publish dietary guidelines intended to promote the health of all Americans, age 2 years and older. The Food Guide Pyramid for Young Children (Figure 5.6), a daily guide for children 2 to 6 years old, is available online at **www.usda.gov/cnpp/KidsPyra** or from the USDA Center for Nutrition Policy and Promotion, Food Guide Pyramid for Young Children, 1120 20th Street, NW, Suite 200, North Lobby, Washington, D.C. 20036.

Using the types and portions of foods recommended in the Food Guide Pyramid for Young Children provides a sturdy foundation for planning meals for children. In addition, use these guidelines as the basis of any nutrition education activities conducted for children, staff, or families.

Nutrition Education

It cannot be overemphasized that early experiences with food have a strong impact on a child's future eating habits and health. Poor diet is associated with the development of many chronic diseases in this country: heart disease, stroke, high blood pressure, some forms of cancer, diabetes, and tooth decay. Nutrition education significantly enriches the lives of children and provides a means for learning about their life and culture. Children who understand themselves and their environment develop a positive self-image, an essential ingredient for effective learning of any kind. Nutrition education teaches young children how to be selective about food and combats misinformation from television advertising. *Dietary habits are established early in life. The habits children learn during their preschool years will significantly affect their future health.*

Figure 5.7 identifies ideas for nutrition education activities that foster the development of positive eating practices and enhance a child's emotional and psychological growth. These learning experiences can be easily integrated into daily routines. Eating together at mealtime and snacktime or during special occasions is an opportunity for children to socialize. Visits to farmers' markets or nearby farms put children in touch with their neighborhoods and creates an awareness of where and how food is grown and sold in places other than a supermarket.

The cultural and ethnic customs of our society influence the food we eat and many mealtime traditions. In fact, cultural heritage may determine whether a particular food is eaten, regardless of its nutritional value. Including a wide variety of experiences with food and traditions of other cultures can be interesting and fun for children.

Involve families

Family involvement is essential so that children receive reinforced messages at home. Families and teachers need to educate themselves and collaborate to be sure children receive the types and amounts of food necessary for good nutrition. Here are some suggestions to involve families.

- Ask them to assist in planning menus. If they are interested, schedule an educational meeting on the principles of good nutrition involved in menu planning for young children.
- Include nutrition articles in your newsletter or post announcements about your nutrition education activities. Ask families for ideas for future programs and invite them to participate in classroom activities. Ask them to share creative meal and snack ideas. Have a contest for the favorite idea.
- Send printed menus home with children to show what meals and snacks are planned. Ask families to share their ideas for interesting, developmentally appropriate, and safe foods that can be brought to child care.
- Invite families to attend a potluck dinner with a special ethnic food unique to their culture.
- Talk with families about any eating or nutritional problems you notice. Make appropriate referrals to community nutrition programs and health professionals; provide regular progress reports.
- Sponsor educational programs on nutrition and food consumer issues. Use the USDA dietary guidelines (Figure 5.6 and Figures 5.1 and 5.2) as a starting point.
- Help families understand how they can foster positive eating habits at home. Encourage good eating behaviors such as always sitting down for snacks and meals.
- Remind families about ways to involve their child with food in the home, such as
—helping prepare food with age-appropriate, safe kitchen tasks
—sharing in cleanup activities
—encouraging talk about food.
- Make available a list of community food and nutrition services, including school nutrition

programs, food stamps, WIC (Supplemental Nutrition Program for Women, Infants and Children), Commodity Supplemental Food Program (CSFP), and emergency feeding agencies.

Community Nutrition Resources

Familiarity with community nutrition programs, local nutritionists, and emergency food agencies will help you make appropriate referrals when necessary.

Child and Adult Care Food Program

The Child and Adult Care Food Program (CACFP) is a federally sponsored program that helps provide nutritious meals to economically qualified children enrolled in child care centers and family child care programs throughout the country. It also introduces young children to many different types of foods and helps teach them good eating habits. Further, the CACFP provides excellent materials and training for food service staff and nutrition education materials for staff and families. While the training may be available only to participating child care programs, the materials can be used by any child care program.

The CACFP is funded and administered by the U.S. Department of Agriculture but in most cases is operated by the state's department of education or health. The program is limited to public and private nonprofit organizations providing licensed or approved nonresidential child care services. Some private, for-profit programs qualify under certain circumstances. Child care and after-school programs are eligible either independently or through a sponsoring organization that accepts final administrative and financial responsibility for the program. Family (home-based) child care programs must participate under a sponsoring organization; they cannot enter the CACFP directly. All participating institutions must serve meals that meet USDA nutritional standards.

Child care providers may receive reimbursement for up to three meals per child per day; one of them must be a snack. Payments are generally limited to the number of meals served to enrolled children multiplied by the appropriate rates for reimbursement. The rate of payment varies according to children's family size and income. Some state-administering agencies base payment on the maximum rates or actual costs, whichever is less. Meals served by home-based providers are paid for at different rates for each type of meal. The sponsoring organization must pass the full food-service payment to the provider, unless the organization provides part of the food service. Providers receive payment for meals served to their own children only when (1) their children meet the family size and income standards and participate in the CACFP, and (2) other nonresident enrolled children are present and participating in the program. Separate administrative funds are provided to sponsoring organizations based on the number of homes in the program they administer.

To obtain information about participation in or access to the educational resources of the CACFP in your area, write or call Director, Child Nutrition Division, Food and Nutrition Services, U.S. Department of Agriculture, 3101 Park Center Drive, Alexandria, VA 22302 (703-756-3590). You can also visit the USDA Website at **www.fns.usda.gov/fns**.

Food Distribution Program

Through the Food Distribution Program, the USDA purchases commodity foods, including surplus foods from U.S. markets, and distributes them to state agencies for use by eligible local agencies. The foods go to schools and institutions participating in the child nutrition programs (school lunch, school breakfast, summer feeding, and after-school programs); to nutrition programs serving the elderly; to low-income families on Indian reservations; to low-income pregnant, breastfeeding, and postpartum women and then infants, and children; and to soup kitchens, food banks, and disaster feeding organizations.

Licensed child care programs are eligible to participate in the food distribution program. Programs enrolled in CACFP automatically receive an application for the Food Distribution Program. If their applications are approved, they can elect to receive commodities or cash.

Food Stamp Program

The Food Stamp Program helps low-income households purchase the foods they need for good health. Participating families get coupons or an EBT card that they use to purchase food at authorized stores. People can apply at their local food stamp office.

Special Supplemental Food Program for Women, Infants and Children

The Special Supplemental Nutrition Program for Women, Infants and Children, commonly known as WIC, is a federally funded program that provides supplemental foods, nutrition education, and access to health services to low-income pregnant, postpartum, and breastfeeding women and then infants and children up to age 5 who are at nutrition risk. Federal funds are provided to WIC state agencies (health departments or comparable agencies) to pay for foods, nutrition counseling, and education and administrative costs.

Most WIC state agencies issue monthly checks or vouchers to participants to purchase specific foods designed to supplement their diets. A few agencies distribute the WIC foods through warehouses or deliver the foods to participants' homes. The foods provided are high in one or more of the target nutrients (protein, calcium, iron, and vitamins A and C) frequently lacking in the diets of the target population. A variety of food packages are provided and may include iron-fortified infant formula and infant cereal, iron-fortified adult cereal, vitamin C-rich fruit or vegetable juice, milk, eggs, cheese, peanut butter, dried beans/peas, tuna fish, and carrots. Special therapeutic infant formulas and medical foods are provided when prescribed by a physician for a specified medical reason.

WIC has historically promoted breast milk as the optimal infant food, unless medically not advised. WIC mothers choosing to breastfeed receive counseling, breastfeeding educational materials, and sometimes equipment and supplies such as breast pumps. Mothers who are exclusively breastfeeding receive an enhanced food package.

Team Nutrition Training Grants

Team Nutrition Training Grants are competitively awarded to states for dissemination of nutrition information to children and for inservice training of teachers and food service personnel. State agencies that administer the National School Lunch Program or the CACFP are eligible to apply. In turn, they may award a portion of the grants to local school food authorities or CACFP sponsors' agencies. Contact your state agency to see if your program is eligible for a subgrant or minigrant for training your food service staff or for providing nutrition education to children and their families. Visit **www.fns.usda.gov/tn** to see the many resources available.

Expanded Food and Nutrition Education Program

EFNEP serves limited-resource youth and families with young children. It is regarded as the nutrition education component of the Food Stamp Program. Home economists and nutrition specialists teach paraprofessionals who, in turn, teach participants about food purchasing and budgeting, storage, preparation, healthy foods, meal planning, and sanitation. For more information, contact your local county extension office, your state land-grant university, or the Extension Service at the USDA, Washington, DC 20250.

Running a Food Service

Operation of a food service program for young children involves menu planning, food purchasing and preparation, food service, and a number of issues related to environmental health, sanitation, and infectious disease control. Even if all foods served are brought from home, the program is running a food service. Many issues must be addressed when food is brought from home:

- selection of foods
- preparation of foods
- transportation of foods
- labeling of foods and containers
- safe storage in child care until foods are served
- method of serving the foods to children at the time foods are to be eaten
- sanitation in handling foods and food containers brought from home.

For more detail about how to run a food service, child care providers should consult other references. The National Child Care and Adult Food Program has excellent materials. Visit the CACFP nutrition resources online at **www.nal.usda.gov/childcare/index.html** for recipes, information on preparing nutritious meals, and food safety. Also, chapter 4 of *Caring for Our Children* provides information, includ-

Figure 5.8. Menu Planning Worksheet

Use with USDA recommended meal and snack pattern	Monday	Tuesday	Wednesday	Thursday	Friday
Breakfast					
Morning snack					
Lunch or supper					
Afternoon snack					

ing current references for more detailed guidance on running a food service. Tables listing meal patterns, food storage guidelines, food service cleaning routines from the appendix of *Caring for Our Children* are included in this manual for convenience. They are handy references for centers and home-based programs that offer food service (see Figures 5.1, 5.2, 5.7, 5.8, and 5.9).

Menu planning

Plan your menus around the nutritional and developmental needs of young children by using the meal pattern developed by the USDA Child and Adult Care Food Program as a minimum standard (see Figures 5.1 and 5.2). Figure 5.8 provides a sample menu planning worksheet to translate the USDA recommended meal pattern into meals and snacks. You may find it helpful in menu planning to use the Team Nutrition Website (**www.fns.usda.gov/tn**), which provides "Building Blocks," a menu planner for centers, and "Menu Magic" for use in family child care homes. Prepare weekly written menus and post them for staff and families. Vary menus by season and avoid repeating weekly menus more than once a month. Provide nutritious snacks mid-morning or mid-afternoon for children who attend less than four hours. When children stay for 4 hours or longer, either the program or the families must provide meals in addition to snacks.

Give children nutritious foods they like and can eat easily:

- Fibrous foods like raw broccoli are difficult for young children to chew and swallow.
- Preschoolers usually do not like food that is very hot, very cold, or very spicy.
- Cut foods into bite-size pieces to avoid choking.
- Serve a variety of finger foods or foods that can be easily picked up.
- In cooking, try to preserve natural colors and textures so food looks appealing.

Centers should consider setting up a menu planning committee. This committee might consist of the program director, teacher or teacher's assistant, cook, parent(s), and nutritionist. If you use cyclical menus, the committee may only have to meet once a month or every 6 weeks.

Food purchasing

- Be sure that suppliers of food and beverages meet local, state, and federal codes.

- Be sure that the meats and poultry you purchase have been inspected and passed tests for wholesomeness by federal or state inspectors.
- Use only pasteurized milk and milk products. If you use dry milk for cooking, prepare it in a clean container and immediately refrigerate or use it.
- Do not use home-canned foods or food from dented, rusted, bulging cans, or cans without labels.

Food storage

- Store all perishable foods at temperatures that will prevent spoilage (refrigerator temperature, 40 degrees F or lower; freezer temperature, 0 degrees or lower).
- Place thermometers in the warmest part of the refrigerator and freezer (near the door) and check them daily.
- Set up refrigerators to allow for air circulation around shelves and walls. This helps maintain proper food temperatures.
- Always examine food when it arrives to make sure it is not spoiled, dirty, or infested with insects.
- Store unrefrigerated foods in clean, rodent- and insect-proof, covered metal, glass, or hard plastic containers. (Check local bakeries for containers that they consider disposable or get them from restaurant equipment suppliers.)
- Store food containers above the floor (about six inches) on racks or other clean slotted surfaces that permit air circulation.
- Keep storerooms dry and free from leaky plumbing or drainage problems. Repair all holes and cracks to prevent insect and rodent infestation.
- Keep storerooms cool (about 60 degrees F) to increase the food's shelf life.
- Store all food items separately from nonfood items.
- Use an inventory system: *The first food stored is the first food used.* This ensures proper rotation. Inspect food daily for spoilage. Use the Food Storage Chart (Figure 5.9) as a guide to keeping foods safely in a refrigerator or freezer.

Preparing and handling breast milk and infant formula sent from home

Staff should thoroughly wash their hands prior to preparation of all infant feedings. Only cleaned and sanitized bottles and nipples, or equivalent factory-prepared nursing bottle bags, should be used. Only

Figure 5.9. Food Storage Chart

This chart has information about keeping foods safely in the refrigerator or freezer. It does not include foods that can be stored safely in the cupboard or on the shelves where quality may be more of an issue than safety.

FOOD	IN REFRIGERATOR	IN FREEZER
Eggs		
Fresh, in shell	3 weeks	Don't freeze
Raw yolks, whites	2-4 days	1 year
Hardcooked	1 week	Don't freeze
Liquid pasteurized eggs or egg substitutes, opened	3 days	Don't freeze
unopened	10 days	1 year
Mayonnaise		
Commercial, refrigerate after opening	2 months	Don't freeze
TV Dinners, Frozen Casseroles		
Keep frozen until ready to heat and serve		3-4 months
Deli and Vacuum-Packed Products		
Store-prepared or homemade egg, chicken, tuna, ham, macaroni salads	3-4 days	Don't freeze
Pre-stuffed pork and lamb chops, stuffed chicken breasts	1 day	Don't freeze
Store-cooked convenience meals	1-2 days	Don't freeze
Commercial brand vacuum-packed dinners with USDA seal	2 weeks, unopened	Don't freeze
Hamburger, Ground, and Stew Meats (Raw)		
Hamburger and stew meats	1-2 days	3-4 months
Ground turkey, chicken, veal pork, lamb, and mixtures of them	1-2 days	3-4 months
Hotdogs and Lunch Meats*		
Hotdogs, opened package	1 week	
unopened package	2 weeks	In freezer wrap, 1-2 months
Lunch Meats, opened	3-5 days	
Unopened	2 weeks	In freezer wrap, 1-2 months
Deli sliced ham, turkey, lunch meats	2-3 days	1-2 months
Bacon and Sausage		
Bacon	1 week	1 month
Sausage, raw from pork, beef, turkey	1-2 days	1-2 months
Smoked breakfast links or patties	1 week	1-2 months
Hard Sausage-Pepperoni, Jerky Sticks	2-3 weeks	1-2 months

FOOD	IN REFRIGERATOR	IN FREEZER
Ham		
Canned, unopened, label says keep refrigerated	6-9 months	Don't freeze
Fully cooked - whole	7 days	1-2 months
Fully cooked - half	3-5 days	1-2 months
Fully cooked - slices	3-4 days	1-2 months
Fresh Meat		
Steaks, beef	3-5 days	6-12 months
Chops, pork	3-5 days	4-6 months
Chops, lamb	3-5 days	6-9 months
Roasts, beef	3-5 days	6-12 months
Roasts, lamb	3-5 days	6-9 months
Roasts, pork and veal	3-5 days	4-6 months
Fresh Poultry		
Chicken or turkey, whole	1-2 days	1 year
Chicken or turkey pieces	1-2 days	9 months
Giblets	1-2 days	3-4 months
Fresh Seafood		
Fish and shellfish	2 days	2-4 months

*Uncooked salami is not recommended because recent studies have found that the processing does not always kill the E. coli bacteria. Look for the label to say "Fully Cooked."

Source: Appendix R, *Caring for Our Children.*

human milk and formula in factory-sealed containers can be brought into the facility (transport time and uncertainties about preparation and holding temperatures until the formula arrives make it unacceptable to use formula prepared at home). Expressed human milk should be refrigerated or frozen at home and transported in a container that keeps the milk cold until arrival at the child care facility. Unlike formula, human milk has antibacterial components that help protect it from spoiling during transport. No matter what type of milk is used, discard any remaining in the bottle after a feeding (bottled milk that has been fed will have been contaminated with saliva and bacteria).

Expressed human milk. The milk should be placed in a clean and sanitary bottle with nipple fitted tightly to prevent spilling. All containers of human milk should be of the ready-to-feed type, identified with a label that won't come off in water or handling, bearing the date of collection and the child's full name. Labels should be resistant to loss of the name and date when washing and handling. This is especially important when a frozen bottle is thawed in running tap water; there may be several bottles from different mothers being thawed and warmed at the same time in the same place. Chilled or frozen human milk may be transported from home to the child care facility in a cooler bag (at a temperature at 40 degrees F or less) as long as the ambient temperature is below 86 degrees F and the out-of-refrigerator time is less than two hours.

The bottle or plastic bag that fits into a bag-holding feeding unit should immediately be stored in the refrigerator (or freezer if frozen) on arrival at the child care facility and kept there until prepared for a feeding. Discard expressed milk if it is in an unsanitary bottle, has been unrefrigerated in transit for more than two hours or at the facility for an hour or more, or if the bottle has been fed to a baby over a period that exceeds an hour from the beginning of the feeding.

Unused (never-fed) containers of expressed human milk must be discarded after 48 hours if refrigerated, or by three months if frozen and stored in a deep freezer at 0 degrees F. Unused frozen breast milk that has been thawed in the refrigerator must be used within 24 hours. Thaw frozen milk under running cold water or in the refrigerator. Human milk contains components that are damaged by excessive heating during or after thawing. It should never be thawed in a microwave oven. Excessive shaking of human milk may damage some of the cellular components that are valuable to the infant, so gentle mixing during or after warming is best.

Because it is difficult to consistently maintain 0 degrees F in a freezer compartment of a refrigerator or even in a free-standing freezer, caregivers should carefully monitor the temperature with an appropriate working thermometer.

Since human milk is a body fluid that can carry viral disease to an infant, caregivers need to be sure that a mother's milk is fed only to her own child. In the event human milk from one infant's mother is inadvertently fed to another infant, the facility must follow a protocol to address the possibility of infection of the infant (consult *Caring for Our Children*).

Preparing infant formula. Formula provided by parents or by the facility should be in a factory-sealed container. Infants should be fed the same brand at child care and at home. Formula comes in ready-to-feed strength, concentrated liquid, or powder. Prepare all forms according to the manufacturer's instructions, using water from a source approved by the health department. Unless local health authorities recommend otherwise, water should be brought to a rolling boil before being used to make formula from concentrate or powder. A safe source of water (usually tap water prepared fresh daily by being brought to a rolling boil) can be kept at room temperature in a clean container for use in preparing formula during the day.

Powdered formula is the least expensive type of formula. Make up bottles when needed by adding the powdered formula to a bottle of water just before feeding. Bottles made in this way do not require refrigeration or warming and are promptly ready for feeding. Caregivers should only use the scoop that comes with the can (the volume of scoops varies from manufacturer to manufacturer and product to product).

Concentrated infant formula, not ready to feed, must be diluted with water. Sealed, ready-to-feed bottles are easy to use, but they are the most expensive approach to feeding formula. Infant formula made up from concentrate or powder must be refrigerated if not being fed immediately. Label bottles of formula prepared from factory-sealed products with the child's name and date of preparation. Discard these bottles if not used within 48 hours. An open container of ready-to-feed or concentrated formula can be covered and refrigerated, but it too must be discarded after 48 hours if not used.

Warming formula bottles and infant foods

Caregivers may warm infant formula bottles and infant foods if babies do not accept them at the refrigerated or room temperature at which they were stored. (Many babies are quite happy with cold bottles and room temperature infant foods.) When formula or food is warmed, use running warm tap water or place in a container of water no warmer than 120 degrees F. Don't leave bottles in water to warm for more than five minutes. When bottles of milk or infant foods are warmed at room temperature or in warm water for an extended time, they provide an ideal growth medium for bacteria.

After warming, mix bottles gently and test the temperature of the milk before feeding. Stir infant foods to distribute the heat evenly. You need two hands to safely prepare food and test food temperature. Mishaps occur easily while holding a child and working with food, hot water, or hot surfaces. It's also harder to perform proper handwashing, prepare food, and keep food and utensils off unsanitary surfaces when you're juggling a child and food at the same time.

If a slow-cooking device, such as a crock pot, is used for warming infant formula, human milk, or infant food, the device and its cord should be out of children's reach. The water should not exceed 120 degrees F. Some infants have received burns from water dripping from a bottle removed from a crock pot or when they pulled on a dangling cord and the crock pot came down on them. Keep a thermometer in the slow-cooking device to check the temperature when food is put into it. Empty, sanitize, and refill with fresh water daily.

Microwave ovens are not appropriate for warming bottles and infant foods because uneven heating of the mixture creates hot spots. Microwave heating involves agitation of molecules that go on generating heat for up to five minutes after power cuts off. Thus, a caregiver in a hurry could burn a child. Microwave ovens are best used away from children and for purposes other than infant food preparation.

Preparing and handling table foods

The following guidelines apply to all foods, whether they are prepared at the facility, brought to the facility by a catering service, or brought from home.

- Wash all raw fruits and vegetables before use. Wash tops of cans before opening.

- Thaw frozen foods in the refrigerator or put quick-thaw foods in plastic bags under cold running water for immediate preparation. DO NOT thaw frozen foods by allowing them to stand at room temperature.

- Use a thermometer to check internal temperatures of the following foods to be sure they have been cooked evenly and held at safe temperature until they are served:
  —poultry: heat to a minimum of 165 degrees F
  —stuffing: heat to a minimum of 165 degrees F in a separate pan (do not cook inside poultry)
  —pork and pork products: heat to a minimum of 160 degrees F.

- Prepare potentially hazardous foods (meat salads, poultry salads, egg salads, seafood salads, potato salads, cream-filled pastries, and other prepared foods containing milk, meat, poultry, fish, and/or eggs) as quickly as possible from chilled products, serve immediately, and refrigerate leftovers immediately.

- Prevent growth of bacteria by maintaining all potentially hazardous foods at temperatures lower than 40 degrees F or higher than 140 degrees F during transportation and while holding until service. Bacteria multiply most rapidly between 40 and 140 degrees F.

- Cover or completely wrap foods during transportation.

- Never reuse a spoon that has been used even once for tasting.

- Make sure each serving bowl has a spoon or other serving utensil.

- Reserve food for second servings at safe temperatures in the kitchen (below 40 degrees F or above 140 degrees F).

- Throw away leftover food from serving bowls on the table with these possible exceptions:
  —whole raw fruit and cut or raw vegetables that can be thoroughly washed, and
  —packaged foods that have not been unwrapped and do not spoil.

- Place foods to be stored for reuse in shallow pans and refrigerate or freeze immediately to rapidly bring temperature to 40 degrees F or lower.

- Discard leftovers or prepared casseroles in the refrigerator after 2 days.

- Do not send leftovers home with children or adults because of the hazards of bacterial growth during transport.

Figure 5.10. Sample Food Service Cleaning Schedule

TASK	HOW OFTEN?					COMMENTS
	After each use	Before & after each use	Daily	Weekly	As necessary	
RANGE						
Clean grill and grease pans	√					
Clean burners	√					
Clean outside			√			
Wipe out oven				√		
Clean edges around hood				√		
Clean hood screening and grease trap				√		
REFRIGERATOR AND FREEZER						Or when more than 1/4-inch frost develops or temperature exceeds 0°F.
Defrost freezer and clean shelves					√	
Wipe outside			√			
Dust top				√		
Clean inside shelves in order				√		
MIXER AND CAN OPENER						
Clean mixer base and attachments	√					
Clean and wipe can opener blade	√					
WORK SURFACES						
Clean and sanitize		√				
Organize for neatness			√			
WALLS AND WINDOWS						
Wipe if splattered or greasy					√	
Wipe window sills					√	
Wipe window screens					√	
SINKS						
Keep clean	√					
Scrub			√			
CARTS (if applicable)						
Wipe down	√					
Sanitize			√			
GARBAGE						Or more often, as needed.
Take out			√			
Clean can					√	
TABLES AND CHAIRS						
Clean and sanitize		√				
LINENS						
Wash cloth napkins	√					
Wash tablecloths and placemats	√ if plastic		√ if cloth			
Wash dishcloths			√			
Wash potholders				√		
STORAGE AREAS						
Wipe shelves, cabinets, and drawers					√	

Source: Appendix S, *Caring for Our Children.*

- Keep lunches brought from home in the refrigerator until lunchtime. Encourage parents to use cold packs to transport any perishable food at safe temperatures. (Spot-checking whether food was transported at safe temperatures is simple: Put a food thermometer in the perishable food just before putting the lunch box in the facility's refrigerator.) Remember, outsides of lunch boxes are not sanitary; put the contents, not the lunch box itself, onto a sanitized table where children eat.
- Let the children choose what to eat from the contents of the lunch boxes, but put out the most nutritious foods first.

Storage of Nonfood Supplies

- Store all cleaning supplies (including cleaning agents) and other poisonous materials in *locked* compartments or in compartments well above the reach of children and separate from food, dishes, and utensils.
- Store poisonous and toxic materials (other than those needed for kitchen sanitation) in *locked* compartments *outside* the kitchen area.
- Store insect and rodent poisons in *locked* compartments in an area apart from cleaning materials to avoid contamination or mistaken usage.
- Make sure any bait put into food storage areas is boxed, labeled, and separated to prevent possible contamination of food supplies.
- Keep all poisonous materials in their original containers and use them only according to the manufacturer's instructions.

Cleaning and Care of Equipment

- Throw away cracked or chipped dishes or utensils that may harbor bacteria. Avoid utensils with chipped or painted handles.
- Wash dishes using a method approved by the local department of health.
- Set up a cleaning schedule to prevent contamination of food according to the schedule in Figure 5.10.
- Be sure there are sufficient garbage cans to hold all garbage and that they have tight-fitting lids and are leakproof. Line the cans with plastic liners; empty and clean cans frequently. Keep the garbage area clean at all times.

Insec

- For f
  only
  flysw
  conta
  equip
  with a
  insect

- Insectic
  only by
  training
  variable,
  insecticic
  preparati
  contamina

- Be sure all
  good cond

- Close all o
  dents and i

Suggested

- Assess the m
  the menu ag
  children actu
  Adult Food Pr
  snacks to see w
  served meet th

- Observe the foo
  in a child care c
  against the guid
  Which requireme
  What change in
  meet the requirer
  gram additional n
  without additional

- Observe food prepa
  tation and food han
  staff using? Use a th
  tor and freezer temp
  eter to check peris
  brought from home. L
  and stored. Do you se

- At a facility you visit, a
  involved in ensuring go
  How could this involve
  children and families ha
  disrupting the program'

Chapter 6

Promoting Health through Oral Health, Mental Health, and Health Education

Children depend on adults for protection from harm and for health promotion. Infection and physical injury are commonly recognized as the types of harm from which young children need the most protection. Other health problems that may be less evident can be identified early in a child's life, when corrective actions are likely to be effective.

Since the roots of lifetime healthy behaviors and emotional resiliency are planted in the early years, early childhood educators have unique opportunities to include positive experiences for children on a day-to-day basis. In addition, they should be mindful of the importance of the early identification of health problems and share their sources of information and services with families to assist them in identifying and solving problems early. One area of early problems that may be less evident is nutrition, discussed in the previous chapter. This chapter addresses three other areas in which the choices that parents and other caregiving adults make for children have a powerful influence on child health: oral health, mental health, and health education.

Oral Health

The type of oral hygiene and dental care children receive, along with diet and heredity, often determines their oral health throughout life. Child care programs can help prevent dental disease by

Major Concepts

- Child care providers are members of the preventive health team that helps families keep children well.
- Oral health contributes to good nutrition, speech, self-image, and a sense of well-being.
- Mental health promotion is the cornerstone of child development. Mental health services support the emotional, cognitive, and social development of children. Mental health is monitored through child behaviors viewed in the context of child care arrangements, families, and communities.
- Health education is taught daily through teachable moments as well as planned activities for staff, parents, and children.
- Use credentialed, credible sources for health information to avoid spreading misinformation.

- serving nutritious food, limiting sugared and sticky foods
- ensuring that children get the right amount (and not too much) of fluoride through a variety of means (drinking water, rinses, toothpastes, professionally applied tooth varnish, tablets, or drops
- teaching children and staff about good oral health care by having them brush their teeth during the day
- identifying children with evident dental problems and referring them to oral health professionals.

Healthy foods for teeth

High-sugar foods and frequent eating are clearly linked to tooth decay. Caregivers should help children preserve their teeth by avoiding or limiting sweet drinks, candy, jelly, jam, cake, cookies, sugared gelatin, and sweetened, canned fruit. Fresh fruit and vegetables make great snack or dessert alternatives.

Mealtimes in group programs can promote oral health. Avoid grazing as a style of eating for children in child care and by adults whom children observe in child care. Infants should be fed on demand, but mealtimes for older children should be at clearly defined intervals. Young children need frequent meals and snacks. When the meal or snack is over, the food should be put away until the next planned feeding time.

Here are some important facts about sugar and teeth.

- Natural sugars (such as maple syrup and honey) are just as harmful to teeth as refined sugar.

- Sticky sweets (such as caramel) are particularly harmful because they remain on the teeth longer than other sweets.

- Eating a sweet all at once is better than eating one over a period of time (such as a lollipop) or eating sweets often (such as mints or hard candies throughout the day).

- Sweet sticky fruits, such as raisins and dates, should be eaten with a meal.

- Because teeth are attacked by the decay process each time food is put in the mouth, frequent eating or snacking can cause problems.

- Toothbrushing or rinsing with water after eating reduces the time teeth are exposed to the decay process.

- Babies should not be put to bed with a bottle. Milk, formula, sweetened liquids, or fruit juices all contain sugars. Prolonged feeding can result in serious decay, called nursing bottle mouth or baby-bottle tooth decay. (Putting babies to bed or in a lying-down position with a bottle also increases the risk of ear infection and choking.)

- Rewarding good behavior with candy or other sweets teaches children to reward themselves with sugary foods.

Fluoride

Fluoridation of public water supplies is the single most effective method to prevent tooth decay. When children have fluoride in their drinking water, or fluoride supplements from birth, tooth decay can be reduced about 50 percent! Know whether your community fluoridates its water and whether the children in your care drink this fluoridated water. Certain types of home water filters remove fluoride; others do not. Many families buy bottled water in the false belief that it is better than their community water source. (Since the bottled water industry is unregulated, the safety and content of any particular container of bottled water is unknown.)

Children also may be consuming other sources of fluoride. Some commercially prepared foods and beverages are made with fluoridated ingredients, a fact usually not indicated on the label. Consequently, it is hard to know whether or not children who consume a lot of commercially prepared or packaged foods (rather than those prepared from fresh ingredients) are receiving significant amounts of fluoride.

Most toothpaste now has fluoride. Adults should monitor the amount of toothpaste that children use. Half a pea-sized dab is about right for young children. Excess ingestion of fluoride can lead to staining of the teeth called fluorosis. While this staining does not make teeth weak, it can be unattractive. Depending on their assessment of a child's individual situation, dentists may prescribe fluoride drops or tablets, or paint the teeth with a fluoride varnish.

Brushing teeth

Very young children can learn good oral hygiene habits that will last into adulthood. Routine brushing after lunch and snacks has the double benefit of cleaning teeth *and* establishing a good habit. If organized well, brushing probably will not take more than five minutes. Here are some points to remember:

- Each child must have her or his own toothbrush, labeled by name, and it must *never* be shared.

- A sink is not necessary for toothbrushing. In fact, using a sink for a group of children is very difficult. Instead, give each child a cup of water to wet the toothbrush, take a mouthful of water to swish, and then spit the swished mouthful back into the cup.

- Store toothbrushes so they stay clean and open to the air. The bristles should not touch any surface. While commercial toothbrush holders are available for child care programs, you can make your own. One effective holder is a sanitized Styrofoam egg carton. Clean the carton and spray the surfaces with the sanitizing bleach solution, turn the carton upside down, and punch a hole in the bottom of each egg compartment. Store the brushes bristle-side up so they do not touch. Place a tall, clear plastic box over the top to keep dust, dirt, and any insects off the toothbrush heads. Replace the egg carton with a new one when it becomes soiled.

- Many dentists and hygienists recommend a small toothbrush with soft, rounded, nylon bristles. The type should be determined by whatever is easiest for the child to brush every tooth. (At home, parents might invest in an inexpensive electric toothbrush to get the job done better and faster than a young child can manage.) When the bristles become bent, the brush should be replaced. Routinely replace brushes about every three months.

- Caregivers should brush their own teeth with the children as well as supervise. When adults model good toothbrushing, children learn the importance of this lifetime habit. Because of limited motor skills, some children may need an adult's help to reach all their teeth.

- Model proper brushing technique, but don't worry if children do not have the skill to do it well. Use a circular scrubbing motion to cover the teeth from the gums over every biting edge—from all directions and on all surfaces. This technique is easy and effective. Scrub back and forth on the chewing surfaces after brushing the surfaces closest to the tongue and those closest to the cheek. Finish by brushing the tongue. You can make up chants and songs to reinforce this pattern of tooth brushing. Remember, the most effective teaching technique is to actually brush with the children.

Oral health education

Children and families must understand the importance of good oral health. Children can learn effectively through integration of oral education activities with their regular routines. Family education can involve posters, articles in a newsletter, parent handouts about oral health activities the children are doing, or videos. Brochures describing particular problems, conditions, or resources are frequently available from state or local health departments. Many dentists or hygienists are willing to come to child care programs to teach children about oral health and oral health examinations. A field trip to a dentist who enjoys working with young children can be a wonderful introduction to regular dental care.

Dental care

Encourage families to follow healthy oral health routines and to get regular dental care themselves. Taking their children for preventive dental care is essential. Some families have dental health insurance, but many do not. Even those with insurance may only have coverage for a portion of treatment services, not for preventive care. Remind parents of painful dental repair experiences that might be avoided with good preventive care. Offer the names of children's dentists (pediatric dentists/pediadontists) or family dentists who work regularly with young children. Some communities have dental health clinics, dental school clinics, community health centers, and children's hospitals that provide emergency dental care.

A child's first visit to the dentist for preventive services should be before the age of 3. Many dentists who specialize in caring for children want to examine the child's mouth and

Figure 6.1. Dental Referral Criteria

For most children younger than age 3, a visit to a dentist is purely an educational and preventive experience. However, there are other situations when consultation and treatment are needed.

Listed below are some things to look for in young children. If you answer no to any of the questions, you should recommend that the family take the child to a dentist.

SOFT TISSUES (tongue, lips, cheeks, gums)

- Can the child stick the tongue tip completely out of the mouth?
- Can the child swallow with the teeth together (without the tongue pushing through)?
- Are the upper and lower lip the same size?
- Is there a clear distinction between lip and skin of face?
- Is the color inside the cheeks even throughout?
- Are all gum tissues the same color? Are gums free of pimples and/or swelling?

HARD TISSUES (teeth)

Number

- Does the child have at least 1 or 2 teeth by age 1? At least 12 by age 2?
- Are there the same number of teeth on either side of the middle of the jaw?
- Are teeth on either side the same shape?

Bite

- When the child closes her mouth, do the top teeth bite over the bottom teeth? Do the back teeth meet?
- Do all the teeth come in contact when the jaw is closed?
- Are the teeth spaced out, not crowded?

Color

- Are the teeth milky white? Are they all an even color?
- Do any stains and colors come off easily with a toothbrush?
- Are there any dark spots or pits on the teeth?

ORAL HYGIENE

- Are the teeth clean?
- Does the mouth have a clean, sweet odor?

provide advice about oral health to families as soon as the first tooth erupts. By 3, most children have all 20 of their primary (baby) teeth showing for an oral health professional to check. In addition to preventive care, certain observations that caregivers can make should lead to a visit to a pediatric dentist (see Figure 6.1). Most children need little treatment at this stage, so the dentist can form a friendly and relaxed relationship with a child. The dentist also can look for early signs of future problems such as overcrowding or poor dental hygiene.

Help families make a dental visit an appealing new experience. A good first trip will help mold children's feelings for many years. Explain to children that the dentist is a friendly doctor who will help keep their teeth and mouth healthy. Talk about the visit in a positive, matter-of-fact way as you would any new experience. Avoid statements that suggest the visit may be unpleasant, such as, "It won't hurt." If you are fearful about dental visits, do not pass on the fear to the children. Most adult fears come from treatment for problems that could have prevented by routine dental care and good personal oral health habits in childhood.

Common dental problems

Broken tooth. Contact the family and make sure a dentist is contacted immediately. If a broken, permanent tooth is not cared for in a very short time, it can be lost. Even if a tooth appears to be hanging by a thread, don't pull it out. Get in touch with the dentist right away.

Knocked out tooth. Contact the family and dental provider immediately and *save the tooth!* Examination of a baby tooth may reveal a retained fragment. A permanent tooth sometimes can be replanted. If the tooth has a lot of dirt on it, hold it by the chewing surface and gently swish in a cup of water or milk, then put it into a cup of milk for transport to the dentist. If the tooth is a permanent tooth, try to put the tooth back into the socket right away, and have the child bite on a piece of cloth to hold it in place. (Do not do this with primary [baby] teeth.) Rush the child and the tooth to the dentist (within 30 minutes if possible). The sooner the child sees the dentist, the better the chance of saving the tooth.

Toothache, swelling, redness or bleeding of the gums. Ask the parent to call the dentist at once. The dentist can find the cause of the toothache or soft tissue irritation and reduce the pain. There are

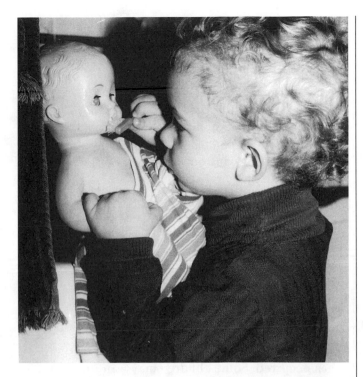

temporary emergency measures to use only when a child is in extreme pain. If a cavity can be seen in the tooth that aches, flush out any food particles with warm water. Parents can apply oil of clove directly on the aching tooth and give the child acetaminophen for temporary relief of pain. They should arrange a dental appointment immediately.

Thumb, finger, or pacifier sucking. Sucking the thumb, fingers, or pacifier often gives a baby a feeling of pleasure and security. During the first several years, it should cause no concern. However, if the child continues this habit beyond the age of 5, or when permanent teeth begin coming in, it can affect the position of the incoming teeth and the shape of the jaws. The pressures of sucking may push the teeth out and narrow the dental arches. Eventually orthodontic care may be needed. Work with the parents and their clinician to help the child find a caring way to eliminate this habit.

Baby-bottle tooth decay. Baby-bottle tooth decay is a condition that can destroy the teeth. It is caused by the frequent and lengthy exposure to liquids containing sugars (milk, formula, fruit juice, and other sweetened liquids). The teeth most likely to be damaged are the upper front teeth, but others also may be affected. The tongue lies over the lower teeth and protects them more than the upper teeth from the exposure to the sugary liquids.

Bleeding around a tooth after an injury. Apply ice to the area as soon as possible and for as long as possible to minimize bleeding into the tooth and discoloration. Have the child suck on a Popsicle or hold an ice cube with a clean cloth on a fresh injury. The family should consult a dentist to be sure the tooth or teeth do not need treatment.

Mental Health

Sound child development practice fosters good mental health. Unlike physical health needs, mental health cannot be achieved by focusing on the child alone. The child is a part of a family, a child care group, and a social structure that all affect the child's mental health. Caregivers often notice or call attention to problem behaviors before parents do; they have the opportunity to compare a child's behavior with that of typically developing peers. Since parents are the reporters to the child's clinician about problem behaviors, the clinician may not know of a problem unless the child care provider brings the symptoms to the attention of the family and asks the family to share the caregiver's observation with the clinician.

When do children develop behavior problems?

Sometimes healthy and well-adjusted children experience environmental stress, which leads to behavior problems. When you are aware of these stresses, monitor the child closely and note any changes in mood or behavior. Children's responses to stress vary greatly, some mild, some severe. High-quality, consistent, and supportive relationships with family and child care providers may lessen the effects of stress.

Other children can exhibit behavior problems for no apparent reason. These problems also vary from mild to severe. Do not assume that the family is the root of behavior problems.

Stressful situations that call for closer monitoring of child behavior

- *Changes in the family or caregiver.* If a loved one becomes ill, is hospitalized, or dies, or if parents separate or divorce, the child loses physical contact and emotional support. Even seemingly positive changes can be stressful for children. For example, the birth of a sibling, adoption, or blending of families may increase a child's number of playmates, but it can also be stressful. When parents or caregivers have problems at work or lose their job, both children and adults may feel stress. When a family moves, children miss their old home and friends or may experience stress adapting to a new culture and language.

- *Problems in family relationships.* Conflict between parent figures or between parent and child are very stressful. Conflict often accompanies problems of communication. Domestic violence can spread and children become victims of abuse, sometimes physical, sometimes sexual, sometimes emotional or psychological abuse, such as when the child feels completely rejected or is repeatedly terrified.

- *Inadequate care.* Some parents or caregivers do not adequately supervise a child, respond to his needs, or place reasonable limits on behavior. They may be harsh in discipline, too permissive, or inconsistent. Others may overprotect a child and not let her do what other children are doing at that age.

- *Problems of individual family members.* If a parent has a serious illness, the condition may affect his or her ability to care for and nurture the child. Similarly, mental problems or alcohol or drug abuse can impair the competence of adults. Physical or mental health problems of siblings also affect the parents and other children. Some parents have difficulty with reading and the children also experience stress when the parent must read.

- *Community conditions.* Sometimes the source of stress is one or more conditions in the community. Too many families face poverty. Some experience social discrimination or isolation. Housing or schools may not be adequate. There may be considerable violence on the streets or fear of violence. In an unsafe neighborhood, where families may not allow their children to go outside to play, the children cannot interact with peers and discharge their energy. Children become particularly distressed if they witness violence. The associated stress of living in poverty increases the risk of behavior and emotional problems.

Common behavioral or emotional problems in young children

Children respond to environmental stress and challenge in different ways, depending upon chronological age, developmental stage, and the child's own intrinsic vulnerability. Many children demonstrate difficult behaviors for hours or days at a time. The following behaviors and emotions are serious problems when they occur over long periods of time or are extreme.

- *Emotions and moods.* Children may cry often for no obvious reason. They may have quick changes of moods. They may become sad or withdrawn and refuse to play with other children or talk with adults. They may get no pleasures out of play.

- *Activity level and attention.* Some children are very active and disorganized. They may not be able to concentrate on games or stories.

- *Negative behavior.* Children may throw frequent temper tantrums. They also may get angry easily. They may fight with their friends. They may refuse to do the things adults ask of them. They may strike out at caregivers who are trying to comfort them. These behaviors are particularly of concern in children over the age of 3 years.

- *Problems in eating, elimination, and sleep.* Some children refuse to eat; others eat too much. Some lose control of their bladder after toilet learning has occurred. Some children may want to sleep more than usual; others have difficulty relaxing for a nap or falling asleep at night. Sleep deprivation may add to other behavioral difficulties.

- *Problems with relationships.* Children may show dramatic changes in how they relate to others. They may become extremely distressed when a parent or child care provider has to leave. This may make it very hard for parents to leave their children at the child care setting. Children may become very clingy. They may become afraid of being alone. On the other hand, some children become indifferent. They may go to anyone, an adult they trust or a stranger. Some children avoid eye contact, stare, and refuse to let others help them. They may isolate themselves from their friends and caregivers.

- *Developmental problems.* Children may lose developmental skills they previously mastered. For example, a child who has been using the toilet may need to go back to diapers, a child who can speak in sentences reverts to single words, a child able to feed herself independently suddenly demands adult help, a child who played independently or with other children is not able to play alone or socialize.

What parents and other caregivers can do

To help a child showing behavior that is not typical for either the specific child or the age of the child, a caregiver can try several approaches.

Figure 6.2. Behavioral Data Collection Sheet

This sheet is intended to be used by caregivers to document a child's behavior that is of concern to them. The behavior may warrant evaluation by a health care provider, discussion with parents, and/or consultation with other professionals.

Child's name: _____   Date: _____

1. Describe behavior observed: (see below for some descriptions)

    _____

2. Behavior noted from: _____ to _____
                                 (time)   *(time)*

3. During that time, how often did the child engage in the behavior (e.g. once, 2-5 times, 6-10 times, 11-25 times, >25 times, >100 times)

    _____

4. What activity(ies) was the child involved in when the behavior occurred? (e.g. was the child involved in a task? Was the child alone? Had the child been denied access to a special toy, food, or activity?)

    _____

5. Where did the behavior occur? _____

6. Who was around the child when the behavior began? (list staff, children, parents, others)

    _____

7. Did the behavior seem to occur for no reason? Did it seem affected by changes in the environment? _____

8. Did the child sustain any self-injury? Describe. _____

9. Did the child cause property damage or injury to others? Describe. _____

    _____

10. How did caregiver respond to the child's behavior? If others were involved, how did they respond?

    _____

11. What did the child do after caregiver's response? _____

12. Have parents reported any unusual situation or experience the child had since attending child care?

_____

Child Care Facility name: _____

Name of caregiver completing this form: _____

Behaviors can include:
- *repetitive, self-stimulating acts*
- *self-injurious behavior (SIB) such as head banging, self-biting, eye-poking, pica (eating non-food items), pulling out own hair*
- *aggression / injury to others*
- *disruption such as throwing things, banging on walls, stripping*
- *agitation such as screaming, pacing, hyperventilating*
- *refusing to eat / speak; acting detached / withdrawn*
- *others*

Check a child's developmental stage before labeling a behavior a problem. For example, it is not unusual for a 12 month old to eat non-food items, nor is it unusual for an 18 month old to throw things. Also note how regularly the child exhibits the behavior. An isolated behavior is usually not a problem.

Source: Reprinted with permission of the Pennsylvania Chapter, American Academy of Pediatrics.

Figure 6.3. Special Care Plan for a Child with Behavior Problems

*This sheet is intended to be used by health care providers and other professionals
to formulate a plan of care for children with severe behavior problems
that parents and child care providers can agree upon and follow consistently.*

Part A: To be completed by parent/custodian

Child's name: _____ Date of birth: _____

Parent name(s):_____ _____

Parent emergency numbers: _____ _____

Child care facility/school name: _____ Phone: _____

Health care provider's name: _____ Phone: _____

Other specialist's name/title: _____ Phone: _____

Part B: To be completed by health care provider, pediatric psychiatrist, child psychologist, or other specialist

1. Identify/describe behavior problem: _____

2. Possible causes/purposes for this type of behavior: (circle all that apply)

   medical condition _____   tension release

                      (specify)   developmental disorder

   attention-getting mechanism   neurochemical imbalance

   gain access to restricted items/activities   frustration

   escape performance of task   poor self-regulation skills

   psychiatric disorder _____   other:

   _____

                      (specify)

3. Accommodations needed by this child: _____

   _____

4. List any precipitating factors known to trigger behavior: _____

   _____

5. How should caregiver react when behavior begins? (circle all that apply)

   ignore behavior   physical guidance (including hand-over-hand)

   avoid eye contact/conversation   model behavior

   request desired behavior   use diversion/distraction

   use helmet*   use substitution

   use pillow or other device to block self-injurious behavior (SIB)*

   other: _____

   _____

   *directions for use described by health professional in Part D.

6. List any special equipment this child needs: _____

    _____

7. List any medications this child receives:

    Name of medication: _____   Name of medication:_____

    Dose: _____   Dose: _____

    When to use: _____   When to use: _____

    Side effects:_____   Side effects:_____

    _____   _____

    Special instructions:_____   Special instructions:_____

    _____   _____

8. Training staff need to care for this child: _____

    _____

9. List any other instructions for caregivers: _____

    _____

Part C: Signatures

Date to review/update this plan: _____

Health care provider's signature: _____ Date: _____

Other specialist's signature: _____ Date: _____

Parent signature(s): _____ Date: _____

_____ Date: _____

Child care/school director: _____ Date: _____

Primary caregiver signature: _____ Date: _____

Part D: To be completed by health care provider, pediatric psychiatrist, child psychologist, or other specialist

Directions for use of helmet, pillow, or other behavior protocol: _____

_____

_____

_____

_____

_____

_____

_____

Source: Reprinted with permission from S. Bradley, Pennsylvania Chapter, American Academy of Pediatrics, reviewed by J. Hampel and R. Zager.

- *Discuss the issues.* Speak with other staff who observe the child and the family about the child's behavior early in the process. Do not wait until the child's behavior or moods seriously deteriorate. Begin with a description of what changes you are observing. You might say to a parent, "I notice that your child is crying a lot at school. It is difficult for me to comfort him." If you know why the child is experiencing anxiety or stress, you might say, "Since her father has been in the hospital, Sarah has been eating poorly at school. What do you see at home?"

- *Be supportive of the child.* Remain calm. Use supportive language; "I know you feel sad, but please try to eat a little." Provide comfort when possible. Praise the child when she does something appropriate. Be gentle. It is easy to arouse children who are under stress.

- *Maintain the structure of the program.* Children may find routines and the usual schedules very reassuring. Keep a predictable program. Do not insist that the child participate fully. Gently remind the child that she is welcome in the group.

- *Encourage communication.* Allow the child to talk about the problems. Play is the language of young children. Sometimes a child will act out the stress in play or in an art activity. Use play to demonstrate some ways to handle stress. For example, use a doll to express in words *sad* or *angry* feelings. Provide positive reinforcement when the child's behavior is appropriate.

- *Limit dangerous or hurtful behaviors.* Provide clear messages that tantrums, aggression, and other negative behaviors are not acceptable. Give the child acceptable alternatives. For example, remind him "Say how angry you are in words, but do not hurt your friends." Use positive guidance and create environments that reduce *mistaken behavior.* Time-out should be used sparingly when necessary to help a child regain self-control or prevent harm to self or others. Young children should be separated from the situation but never left alone; it should be clear that the adult is taking care of the child.

- *Reassure the child that she will be safe and that her needs will be met.*

- *Keep an accurate log of problem behaviors.* It is difficult to remember when the problem behaviors occurred, what happened before the problem, and what helped the child. Keep a diary of the behaviors. Consider using the Behavioral Data Collection Sheet in Figure 6.2.

When a child needs further evaluation

When should a child care provider refer a child for further evaluation? Several factors may trigger a referral.

- The problems have lasted several weeks to months.
- The problems are severe or getting worse.
- Your supportive care and interventions do not help.
- The child is unable to function well in the child care setting.
- The child is not achieving age-appropriate developmental levels and tasks.
- The family is extremely distressed or the stresses are getting worse.

Whom you refer to depends on the child's condition and the resources in your community. The primary care clinician is always a good starting place. The clinician may know of the family's circumstances and may be able to provide additional support. It is also easier in many cases to refer the child to a pediatrician or family doctor than to a psychiatrist or psychologist. However, some families appreciate an immediate referral to a mental health professional.

Know the names of professionals in your area who work with children. If the parent gives you permission, provide the professional notes of your observations and concerns. The Behavioral Data Collection Sheet (Figure 6.2) is an easy-to-use format. Send along the Special Care Plan for a Child with Behavior Problems (Figure 6.3) to help the clinician formulate suggestions that the child care program and family can implement.

With parent permission it may be best to arrange a conversation with the clinician to clarify observations and recommendations. If you make a referral to a mental health professional, try to maintain the child in your program. This stability may be very helpful to the child and family. You may be able to arrange for behavioral consultation in your community so that you can improve your interventions with the child and family. This guidance on when a child care provider should refer a child for further evaluation is based on material prepared by Dr. Heidi Feldman, a developmental pediatrician at the UCLID Center at the University of Pittsburgh. Developmental pediatricians provide consultation on behavioral problems that a primary care pediatrician cannot handle. See related fact sheets online at the Pennsylvania Chapter of the American Academy of Pediatrics Website (**www.paaap.org**). Behavior issues covered

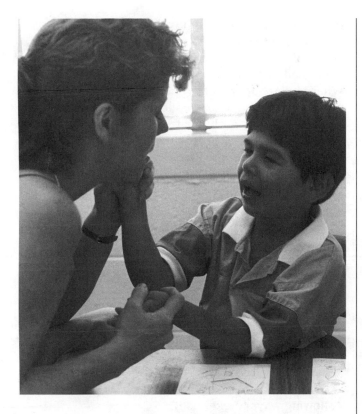

included discipline, biting, repetitive behavior, and attention deficit hyperactivity disorder.

These fact sheets provide helpful information that caregivers can use and also share with families. For further information about specific behavior problems in children, refer to *The Classification of Child and Adolescent Mental Diagnoses in Primary Care: Diagnostic and Statistical Manual for Primary Care (DSM-PC) Child and Adolescent Version* (American Academy of Pediatrics 1996).

Adult mental health

Caregiving is a stressful occupation. Good caregiver mental health is key to addressing the mental health of children. Without caring for the caregiver, there is no hope of quality child care. Caregiving may require that mentally healthy adults defer meeting their own immediate needs so they can provide competent care of children. Child care providers have sources of personal stress outside their jobs just like everyone else. Family problems, upsets in plans, and the impact of events in the community and in society all take their toll.

Coworkers and administrators in child care provide an essential support group for each other. Usually this support enables the effective operation of the child care program. Sometimes professional

mental health resources are needed. In such instances the administrator or supervisor can help staff find and use a competent mental health professional. Insurance coverage for mental health services varies widely. Finding sources of community mental health services for a staff member often requires persistence and patience. It is sometimes very difficult and frustrating for those around stressed and mentally ill adults to find a way to help.

Community mental health resources

Community mental health professionals who are skilled in working with young children are in high demand and may be scarce. Access to developmental pediatricians, pediatric psychiatrists, and social workers who specialize in working with mental health problems in children is reserved for the most difficult cases. For the most part, the child's usual source of medical care will be the initial resource to formulate a behavioral management plan. Observations of the child's behavior during a reasonable period specified by the plan will usually form the basis of a decision whether to seek a mental health professional's help.

Most mental health professionals are affiliated with hospitals, clinics, mental health agencies, or—for children—early intervention services. The United States has been organized into geographic regions for mental health services. Most of these services are targeted to older children and adults. To locate local community mental health services, look under human services in the state or local agency section of your telephone directory.

Occasionally mental health professionals skilled in working with young children's problems can provide training for child care providers. However, many are frustrated about their inability to make themselves more available. Most have long waiting times for evaluation of children and limited time to coordinate implementation of their recommendations. Child care providers and mental health professionals must do the best they can with the resources available to them and continue to advocate on behalf of children for needed services.

Health Education for Staff, Families, and Children

This manual mentions many opportunities and responsibilities for health education. During the early childhood years, children form habits and attitudes that can last a lifetime. We know that health education can help establish good habits such as eating healthy foods, exercising regularly, wearing seat belts, crossing streets safely, avoiding poisons, and choosing other positive health behaviors.

Health education works best in a healthy environment in which adults consistently demonstrate healthy behavior. A child care program must follow healthy routines such as frequent handwashing and toothbrushing. Activities should be safe and organized so that children feel secure and cared for. All people—adults and children—must respect and care for other people and the environment.

To create a healthy environment, all staff should be models of good behavior. If adults talk about how we need to take care of our bodies, but smoke, drink soda, and munch candy, children will recognize the contradiction. Adult behavior, attitudes, and appearance are the most powerful tools for children's learning.

Your program can promote good health by providing evidence-based, credible information and activities for children, staff, and families, addressing the same topic with all three groups at the same time. Child health curriculum is more successful if all adults who are part of the children's lives are involved in the process, reinforcing the ideas and practices being taught. At the same time, the adults themselves will gain valuable health and child development knowledge.

Do not spread misinformation. Information from the Internet or print media is not always credible, or based on scientific information. It may come from a well-meaning but ill-informed group with a scientific-sounding name. A reliable place to start a search for evidenced-based, credible health information is **www.healthfinder.gov**, which offers links with many reliable sources of current health information.

Health curriculum for children

Health activities should fit into the natural flow of the program throughout the year. An occasional puppet show or filmstrip is not enough. Routines such as brushing teeth, handwashing, careful food handling, good nutrition, and use of child passenger safety seats should happen every day.

When you know what you want to teach, you can capture the teachable moments when children are most likely to learn. For example, when a child with the sniffles sits in your lap, talk about taking good care of your body when sick (rest, drink liquids). When a child is going into the hospital, set up a hospital corner and read hospital books. Spring is a natural time to talk about growing and eating good foods; plant a vegetable garden if you can. Talk about sticky and sweet foods while you're brushing teeth. When you are approaching, and actually on, the playground, give and ask children to repeat and show how they comply with positive rules about using play equipment. Practice proper use of car seat restraints, then follow-through by helping parents make sure they and their children are safely buckled up.

Learning always has more meaning when it is

- concrete
- geared toward the skills and interests of the children
- a good fit with the rest of the children's learning and understanding
- presented in many different ways—books, conversations, free play, group activities, field trips, films/videotapes
- tied into all areas of the curriculum—science (such growing food), cooking, dramatic play (like hospital play), art (such as making a collage of pictures showing ways to exercise)
- strengthened through practice.

Health education should be interpreted in the broadest sense: teaching children about well-being. Focus not only on physical health and safety but also on topics such as emotional health, growing and changing, and the environment. Provide children with an opportunity to learn about personal health, the health of those around them, and their world. Ideally, try to involve other teachers, parents, nutritionists, mental health specialists, special needs staff, community agencies and community resources. Many groups have materials and teaching ideas targeted especially for young children.

Here are some broad topic areas that can be included in your health curriculum:

- growth and development
- similarities and differences
- families (including cultural heritage)
- expression of feelings (verbal and physical)
- nutrition
- oral health
- personal hygiene
- safety
- physical health
- awareness of disabilities
- environmental health

Figure 6.4. Sample Integrated Objectives: Mental/Family Health

FOR CHILDREN

- Know that it is healthy and normal to express feelings.
- Acknowledge that feelings can be expressed in ways that are not dangerous or traumatic to self or others.
- Know that everyone has feelings and everyone needs to have opportunities to express them.
- Understand *same* and *different* and learn to interact with all kinds of people.
- Experience success in daily activities and thereby develop self-confidence.
- Recognize they are part of a family and group.
- Be aware of their bodies and respond appropriately.

FOR STAFF

- Provide effective developmental assessment of children.
- Recognize and support the importance of children's secure home base.
- Be familiar with children's normal reactions to strange situation.
- Provide psychologically safe environment for children, staff, and families.
- Model positivism and acceptance.
- Be aware of own attitudes concerning family, emotional expression, cultural differences, sexual curiosity of children.
- Develop partnership with families, using resources of home and community.
- Learn when to refer a child for medical and/or mental health consultation.

FOR FAMILIES

- Develop skills in observing children's feelings and needs.
- Recognize importance of secure home base for children.
- Develop stable relationship with children's program and community health care providers.
- Develop self-confidence through participation.
- Learn effective communication and behavior management techniques.

Health education for staff and families

Knowledge is power. Having good information is one of the best ways to feel confident and in control. When you know what to do—whether it is taking a temperature, giving first aid, or keeping a child relaxed during an asthma attack—both you and the child benefit from your knowledge. You can provide the necessary care, remain calm, and maintain control. Lack of information often leads to panic in emergencies or to improper care, such as spreading disease by not washing hands appropriately.

Keys to getting the message across. Some basic ways that program administrators to teach staff, families, and volunteers about health include

- modeling good health behaviors—practice what you preach!
- establishing good health routines such as toothbrushing, serving only healthy foods, handwashing
- posting routines and suggestions as reminders—emergency plans, handwashing techniques, diapering instructions.
- teaching children good habits (and then they will remind you!)
- using a variety of media and training techniques such as staff meeting discussions, workshops or guest speakers, newsletters, site visits (for example, a hospital emergency room), newspaper and magazine clippings, posters, pamphlets, and audiovisual materials.

Selecting health education topics. Many state licensing agencies require specific caregiver training in topics such as approved first aid procedures and fire safety. Beyond that, how do you plan for staff/family health training? Decide first what is most important for your group this year. Here are some ideas to help you plan:

- Ask a supervisor or health consultant to observe the program, consider families' needs and strengths, and suggest health education topics for immediate and long-term concern.
- Ask staff and families about what they want to learn. Present a list of suggested topics with an opportunity for them to suggest others as well. You might ask them to set priorities for their choices.
- Find out the most convenient time to meet with families.
- Try to get a sense of the learning style of the parents and staff. Plan something for everyone

(such as speakers, written materials, hands-on experience, and videos).

- Plan a yearly training schedule based on the priority topics. Revise and update your schedule each year. Some suggested topics are orientation to your health policies, preventive health practices, nutritional needs of children, safety/injury prevention (including transportation safety and site surveys), first aid, management of minor illness, child growth and development, observing and recording health signs and symptoms, child abuse/neglect, cultural views of health, how to be a good consumer of health services, how to advocate for better community health services, health education for young children, value and meaning of health screening results, chronic illness/special needs, parenting, discipline and talking with children.

Figure 6.4 will help you identify objectives to integrate into your health program for children, staff, and families.

Suggested Activities

- Visit a child care facility and look for oral health practices and missed opportunities for oral health promotion. What resources would be needed to improve oral health promotion in the program?

- Find a community oral health professional who will work with you to plan an oral health education activity for a preschool group. Ask the staff to evaluate whether any of the children or adults changed their practices after this activity.

- Look up the mental health resources listed under Human Services in the telephone book and call one or two to ask how they would handle a request for mental health assessment of a 3-year-old whose difficult behavior makes inclusion a burden for child care staff.

- Ask a program director who has held her position for at least a few years how children's behavior problems that are beyond typical developmental expectations affect the program. Ask if and how mental health problems of staff have affected the program in the past.

- Research a health education topic and prepare a presentation for your peers. If appropriate, prepare and present a simplified version of the same topic to a group of children and then to their families.

Chapter 7

Medical Care—Clinical Health Services for Children

Major Concepts

- Regularly scheduled clinical health service visits are essential to maintain children's health. They should include assessment, screening, and immunization to identify and treat correctable child health problems.
- Health is assessed through evaluation of health histories, screening tests, and selective laboratory examinations.
- Families may need help to find a *medical home* in which they can obtain routine preventive care, or medical care for illness evident to them or identified by routine health supervision to restore health and function.
- Child care providers are key guardians of a safety net that identifies young children (and families) who need clinical health services or referral to other community resources.
- Families may need help to find health insurance coverage for their child.

Health is defined by the World Health Organization as "a state of complete physical, mental, and social *well-being* and not merely the absence of disease or infirmity." This total state of wellness is affected by the interrelationships between each area of a person's development. For example, when children are ill, tired, hungry, or poorly fed, they cannot function well; they may be cranky or inattentive. A child who has an undetected medical condition or who is neglected may become depressed or withdrawn. A child with a physical problem also may develop emotional or learning problems; a child who has emotional upsets may develop physical symptoms. As children grow, their health needs constantly change, particularly during their early years.

Young children are at risk for developing a number of health problems, such as hearing or vision difficulties, lead poisoning, developmental delay, and injury. The goal of preventive care is to keep children well and safe. Additional clinical health services are necessary to treat them if they become sick or hurt.

Health Care

Health care should take place in a *medical home*. A medical home is not a place; it is an arrangement that provides health care that is

- accessible
- comprehensive
- compassionate
- continuous 24 hours a day, 7 days a week, every day of the year
- coordinated
- culturally competent
- family centered.

A medical home reaches out to families to support them in doing what is in the best interests of their children. Ideally, clinicians from a medical home look for children and families who do not come for routine and follow-up visits. Access to comprehensive health insurance coverage for medical-home services is a barrier to care for many families. Nonetheless, having a medical home for every child is a goal for families, health professionals, and all child advocates. Child care programs should be familiar with the state Medicaid program and state Child Health Insurance Program (CHIP) referral resource telephone numbers to assist families who lack health insurance as well as local clinicians whose services most closely resemble a medical home.

Child care providers play an important role in promoting the use of a medical home for every child. By checking whether children have had universally recommended preventive health services (checkups with appropriate immunizations and screenings), child care providers identify children who have been missed by the health care system. For children who have special needs, it is especially important for child care providers to collaborate with families and clinicians to ensure that the child has and uses a medical home. (For more about children with special needs, see chapter 11.)

Preventive health services are intended to

- detect medical conditions that may not be easily recognized but require medical attention (for example, fluid in the ear, anemia, or "lazy eye"). Early identification and treatment of such problems may completely resolve them, or at least limit later disability, while a delay in attention can result in more—or permanent—damage.
- identify children who may be at high risk for developing diseases due to hereditary factors, family health habits, or environmental factors.
- identify and follow signs in growth patterns, behavior, or development that provide clues to current or future health problems.
- evaluate the effectiveness and adjust past or current treatments, such as tubes in ears, antibiotics, or patching an eye, medication for prevention of asthma episodes.

Routine checkups

- promote health through counseling, education, and guidance for anticipated problems
- provide highly effective preventive measures such as immunizations
- identify potential health problems through screenings such as measurements of growth, vision, hearing, lead levels, red blood cells or hemoglobin (for anemia)
- provide early detection and treatment of illnesses with symptoms (for example, strep throat) to prevent complications
- prevent and reduce disability from chronic diseases

Children need to be seen by pediatric clinicians at recommended intervals. The pediatric clinician who provides this care is often called a primary health provider. Primary health providers for children include pediatricians, family practice physicians, and nurse clinicians or nurse practitioners. Since care of children requires specialized training, families should be encouraged to select a pediatrician who provides a medical home for routine checkups, management of common illnesses, and follow-up care.

The majority of pediatricians in the United States are members of the American Academy of Pediatrics (AAP). Experts organized by the AAP set the nationally accepted, minimum guidelines for routine health care for children. AAP and public health guidelines are usually the same or have only minor differences. AAP guidelines are reviewed and updated as new information about valuable preventive health measures becomes available. The guidelines in use at the time this manual was printed are shown in Figure 7.1 (available online at **www.aap.org/policy/re9939.html**). Check the AAP website at least once a year to be sure you are using the most current version of the schedule. Note that the guidelines are minimum requirements for healthy children receiving competent parenting and having no significant health problems. When a child has a special situation, more frequent visits may be required.

Some doctors and clinics do not follow the AAP guidelines. Some health programs do not pay for preventive health care that meets the schedule guidelines. Acting in the best interest of children, child care providers should encourage families to seek clinicians who do follow the guidelines and urge them to seek insurance coverage from public insurance, from their employers, or pay for those services that are not covered.

Some families fragment their children's health care by using different sources of care without coordination or use emergency rooms for minor illnesses. As a result, their children are more likely to have poor health. When the child's regular sources of care do not provide all the routine minimum services as outlined in Figure 7.1, every effort should be made to find community agencies and providers who will fill in the gaps. Information obtained from gap-filling special screening programs should always be forwarded (with parental consent) to the child's usual source of health care. Coordination of service among clinicians for children is essential to approximate the quality of care that a medical home should provide.

Figure 7.1. Recommendations for Preventive Pediatric Health Care (RE9535)

Committee on Practice and Ambulatory Medicine

Each child and family is unique; therefore, these **Recommendations for Preventive Pediatric Health Care** are designed for the care of children who are receiving competent parenting, have no manifestations of any important health problems, and are growing and developing in satisfactory fashion. **Additional visits may become necessary if circumstances suggest variations from normal.**

These guidelines represent a consensus by the Committee on Practice and Ambulatory Medicine in consultation with national committees and sections of the American Academy of Pediatrics. The Committee emphasizes the great importance of **continuity of care** in comprehensive health supervision and the need to avoid **fragmentation of care.**

AGE[5]	INFANCY[4] PRENATAL[1]	NEWBORN[2]	2-4d[3]	By 1mo	2mo	4mo	6mo	9mo	12mo	15mo	18mo	24mo	EARLY CHILDHOOD[4] 3y	4y	5y	MIDDLE CHILDHOOD[4] 6y	8y	10y	ADOLESCENCE[4] 11y	12y	13y	14y	15y	16y	17y	18y	19y	20y	21y
HISTORY Initial/Interval	●	●	●	●	●	●	●	●	●	●	●	●	●	●	●	●	●	●	●	●	●	●	●	●	●	●	●	●	●
MEASUREMENTS Height and Weight		●	●	●	●	●	●	●	●	●	●	●	●	●	●	●	●	●	●	●	●	●	●	●	●	●	●	●	●
Head Circumference		●	●	●	●	●	●	●	●	●	●	●																	
Blood Pressure													●	●	●	●	●	●	●	●	●	●	●	●	●	●	●	●	●
SENSORY SCREENING Vision		S	S	S	S	S	S	S	S	S	S	S	O[6]	O	O	O	O	O	S	S	S	S	S	S	S	S	S	S	S
Hearing		O[7]	S	S	S	S	S	S	S	S	S	S	S	O	O	O	O	O	S	S	S	S	S	S	S	S	S	S	S
DEVELOPMENTAL/ BEHAVIORAL ASSESSMENT[8]		●	●	●	●	●	●	●	●	●	●	●	●	●	●	●	●	●	●	●	●	●	●	●	●	●	●	●	●
PHYSICAL EXAMINATION[9]		●	●	●	●	●	●	●	●	●	●	●	●	●	●	●	●	●	●	●	●	●	●	●	●	●	●	●	●
PROCEDURES-GENERAL[10] Hereditary/Metabolic Screening[11]		↕	●	●																									
Immunization[12]		●	●	●	●	●	●		●	●	●			●	●				●	●									↕
Hematocrit or Hemoglobin[13]						★		★	★	↕—★	★	★			●				↕		14			•[15]					↕
Urinalysis															●														
PROCEDURES-PATIENTS AT RISK Lead Screening[16]								★	★	★	★	★	★																
Tuberculin Test[17]									★		★	★	★	★	★	★	★	★	★	★	★	★	★	★	★	★	★	★	★
Cholesterol Screening[18]													★	★	★	★	★	★	★	★	★	★	★	★	★	★	★	★	★
STD Screening[19]												★	★	★	★	★	★	★	★	★	★	★	★	★	★	★	★	★	★
Pelvic Exam[20]																			↕————————————————20—————————————↕										
ANTICIPATORY GUIDANCE[21] Injury Prevention[22]	●	●	●	●	●	●	●	●	●	●	●	●	●	●	●	●	●	●	●	●	●	●	●	●	●	●	●	●	●
Violence Prevention[23]	●	●	●	●	●	●	●	●	●	●	●	●	●	●	●	●	●	●	●	●	●	●	●	●	●	●	●	●	●
Sleep Positioning Counseling[24]	●	●	●	●	●	●	●																						
Nutrition Counseling[25]	●	●	●	●	●	●	●	●	●	●	●	●	●	●	●	●	●	●	●	●	●	●	●	●	●	●	●	●	●
DENTAL REFERRAL[26]												↕	●																

1. A prenatal visit is recommended for parents who are at high risk, for first-time parents, and for those who request a conference. The prenatal visit should include anticipatory guidance, pertinent medical history, and a discussion of benefits of breastfeeding and planned method of feeding per AAP statement "The Prenatal Visit" (1996).

2. Every infant should have a newborn evaluation after birth. Breastfeeding should be encouraged and instruction and support offered. Every breastfeeding infant should have an evaluation 48-72 hours after discharge from the hospital to include weight, formal breastfeeding evaluation, encouragement, and instruction as recommended in the AAP statement "Breastfeeding and the Use of Human Milk" (1997).

3. For newborns discharged in less than 48 hours after delivery per AAP statement "Hospital Stay for Healthy Term Newborns" (1995).

4. Developmental, psychosocial, and chronic disease issues for children and adolescents may require frequent counseling and treatment visits separate from preventive care visits.

5. If a child comes under care for the first time at any point on the schedule, or if any items are not accomplished at the suggested age, the schedule should be brought up to date at the earliest possible time.

6. If the patient is uncooperative, rescreen within 6 months.

7. All newborns should be screened per the AAP Task Force on Newborn and Infant Hearing, "Newborn and Infant Hearing Loss: Detection and Intervention" (1999).

8. By history and appropriate physical examination; if suspicious, by specific objective developmental testing.

9. At each visit, a complete physical examination is essential, with infant totally unclothed, older child undressed and suitably draped.

10. These may be modified, depending upon entry point into schedule and individual need.

11. Metabolic screening (eg, thyroid, hemoglobinopathies, PKU, galactosemia) should be done according to state law.

12. Schedule(s) per the Committee on Infectious Diseases, published annually in the January edition of Pediatrics. Every visit should be an opportunity to update and complete a child's immunizations.

13. See AAP Pediatric Nutrition Handbook (1998) for a discussion of universal and selective screening options. Consider earlier screening for high-risk infants (eg, premature infants and low birth weight infants). See also "Recommendations to Prevent and Control Iron Deficiency in the United States. MMWR. 1998;47 (RR-3):1-29.

14. All menstruating adolescents should be screened annually.

15. Conduct dipstick urinalysis for leukocytes annually for sexually active male and female adolescents.

16. For children at risk of lead exposure consult the AAP statement "Screening for Elevated Blood Levels" (1998). Additionally, screening should be done in accordance with state law where applicable.

17. TB testing per recommendations of the Committee on Infectious Diseases, published in the current edition of Red Book: Report of the Committee on Infectious Diseases. Testing should be done upon recognition of high-risk factors.

18. Cholesterol screening for high-risk patients per AAP statement "Cholesterol in Childhood" (1998). If family history cannot be ascertained and other risk factors are present, screening should be at the discretion of the physician.

19. All sexually active patients should be screened for sexually transmitted diseases (STDs).

20. All sexually active females should have a pelvic examination. A pelvic examination and routine pap smear should be offered as part of preventive health maintenance between the ages of 18 and 21 years.

21. Age-appropriate discussion and counseling should be an integral part of each visit for care per the AAP Guidelines for Health Supervision III (1998).

22. From birth to age 12, refer to the AAP injury prevention program (TIPP) as described in A Guide to Safety Counseling in Office Practice (1994).

23. Violence prevention and management for all patients per AAP statement "The Role of the Pediatrician in Youth Violence Prevention in Clinical Practice and at the Community Level" (1999).

24. Parents and caregivers should be advised to place healthy infants on their backs when putting them to sleep. Side positioning is a reasonable alternative but carries a slightly higher risk of SIDS. Consult the AAP statement "Positioning and Sudden Infant Death Syndrome (SIDS): Update" (1996).

25. Age-appropriate nutrition counseling should be an integral part of each visit per the AAP Handbook of Nutrition (1998).

26. Earlier initial dental examinations may be appropriate for some children. Subsequent examinations as prescribed by dentist.

NB: Special chemical, immunologic, and endocrine testing is usually carried out upon specific indications. Testing other than newborn (eg, inborn errors of metabolism, sickle disease, etc) is discretionary with the physician.

Key:
- ● = to be performed
- S = subjective, by history
- ★ = to be performed
- O = objective, by a standard testing method
- ↕ = the range during which a service may be provided, with the dot indicating the preferred age.

American Academy of Pediatrics

Assessing Health Status

Many individuals with unique skills and experiences participate in assessing a child's health. The child's physician or another member of the health team should coordinate services of health professionals as the child's special needs or family preference suggests. In many agencies the coordinator of services is called a *case manager*.

In addition to health professionals, the child's health team consists of the child's family, teachers, and others who regularly observe and interact with the child. Various health professionals contribute multiple perspectives on the child's growth, development, and overall health from their specific areas of expertise. This information should be shared with the health team coordinator or care coordinator to create a comprehensive picture of the child's health. Clear designation of the health team coordinator is especially important for children with multiple health and developmental problems. For information about different types of specialists, see the Website representing the particular specialty.

Health assessment and follow-up care are often separated into three categories: screening, diagnosis, and treatment.

- *Screening* is the use of quick, inexpensive, and simple procedures to identify children who may have a problem in a specific area. Health screening tests typically produce one of these three possible results: apparently healthy, no action needed; possibly at risk, repeat screening test; at risk, refer for further diagnosis and possible treatment.

- *Diagnosis* is a more detailed evaluation to find out if there is in fact a health problem and, if so, what it is. When making a diagnosis, the health professional may use health histories, dietary information, laboratory test results, family/teacher observations, X-rays, or physical and psychological examinations.

- *Treatment* is designed to control, minimize, correct, or cure a disease or abnormality (eyeglasses, dental fillings, therapy). *Treatment is the key to an effective program.* Without it, screening and diagnosis are meaningless.

Health histories

Health histories provide important information about the child's prior health experiences and risks for future disease. The family health history may help predict what illnesses the child may inherit or develop. Competent preventive care requires a detailed health history including information about birth, illnesses, hospitalization, all treatments, immunization status, and current health concerns.

Programs for young children also should collect a health history from the family. It needs to cover only major health problems and developmental concerns that can help explain a child's current condition, behavior, and past experience. Most parents can recall many details about their own child. However, unless there is a specific request for it, few parents will systematically review the details of their child's nutritional, immunization, health, and family history to identify patterns that suggest a need for attention. Even the most alert parents may innocently overlook the health needs of a rapidly changing and growing child because of other urgent demands on them.

When a child care program requests a child's health history, the request helps reinforce the family's role in keeping track of important health information. A form that collects the type of information useful to a child care program is presented in Figure 7.2. Use it as a guide to develop a tool to gather appropriate information. Check the information you collect against information shared by the child's clinician on the Child Health Assessment

Form (Figure 2.3 on page 9). If you notice discrepancies, try to clarify the facts with the parents and the clinician so everyone involved has useful information.

Observations

Physical health. Physical health observations include observable signs of health or illness (coughing, vomiting, swelling) and internal symptoms (nausea, headache, stomachache) that must be described to be known to others. Since young children often cannot describe how they feel, objective observations provide needed clues. It is more useful to say "Jeffrey has a frequent dry cough, flushed cheeks, and a runny nose with thick yellow mucus" than to say "Jeffrey looks sick." Report specific observations rather than drawing conclusions or making a diagnosis. For instance, saying "Jennifer has a sore throat and an oral temperature of 102 degrees" is better than reporting "Jennifer has strep throat." Use a form to record symptoms of minor illness to focus attention on significant observations (see Figure 7.3).

Use all your senses (smell, hearing, sight, touch) when making health observations. Observe clues such as the color, temperature, or texture of skin; breath odor; the appearance of a bruise; or the sound of a cough. Observe the group in general and compare individual children. For example, do most of the children of the same age get out of breath while climbing the hill? If a child has difficulty doing what the rest of the group does easily, it is worth noting and asking the family to bring it up with their child's clinician.

Each observer has a different perspective in obtaining health information. Parents compare a child to her or his typical appearance or behavior or to siblings or friends. Teachers can observe children in a group setting with many children of the same age. Child health professionals use knowledge and experience from their medical practice. Each view is valuable but limited; to have a total picture of the child, all observations must be shared and seen as a whole.

Development and behavior. A child's physical health is only one aspect of her or his life. An equally important aspect is the development of language, gross- and fine-motor skills, social-emotional competence, and cognition (thinking). Difficulties in these areas are best managed when they are identified and worked out during the early years.

1. *Developmental milestones.* Knowledge of general child development with in-depth information about children at particular ages provides a general framework to identify children whose abilities fall outside the typical range. These milestones must be viewed flexibly because a child's development is greatly influenced by childrearing styles, culture and ethnic norms, and the child's own temperament.

   Caregivers can use developmental and behavioral screening tools to assess children in their care. These tools serve more than one purpose: identifying the child whose development is outside the range for typically developing children and reinforcing a sense of normal developmental pathways; and helping caregivers to individualize educational activities, some that are comfortable for the child and some that help the child reach for the next level of accomplishment. For information on the relationship of screening to identification, evaluation, and intervention procedures, see *Developmental Screening in Early Childhood: A Guide* (NAEYC). For a list, description, and sources of standardized developmental and behavioral screening tools, see "Developmental Surveillance and Screening of Infants and Young Children," policy statement of the American Academy of Pediatrics, Committee on Children with Disabilities in *Pediatrics* (Vol. 108, No. 1, July 2001) or online at **www.aap.org/policy/re0062.html**.

   Clinicians frequently use standardized checklists as a framework for reviewing a particular child's placement in the range of normal childhood behaviors and developmental skills. Most tools used in routine checkups are not used as the test-developers intended; instead, clinicians tend to abbreviate assessments, because doing more is difficult under the time and compensation constraints of a busy practice. A child care provider's observations over the course of time in the child's daily life yield much valuable information. Caregivers should not hesitate to communicate their observations and concerns to clinicians, with parental consent. (See "Talking to the Child's Physician: Thoughts for the Child Care Provider" on p. 100.)

2. *Observation and documentation.* Write down observations that might suggest problems in a child's development or behavior. (You can keep file cards in your pocket and note on them the day, time, activity, and behavior you observe.) Ask other staff members to also observe and record

Figure 7.2. Developmental Health History

Child's Name _____ Nickname _____
               (Last)   (First)

Birthdate _____ / _____ / _____

PHYSICAL HEALTH

What health problems has your child had in the past? _____

_____

What health problems does your child have now? _____

_____

Other than what you listed above—
Does your child have any allergies? If so, to what? _____

_____

How severe? _____

Does your child take any medicine regularly? If so, what? _____

Has your child ever been hospitalized? If so, when and why? _____

_____

Does your child have any recurring chronic illness or health problem (such as asthma or frequent earaches)?

_____

Has a disability been diagnosed (such as cerebral palsy, seizure disorder, developmental delay)? _____

_____

Do you have any other concerns about your child's health? _____

_____

DEVELOPMENT (compared to other children this age)

Does your child have any problems with talking or making sounds? Please explain. _____

_____

Does your child have any problems with walking, running, or moving? Please explain. _____

_____

Does your child have any problems seeing? Please explain. _____

_____

Does your child have any problems hearing? Please explain. _____

_____

Does your child have any problems using her or his hands (such as with puzzles, drawing, small building pieces)? Please explain. _____

_____

Does your child have any problems with mood or behavior? Please explain. _____

_____

DAILY LIVING

What is your child's typical eating pattern? _____

_____

Write **N/A** (nonapplicable) if your child is too young for the following questions to apply.

What foods does your child like? _____

   dislike? _____

How well does your child use table utensils (cup, fork, spoon)? _____

How does your child indicate bathroom needs? _____

Word(s) for *urination:* _____ Word(s) for *bowel movement:* _____

Special words for body parts: _____

What are your child's regular bladder and bowel patterns? _____

_____

Do you want us to follow a particular plan for toileting? _____

For *toddlers,* please describe use of diapers or toileting equipment (such as potty, toilet seat adapter).

_____

What are your child's regular sleeping patterns? _____

Awakes at _____ Naps at _____ Goes to bed at _____

What help does your child need to get dressed? _____

SOCIAL RELATIONSHIPS/PLAY

What ages are your child's most frequent playmates? _____

Is your child (circle all that apply) friendly? aggressive? shy? withdrawn? _____

Does your child need extra time/preparation to change from one activity to another? _____

Does your child play well alone? _____ What is your child's favorite toy? _____

Is your child frightened by (circle all that apply) animals? rough children? loud noises? new experiences?

   the dark? storms? anything else? _____

Who does most of the disciplining? _____ What works best when you discipline your

   child? _____

With which adults does your child have frequent contact? _____

How do you comfort your child? _____

Does your child use a special comforting item (such as a blanket, stuffed animal, doll)? _____

Parent signature _____ _____ **Date** _____

Figure 7.3. Symptom Record

Child's name:_____

Date: _____ Symptom(s: _____

When symptoms began, how long did they last, how severe, how often?_____

_____

Any change in child's behavior?_____

_____

Child's temperature:_____ (circle: axillary (armpit), oral, rectum, or ear canal)

How much and type of food and fluid the child take in the past 12 hours? _____

_____

How many and how typical/normal was urine and bowel movement in the past 12 hours? _____

_____

Circle or write in other symptoms:

runny nose	sore throat	cough	vomiting	diarrhea	wheezing
trouble breathing	stiff neck	rash	trouble urinating	pain	
itching	trouble sleeping	earache	headache	stomachache	

Other symptoms _____

_____

Exposure to medications, animals, insects, soaps, new foods: _____

Exposure to other people who were sick; and who and what sickness?_____

_____

Child's other problems that might affect this illness: asthma, anemia, diabetes, allergy, emotional trauma

_____

What has been done so far? _____

_____

Advice from the child's clinician: _____

_____

Name of person completing form: _____

_____

_____

Source: Appendix J, *Model Child Care Health Policies*

the child's behaviors. Choose an appropriate developmental screening tool to use in your setting and apply it to children whose development does not seem in line with peers. Document problem behaviors using the Behavior Data Collection Sheet in Figure 6.2. Determine the appropriate next steps to take and plan a meeting to discuss your concerns with the family. Have the documentation in hand that makes the observations of the problem clear.

3. *Communication.* Develop your ability to communicate concerns in a supportive, nonthreatening manner. Parents are experts on their children and should be involved in discussions about concerns as soon as possible. Their input can help you identify which of your observations are appropriate for the family and culture and which are not, and which behaviors or traits are of particular concern to them. Often they may have had questions similar to yours but may not have wanted to bother the staff or appear to be overly anxious. Your dealing with these concerns in a respectful partnership can be a great help and support.

4. *Referral and consultation.* When concerns suggest the need to consult or make a referral, start with the child's pediatric clinician. The problem may be solved at that level, or it may be necessary to seek community resources for referral and consultation. Use the Special Care Plan for a Child with Behavior Problems (Figure 6.3) as a guide. Many communities have a wide array of experts on every aspect of child health and development. A list of local services should be developed and kept at the center so that referrals can be made easily.

Health screenings

The AAP and the U.S. Department of Health and Human Services recommend a schedule that includes periodic assessments with a minimum number of screening tests for sound health care for all children. Head Start requires its programs to meet the well-child assessment requirements of the states' Early and Periodic Diagnosis and Treatment Program (EPSDT) for children who are eligible for Medicaid services. Advocates are working steadily to eliminate the differences between the state EPSDT schedules of services and the national recommendations. By law, states must pay for diagnosis and treatment of any conditions identified in EPSDT screening. To limit spending, some states are reducing their coverage. Other forms of child health insurance

cover more or less of the recommended screening schedule and follow-up diagnosis and treatment for conditions suspected as a result of screening. What the insurance carrier pays for does not affect the child's need to have services. If insurance does not cover these costs, families should be encouraged to arrange to pay out-of-pocket for screening, diagnosis, and treatment—just as they do for other necessities such as clothing and food.

Screening tests look for conditions that, if undetected and untreated, may seriously handicap a child for life. Most conditions respond to early treatment, which is often more effective and less costly than later treatment and may also prevent the development of other problems. For instance, children with undetected hearing loss risk developing language, learning, and behavior problems. Children with eyes that are not straight and children with a marked difference in visual acuity between their two eyes are at risk for developing amblyopia (loss of vision in one eye). If decreased vision is not treated during the early years, treatment in the school-age years is slow and often unsuccessful.

Screening generally involves short and simple procedures because it is intended for large numbers of apparently well children. A good screening may identify some children who do not have a problem, but it misses few who *do* have a problem. Without screening, problems may go unnoticed or, if the signs or symptoms are recognized, their significance may not be understood. An abnormal screening test result is a clue that something is wrong, that a further look is needed. Abnormal results should be interpreted by the child's usual source of health care so appropriate further evaluation can be planned. Premature referral to a specialist may result in overlooking the possibility that the abnormality is part of a multisystem problem.

To be valuable, a screening program must include

- parent education about the screening
- family involvement and consent
- use of a valid, reliable tool appropriate for the age
- a competent screener
- screening and re-screening of children who may have a problem before making referrals
- written information provided to the family when further examination is suggested
- family choice of the health professional to follow up
- information received from the health professional about examination results and treatment plans.

Vision screening

Developmental vision problems may be most effectively corrected during the preschool years. This is especially true in the areas of visual acuity (the ability of each eye to distinguish detail both near and far) and vision skills (the ability to use both eyes efficiently and effectively in a coordinated manner). All children should have an eye examination, from birth, at each check-up visit. By 4 years of age, this eye examination should include not only evaluation of general eye health, but also near and far vision acuity. Some vision problems can interfere with a child's coordination and developmental skills.

Many people believe that preschool children are too young to be tested. Subjective vision screening can be done from birth, but at 3 years of age, most children *can* cooperate with a vision screening program that tests for visual acuity and stereopsis (checking if both eyes work together.) Objective vision screening is done with an age-appropriate, standardized screening tool designed to identify some of the most common problems found in young children. A number of tools are available. Various picture identification tests are generally considered less accurate than tests with crowded letters or specific shapes, but using pictures is better than not testing. Testing for whether the eyes work well together is essential, yet not usually done. Two of these tests, the Random Dot E and the bug or butterfly test, are most popular. If you are interested in doing vision screening, it is important that you receive training and learn the technique, strengths, and weaknesses of the testing methods you will use.

The first priority is for children to receive competent vision screening in a medical home. When this is not possible, ask a pediatric vision screening professional (pediatric ophthalmologist, pediatric optometrist) or a pediatrician to help you find someone who can do competent vision screening or arrange training for the child care staff on how to screen children. For screening purposes, 3-year-olds are expected to pass at 20/40 line on eye charts; 4-, 5-, and 6-year-olds should pass at 20/30; and 7-year-olds at 20/20.

Any screening program is valuable only if follow-up occurs. The first referral should be to the child's usual source of health care, not to a vision specialist. *Do not assume that children will outgrow vision problems.* Some problems get worse. Early detection permits early treatment that will correct the problem more completely and that will cost less than later treatment. Any child who cannot perform well on a primary care clinician's basic vision screening by age 4 should be referred to a vision specialist.

Hearing screening

A child who does not hear clearly will have trouble imitating sounds and developing language skills. Behavior also can be affected. Learning to read and to write will be difficult and thus frustrating for the child. Hearing problems may be hereditary or the result of certain illnesses during pregnancy or early childhood. Temporary or intermittent hearing loss may be caused by chronic ear infection, a heavy buildup of wax in the ear, or chronic fluid in the middle ear.

Hearing loss may be readily observed when the loss is fairly severe. Some signs signal milder loss. Infants who do not hear well will not startle at a sudden noise, will not search with their eyes for the source of a noise, will not respond to a musical toy or their parent's voice unless the parent is seen, and will be slow to imitate sounds or respond to simple commands and the sound of their own names. Older children with hearing problems often have smaller vocabularies, use shorter sentences, speak in an unusual voice, and seem to understand less than other children the same age.

Hearing screening for newborns is now being performed in most states. The equipment used measures the brain response to sound. After birth children need periodic hearing screening because some hearing problems can develop as the child grows.

Pure tone audiometry is the typical hearing test for preschool and older children. It checks a child's ability to hear quiet sounds at four different pitches or frequencies. The test requires that children do some specific action such as putting a toy in a box or raising a hand when a sound is heard through the earphones.

Tympanometry measures the pressure required to move the eardrum (middle ear) and the way the eardrum moves. Fluid in the middle ear may cause negative pressure and decrease the eardrum's ability to move, affecting a child's ability to distinguish sounds clearly. This test is difficult to do on infants because they have sharply angled ear canals.

Acoustic reflex screening measures the control of a muscle in the middle ear in response to a loud sound. If the contraction (reflex) is absent, there may be fluid in the ear or incomplete healing from a recent infection. This test can be done on very young children.

Because children are more comfortable and secure in familiar surroundings with familiar adults, screening may be more successful if screeners come to the child care program. Prepare the children for what to expect, and follow through on referrals. Be sure to notify the child's usual source of health care about any screening results to avoid duplication and to promote coordination of screening results with the rest of the child's health data.

Measuring height and weight

Height and weight should be measured regularly and recorded on a chart that permits comparison with normal growth patterns. These measurements are one of the best ways to detect physical growth patterns that may indicate a serious problem. Head circumference (measurement around the head) should also be measured for children from birth to 12 months of age. Growth measurements are usually taken as part of a routine checkup. They should be graphed over time to show the pattern of the child's growth compared with other children the same age

and the relationship of length/height and head circumference to weight.

Children whose length/height growth percentile differs by more than one percentile curve from their weight/growth percentile, or whose growth data are below the fifth percentile curve, need further evaluation. You should receive this information with the child's physical examination report. If you want to be able to plot the growth data yourself, you can obtain the growth charts online from the Centers for Disease Control and Prevention at **www.cdc.gov/ growthcharts**. For school-age children, you may want to get the charts, make the measurements, and let the children plot their own values. These measurements integrate learning about mathematics, science, self, and health.

Anemia screening

Hematocrit, or hemoglobin measurements, are commonly used to screen children for anemia during early childhood. Anemia results when the body does not have enough circulating red blood cells to carry oxygen from the lungs to the tissues and/or not enough hemoglobin (the chemical carrying oxygen to the red blood cells) in each cell.

Iron is needed to form hemoglobin. Without enough iron, blood cannot carry the oxygen the body needs. There are also other causes of anemia. An anemic child is likely to appear tired, pale, and inattentive, and to be susceptible to infection.

Iron deficiency anemia used to be a common problem among young children, and it is still the most common form of anemia, particularly for children from low-income families or toddlers who did not receive sufficient iron when they were rapidly growing infants. Causes of iron deficiency anemia include

- overconsumption of milk (more than 24 to 32 ounces per day) resulting in low intake of other foods, particularly iron-containing foods
- lack of high-iron, high-nutrient foods in the diet (such as meat, fish, beans, and green leafy vegetables)
- lead toxicity. Iron deficiency and lead poisoning frequently occur together. Iron and lead compete with each other for the same binding sites in the body. Iron deficiency may increase the absorption of lead from the intestine and make the toxic effects of lead worse. Therapeutic doses of iron are often required to correct the iron deficiency when accompanied by lead poisoning.

Normal values for the hematocrit in children vary by race and from one laboratory to another, but it is usually above 33 percent (percentage of the total blood volume occupied by red blood cells); normal values for hemoglobin also vary but are usually more than 11 grams per deciliter of blood.

Urine screening

Urine is produced by the kidney and stored in the bladder until it is emptied by urination. Abnormalities in kidney function, infection in the urine, or biochemical problems in the body can be detected by urinalysis. Pretreated paper strips are dipped into urine to determine the presence of any abnormality. Normally, urine does not contain protein, sugar, more than a few white or red cells, nitrites, ketones, or urobilinogen.

Lead screening

Lead is everywhere, both in nature and in manufactured products, often in underlayers of interior paint and in the soil around buildings painted with lead paint years ago. Ingestion of a small chip of lead paint or lead dust on unwashed hands can raise the blood lead level. Lead screening is extremely important because even very low elevations of blood lead, even without symptoms, can cause permanent problems in learning and behavior.

Two major ways to prevent lead poisoning in children are removal of lead in the environment and lead screening to identify children who must be removed from sources of lead. The current tests for lead recommended by the AAP and CDC are a fingerstick or venous (usually taken from the vein at the inside of the elbow) blood test to most accurately detect elevated lead levels. Ideally, blood level screening should be a part of routine health care for children in most communities. Both the AAP and CDC recommend that risk for possible lead exposure be assessed by at least asking about possible lead exposure at children's health visits between the ages of 6 months and 6 years.

Children at risk are those identified as living in or frequently visiting a house built before 1960 with peeling or chipping paint *or* that is undergoing recent or planned remodeling/renovation; those who have a sibling, housemate, or playmate being treated for lead poisoning; those living with an adult whose job or hobby involves exposure to lead; or those living in an area where lead poisoning is common. In communities where lead is a known environmental problem, blood lead screening of infants and toddlers should be universal.

Medical examinations or health assessments

A medical examination or health assessment is a comprehensive review by a physician or nurse practitioner of all the information gathered from health history, health observations, and screening tests. Although the medical examination is commonly called a "physical," the physical examination of the body by a clinician looking, touching, listening, and so on, is only one part of a medical examination. The examination includes an interview with the parent or guardian to get current health information and a record of immunizations, a complete physical examination, and laboratory and screening tests as necessary. A dentist or eye specialist also may be involved. The results of medical examinations should be reported on the Child Health Assessment Form (Figure 2.3).

If the form is incomplete or does not provide clear picture of the child's needs while in child care, the director or health consultant should obtain parental consent to contact the clinician for additional information. A program's health policies should require that these forms be on file prior to the child's first day of attendance. But if enrollment cannot be delayed until a checkup appointment is available, the grace period for completion of the form should not be extended beyond 6 weeks after enrollment. The forms should be updated at each checkup visit, following the recommended schedule of the AAP. This requires updates every 2–3 months for infants, decreasing frequency of updates for toddlers, and annual updates for children once they reach 3 years of age. School-age children between the ages of 6 and 10 need checkups only every other year. Health information should be considered confidential and should not be disclosed without written consent of parent or guardian.

Tracking and Advocating for Preventive Health Care

One of the services early childhood programs provide is acting as an advocate for families by requiring review of children's health data. Child care providers are receivers, collectors, and distributors of health information. Each child should have a health record maintained in the facility until the child leaves the program. With parental consent, both the administrator and teaching staff who work with the child and family should be familiar with this information. It is easy to assume that a child who appears healthy has no health needs. However, if you do not know the child is allergic to bee stings, you could face a shocking and life-threatening emergency if the child is stung. Or, knowing that a child has had an extended early hospitalization may help you understand separation difficulties or reluctance to become attached to staff.

In addition to obtaining health data for individual children, staff must learn how to address specific needs. For instance, asthma is very common in early childhood. If you have a child with asthma in your program, review the history of treatment and current medications and know when the child is due for the next follow-up visit to the clinician. Recommendations might change at clinician visits. Read about asthma's triggers and signs of distress. Ask the parents how the child responds best during an asthma episode. Ask your health consultant or the child's health provider to give you appropriate information about what you need to know, watch for, and do to prevent and manage an asthma episode. Let the family and the child's clinician know about any changes in the child's condition or response to possible triggers. With adequate information, you become part of the child's health team, helping the family and the child manage the situation with confidence.

Each staff member must be sensitive, conscientious, and systematic in addressing a child's health needs on a daily basis. Most teachers greet a child in the morning and notice such things as a new haircut or outfit. But look closely at the child's appearance. Through daily observation, you can learn a great deal about the child as an individual: typical coloring and appearance, moods and temperament, response to pain and sickness, activity level, and patterns of behavior. Each of these is a vital clue to health. Changes in the child's health from what is typical for a healthy child or for that individual child's typical state should be noted in the health record so that the information can be aggregated over time and shared when appropriate to determine a need for medical care.

While you are expected to be observant, you are not expected to be an expert on health. Observe the child, record relevant data, and then report anything unusual to the appropriate person on your staff and to the family. You cannot and should not offer diagnoses or treatment plans. But health professionals will be able to make better judgments using the information you have provided. Health observation is an important first step before screening, diagnosis, or treatment.

Keeping Health Records

Maintain a complete, up-to-date health record for each child enrolled in the program. The purpose of keeping health data is to make use it for the child's benefit. It does nothing for the child to have information stored in a file that no one reviews. Be sure the child's preventive services and follow-up care are up-to-date. The information should inform the care of the child. Make this health record available to the family when the child leaves the program or if the program closes. Establish clear policies about confidentiality (see below). The program may release no information without specific permission from the parent or guardian.

Health record contents

The health record (or related files) should contain at least the following information:

- telephone numbers where parents or guardians and at least two emergency contacts can be reached at all times (Figure 4.4)
- the name of the child's regular clinician and any other usual sources of health care, including the name of a specific contact person, an address, and telephone number
- child's pre-admission medical examination form, and subsequent updates at each check-up, including immunization status
- developmental health history (physical and developmental milestones as well as significant events)
- results of all screenings and assessments
- notations about allergies, special diet, chronic illness, or other special health concerns
- emergency transportation permission (Figure 4.4)
- all permission slips authorizing nonemergency health care and giving medications
- reports of all injuries or illnesses that occur while child is in the program
- medication logs
- reports of referrals and follow-up action
- notes about any health communication with family or health providers
- written correspondence about the child's health
- health observations of staff

Talking to the Child's Physician: Thoughts for the Child Care Provider

1. Understand the physician's constraints: The physician can only discuss issues concerning *a particular child* if the parents or legal guardian have given permission (a written consent, except for emergencies). Therefore, formalize that permission with the families, ahead of time if possible, by using a simple form. Copy it for your records, and send the original to the physician.

2. Find out the office operating procedures. Most pediatricians have a "call hour." Find out when it is and call then for nonemergency situations. If the issue will take more than 5 to 8 minutes to discuss, set up a phone appointment with the physician. Ask the office staff to pull the child's chart (and permission slip) and have it on the doctor's desk at the time of your call. Don't expect the physician to remember the child without this refresher. Also don't expect the clinician to
   • leave an examination to pick up your call if it's not an emergency
   • try more than twice to return your call if you are unavailable
   • discuss a child without the parent's approval

3. Format your call. Orient the physician. ("I'm calling about *[child's name].* I'm *[your name],* his child care provider for *[a week, a year].*") Say your topic sentence *first* with the appropriate level of urgency or worry: "She's fallen from the slide and appears badly hurt. I think she needs to be seen *now.*" "He has gone back to wetting after full toileting training. Today he seems to be mildly uncomfortable when urinating." "I've been concerned about her language development for at least six months; she isn't up to her peers at all and isn't picking up."

   Physicians like to hear the main point *first,* with substantiating material afterward. Educators and child care providers often like to tell the story from the beginning with descriptive detail. Physicians get distracted and lost with this approach. Hit them with the main point first, and do not add information that is not focused on this issue unless you clearly change subjects (for example, "A second issue concerning Elizabeth is . . .").

4. Clearly state what you would like of physicians; don't make them guess ("I'd like you to see this child now." "Please consider a hearing test next week during your planned visit").

5. Repeat plans or recommendations concisely to ensure that you understand each other, particularly about which of you will convey this information to the family. Listing is a style physicians can understand.

6. When discussing a case, convey observation data as separate from opinion ("David appears ill—he doesn't play actively, clings to the teacher, and is refusing foods"). These clear observations have been shown to be highly reliable indicators of illness—better in many cases than temperature, although that is important too and should be taken before you call about an ill child. "The child feels warm" does not provide enough information.

7. Don't ask physicians about the health issue of any child who is not their patient. This puts them in a bind: They cannot ethically or legally be involved unless the child is under direct care.

8. If you are concerned about the medical care or treatment of a child, share your concerns with the family and provide them with the names of *several* other physicians in your community for a second opinion. Beware of *single* referral suggestions; this can alienate the local professional community, making other physicians reluctant to help and support your center.

9. If your program needs help with health policies, ask a local pediatrician to serve as consultant. Do your homework first, using resources from NAEYC, the American Academy of Pediatrics, and your local public health department to develop drafts of policies or at least an outline of concerns or issues. Your consultant will bring greater enthusiasm and longevity to the project if she or he doesn't have to start from scratch on health policies, procedures, or staff education. Always separate this role from that of health management of individual children in the center.

Child care providers and the child's physician share a common commitment to advocacy for children. A close working alliance is natural. Speaking the same language and understanding each other's needs facilitate clear communication. Ultimately this will result in better care for children.

Source: Adapted from Dixon, S. 1990. Talking to the child's physician: Thoughts for the child care provider. *Young Children* 45 (3): 36-37.

Reviewing health records and tracking when the next services are due is a tedious task. While some software for child care programs include limited health data, such as immunizations, most "reminder" systems built into commercially available software require that child care providers determine and enter the next date when the record needs a new piece of data. You can set up an index card system that accomplishes the same purpose, filing an index card with the child's name and the next service due chronologically. Appointment and immunization tracking and reminder systems are sometimes used by clinicians, but many doctors depend on families to remember when their children are due back. Busy parents may forget or need reminders of when their children are due for their next preventive service.

Using the current schedule of preventive care, child care providers can advocate for each child to stay up-to-date with immunization and screening services given at routine checkups. Unfortunately, children sometimes miss checkups, or when they come for a checkup visit, they have pressing needs that can lead to temporary delays in routine care. Unless everyone involved with the child's care checks that routine services have been received, temporary delays can become permanent gaps. Every child care program should set up a system to review the record periodically to be sure that the child's services are up-to-date and that staff are familiar with his health data.

Confidentiality

Confidentiality of health records must be maintained to protect the child and family. Use the following guidelines when developing or reviewing your program's confidentiality policy.

- Health records must be kept from public access and unauthorized review.
- Information may not be shared with anyone inside or outside the facility without parental review and consent.
- Telephone requests for information from outside parties are not acceptable unless the parent has previously instructed you in writing to release information or gives/has given witnessed telephone consent (by use of an extension line or conference line).
- Information collected by others and forwarded to you with parental consent becomes part of the child's record and thus the responsibility of the program.
- All releases of information should be properly logged.
- Families have a right to see all information in their child's file.
- Families must be made aware of the nature and type of all information collected and how it will be used.
- A family member may ask to speak to you in confidence, but you must receive this information in a responsible manner. This is particularly true if child abuse is suspected. Your primary responsibility is to protect the child.

Make communication with clinicians a two-way street

In providing health care for a child, each family's pediatric clinician gathers information about the child's medical status, development, personality, family strengths and needs. When it is appropriate for the benefit of the child's care, and with parent consent, the clinician should share information with the child's other caregivers. Likewise, clinicians can learn more about the child and the family from the daily observations of caregivers.

To encourage good communication, set up a system to exchange information with community clinicians. One system involves sending by fax, mail, or hand-carried by parents a copy of each child's periodic reports (always with parental permission) to the clinician to share observations from the child care provider's perspective. The health data form used by child care programs to get reports from clinicians should request developmental information and relevant details on health issues and indicate how this information will be used for the child's benefit. Do not send a blank form with no identifying information about the child or the child care provider requesting the information. Form completion is a burden for everyone, but you can indicate a commitment to share the burden by completing all known information before sending the form to the clinician. Doing so is more likely to induce reciprocal communication. See "Talking to the Child's Physician: Thoughts for the Child Care Provider" on page 100 for more helpful tips.

The standards in Chapter 8 of *Caring for Our Children* specify the following topics to include in communications between the child's clinician and the child care program staff:

- identification of the child's medical home with contact information
- developmental variations, sensory impairment, or disabilities that may need consideration in the child care setting
- description of current physical, social, and language developmental levels
- current medications
- special concerns (such as allergies, chronic illness, pediatric first aid information needs)
- specific diet restrictions, if the child is on a special diet
- individual characteristics or personality factors relevant to child care
- special family considerations
- dates of communicable diseases

Remember, all communication concerning individual children must be done only with parents' permission. Who has access to children's records must be explicitly stated to and understood by all the families in the program.

What if medical experts disagree?

Some information about the health of young children in groups is so new that many health care providers have not yet been trained in current recommendations. Some approaches are controversial. Thus, one child's clinician may provide recommendations that differ from the advice of another child's clinician. This can be confusing and frustrating. As with all policy decisions, you will have to weigh the facts and rationale and make the best decision for your program. Work out with your health consultant what to do before difficult situations arise (for example, how to handle diarrhea before an outbreak occurs). Share these policies with parents.

When you receive conflicting opinions, follow this procedure:

1. Ask your consultant to broker differences of opinion for you.
2. If you have additional questions or conflicts (for example, between your health consultant and a child's pediatrician), contact your local department of health or your state department of public health. They have the legal responsibility to make decisions about health issues for groups of people.

Communicating with Families

Teachers and community human service professionals are partners with families to ensure the optimum development of children. Families, who provide the continuity of care for children into adulthood, are the primary observers, advocates, and providers of services their children need. However valuable the intervention, all service providers play only temporary roles in the lives of children and their families. Parents need information about health and safety in programs before, during, and after the decision to enroll children in child care.

Communications should be respectful and interactive, listening to what families want done to protect the health and safety of their children and what they understand (from whatever written or verbal information they have) about what the program requires and does for children. Families should be able to ask questions, express concerns, or suggest changes to improve the program. Child care providers and families need to work together respectfully to handle differences of opinion as they arise.

Both providers and parents of young children function day-by-day under considerable stress. As professionals, child care providers must be able to temporarily set aside their own concerns to see situations from the parents' perspective. Excluding children from child care, for example, puts a burden on families. Helping parents plan for the inevitable illnesses that require exclusion is a pre-enrollment task for programs. On the other hand, programs should not exclude mildly ill children who can participate without making demands on the staff that could pose a threat to the health and safety of other children or staff.

The requirement to give child care providers health data stimulates families to seek the health care their children need—and which they may have overlooked. Asking parents to seek information from their child's clinician may empower them to ask what they should ask of health professionals. On the other hand, asking parents to get notes from clinicians to certify wellness of children is an unfair burden to place on parents and their relationships with clinicians. Clinicians ask parents if the child seems well to determine the well-being of the child. They trust parents to know when their children are no longer acting sick. Except for diseases that require a laboratory test to determine whether the child is contagious, child care providers should base their assessment of the child's readiness to return to child care on what the parent tells them about how the child is behaving.

For many families, child care staff function as extended family. By reflecting on parental concerns and by providing information about alternative approaches, child care providers help families navigate their work and family lives more successfully. Communicating about health issues is one way providers support families as the most important source of continuing care for children.

Just as caregivers need to know from parents at the beginning of each day how the child feels and what, if any, problems to watch for, parents need to know similar information at the end of each day in child care. Illness tends to intensify in the evening, when everyone is tired and access to professional medical care is more difficult. When parents call a medical professional for advice, they will be asked how the child ate, drank, slept, behaved, voided, and defecated during the day. Child care providers need to establish a routine and effective way to communicate this information to parents daily. This may require being able to communicate in another language, using oral or written messages. Passing responsibility for a child from family to caregivers and back again requires diligent attention to sharing key information that guides decisions if the child's status changes.

In addition to daily transfer of information about the child's status, sharing of information among child care providers, family, and the child's clinicians is essential whenever significant health concerns arise. Caregivers and parents make observations and need to share information. This sharing enables competent care not only for the child with the problem but also for other children and staff who may be affected by their proximity to the ill child. Sometimes the situation may involve illness of a family member—as in a case of hepatitis A of an adult in the family of a child who seems well. In such a case, medical intervention must be prompt to protect the child, other children in the group, and staff.

Suggested Activities

- Contact the office manager or administrative staff in the office of a local pediatrician, a public health clinic, and a family practice. Ask what services are typically provided for a 3-year-old's checkup visit. Compare the responses with the AAP's recommended schedule of routine health services. Are they the same? What might happen to a child who does not receive the recommended services?

- Check the state regulations for what child care providers are required to document in the health records of children in the program. Compare this to the requirements in *Caring for Our Children*. Are the state requirements sufficient to ensure children in child care are fully protected against vaccine-preventable disease and have no detectable disabilities that routine screening would uncover?

- Ask the state licensing agency what they check in health records when they visit child care programs. Are they checking both immunizations and screening services? Are they selective about which ones they check or are they checking that the child care program gets information on all the currently recommended preventive health services for children?

Chapter 8

Staff and Consultants for Safe and Healthy Child Care

E nsuring health and safety is a basic responsibility of staff in an early childhood program. Health professionals who consult with child care providers contribute expertise, leadership, and motivation to reach for quality in the program's health component. Adults who work in child care should use best practices in their work. Best practices are described in written standards of nationally recognized organizations and agencies. For authoritative written health information, go online to the Websites of state and local public health agencies, the American Academy of Pediatrics, and oral health, mental health, and nutrition professionals with a pediatric focus.

Program Responsibilities of All Personnel

In the press of day-to-day operations, important elements of health and safety are easily forgotten. Each facility needs written policies and procedures for orientation of new staff, for regular self-evaluation by staff, and for evaluation by supervisors or peer reviewers. Self-study and peer validation such as that included in NAEYC accreditation help highlight areas in which staff may need to improve. Routine checks help raise everyone's awareness of problem areas.

Major Concepts

- All staff have responsibility for ensuring the health and safety of children in the facility.
- Individual staff have responsibilities related to their special task area, such as caregiving, nutrition, transportation, maintenance, administration.
- A health advocate is an on-site staff member empowered to raise health and safety issues and make sure that health is integrated with the other components of the child care program.
- Health concerns play a key role in recruitment, selection, and retention of staff.
- Paid and volunteer staff need training to acquire the knowledge and skills to maintain a safe and healthy child care program.
- All child care providers should identify and work with a child care health consultant to improve health and safety in the program.

Directors and supervisors

In addition to ensuring they are up-to-date with their own training in health and safety, directors and supervisors have a special duty to orient and monitor all adults—staff or volunteers—who work in child care for health and safety performance. Preservice and inservice requirements must be met conscientiously. When family members help out, or when substitutes less familiar with health and safety routines work in the program, directors and supervisors must assume oversight responsibilities.

While many health practices are common sense, some of the special precautions required for group care of children are not intuitive. For example, the extra attention paid to avoiding contamination during diaper changing in group care settings is less critical in a child's home; the number of people who can be made ill by germs from infected diapers is usually small in the home, but in child care, contamination of surfaces during diaper changing can infect caregivers, other children in the facility, and the families of the caregivers and children in that facility.

The health advocate

Every program benefits from identifying and supporting the role of someone willing to be a health advocate at the facility. The role can belong to a teacher, food service worker, maintenance person, member of the administrative staff, family child care provider, parent, or anyone who can take primary responsibility to function as a health advocate in the program. The health advocate is

- interested in the health aspects of the program
- understands the importance of maintaining a healthy environment and activities that prevent harm in the child care setting
- seeks and shares current information on how to ensure health and safety in child care
- has the support of supervisors and all adults who work in the program.

The health advocate is responsible for increasing the awareness of coworkers, families, and health professionals in the community about the potential of the child care program to prevent harm and promote health of children and families. While health advocates do not need to perform all health activities, they must see that health-related tasks are done or brought to the attention of those with the authority and skills to get them done.

Health advocates need the support of other members of the staff and parents. In some programs, the staff nominate the health advocate; in others, the administrator appoints the advocate. In either case, the program administrator should make sure that the health advocate has regular opportunities to report, review, discuss, and lead action teams so that the program pursues health and safety objectives effectively.

Caregivers and food service, transportation, and maintenance personnel

While some personnel in a child care setting have unique assignments, each person has a duty to ensure the health and safety of everyone in the facility. Everyone in a child care facility usually is involved in some way in food handling, so all staff must be aware of safe food temperatures, techniques

involved in safe food handling, handwashing procedures, and so on. Of course, food service staff need to know more about food safety and sanitation than other staff.

All staff should practice passenger and pedestrian safety. Drivers must know and use routines to be sure children are properly using seat restraints, know how to load and unload passengers safely, and must check all hidden spaces to be sure that all the children are out of the vehicle at the end of the ride. Drivers also need to know about vehicle maintenance, and emergency procedures for breakdowns. All staff involved in transportation should be skilled in pediatric first aid in the event of a mishap. While drivers may not be skilled caregivers, they should be developmentally appropriate in their interaction with children.

Maintenance workers should have an appreciation for how the program operates. Even if they do their work after the children and staff leave the building for the evening, they need to know where children eat, crawl on the floor, have their diapers changed, and so on, to give these areas appropriate attention.

Health and Safety Concerns in Recruiting, Selecting, and Retaining Staff

What the program advertises and shares with prospective and on-the job workers should be explicit about the attributes required for each role. Job descriptions help. Otherwise, refusal to hire someone or dismissal of someone with a disability that precludes competent performance of that role in the child care program could be viewed as discrimination. For example, maintenance and caregiving staff should be able to safely handle cleaning chemicals, using gloves as necessary. Those who have severe skin problems that makes them prone to injury from handling cleaning and sanitizing solutions, even when wearing gloves, should be counseled or otherwise helped to seek a different type of job.

Job descriptions

For each role in child care, there are job-related health concerns.

Caregivers. While seeking caregivers with a firm grounding in developmentally appropriate practice, administrators also must be aware of how physical and emotional health can influence job performance. For example, a caregiver who cannot hear well enough to distinguish the often difficult-to-understand speech of a young child may not effectively foster language development A caregiver who cannot see well enough to read may be unable to provide developmentally appropriate reading experiences to children. Caregivers who have frequent illnesses and absences provide discontinuous and unpredictable care.

Caregivers must be able to pick up infants and toddlers, eat the food that the children eat, move quickly enough to intercede in a situation where a child is in danger, and evacuate children in an emergency. Unless the program can provide accommodations for these core performance expectations, the quality of care provided by the entire program will be lessened by adults who are unable to perform because of physical or mental health problems.

Food service personnel. People who have never done quantity cooking are unlikely to have the necessary knowledge and skills to plan and prepare food in a way that prevents food poisoning and provides good nutrition. Food service sanitation and management routines are different for household and group situations. Preparing food for children is also different from cooking in a restaurant. These skills must be learned and practiced under supervision to work in child care.

Maintenance staff. Maintenance staff must provide the level of service required for sanitation and safety in child care. Cleaning of child care facilities requires more attention at the lower levels than does cleaning of office spaces. After cleaning, many surfaces require a separate sanitizing step. Tables, chairs, and other child equipment, floors, door knobs, toilet room and diapering areas all require special attention. Maintenance staff must be able to make prompt repairs, remove broken equipment, or provide barriers to keep children away from hazards that cannot be fixed right away.

Transportation staff. Drivers must have normal hearing and vision as well as the skills to drive whatever vehicle is being used. They must be mature, capable of making wise decisions in unexpected situations, and tolerant and supportive of age-appropriate behavior of children in their vehicles. Child care programs must be certain that drivers are not using medications or other substances that could affect driving.

Gathering necessary information about health concerns

To assess expected levels of illness, ask job applicants about days missed from work or school in the previous year. Asking about mental health problems requires sensitivity, but the question is essential. Frequent intermittent bouts of depression, episodes of unusual anxiety, and other mental health problems that are poorly controlled by medication are disabilities that should preclude professional work as a caregiver.

Eagerness to be involved in child care may make applicants or current staff reluctant to acknowledge disabilities or health problems of a less obvious nature. For the sake of the children, volunteers, applicants, and staff members should report these problems verbally to a supervisor.

Health assessments of staff and volunteers

The foundation for adult health in child care is the requirement that all adults (staff and volunteers) who work or wish to work in the program have periodic health exams. Such exams should be required before employment for adults who work 40 hours or more per month, but adults working fewer hours should be encouraged to have these exams too. Subsequent exams need to be performed routinely every 2 years and more often if there is any question that the adult's health is affecting performance on the job. The results of such exams are strictly confidential and can be given to the employer only with the staff member's permission. However, sharing of confidential job-related health information should be a condition of working in a child care setting. The child care program should specify the following for these occupational health examinations:

- content of the exam
- who can perform the exam
- how often it must occur
- special examinations for special roles, if any
- who receives the findings
- where the examinations can be performed
- who pays for the exam.

For examinations to be effective, the health professional conducting the exam must know the nature and demands of the adult's job. For instance, a chronic lower back problem may not be as critical to the job performance of a social worker as to the teacher of a toddler group. A sample adult health assessment form is in Appendix U of *Model Child Care Health Policies,* available from NAEYC and in *Caring for Our Children* from AAP.

Ideally, the results of a health exam should be received *before a job offer is made final and before contact with the children.* It is hard to deal with health concerns after an individual has begun to develop relationships or after the children and others have already been exposed. Of course, new health problems may develop after employment. This is why both regular exams and exams when health problems are suspected are important. Information about disabilities should be used to accommodate an otherwise qualified child care worker, but some health problems are incompatible with the requirements of a particular job.

Adult health assessments for child care work should include

- health history, physical examination, and laboratory findings as they relate to the individual's physical and emotional fitness for the job
- confirmation that the person is free of contagious diseases, including tuberculosis (TB). TB skin testing is needed on first entry into the child care field using the Mantoux method (a test performed with syringe and needle, *not* a multipuncture test). Adults residing in a family child care home must be TB skin tested also. Repeated skin testing should be required for those who have increased risk of TB because of HIV, chronic cough that could be from TB, foreign travel, or contact with homeless people, prison populations, or individuals with active TB. Those who do not have these risk factors do not require repeat skin testing after their first test on entry into the field
- immunization status and history of childhood infectious diseases, including measles, mumps, rubella, diphtheria, tetanus, polio, and chicken pox
- assessment of need for immunizations against influenza, pneumococcus, hepatitis A, and hepatitis B; and, if of childbearing age or if anticipating pregnancy, from risk of exposure to chicken pox, cytomegalovirus (CMV), and parvovirus (Fifth Disease). Annual influenza vaccination should be strongly considered for child care workers, not only for their own sake but also because of evidence that child care plays a role in spread of influenza in the community.
- condition(s) that might require emergency care
- limitation(s) in common situations such as difficulty being outdoors, skin conditions affected by frequent handwashing, allergy to art materials
- medication or special diet requirements that might affect job performance
- household members and their status regarding infectious diseases (for family child care or group home care)
- functional implications of visual acuity and hearing screening.

The current recommendations for TB screening of adults who work in child care are based on studies of the value of routine administrative screening. The Centers for Disease Control and Prevention advises that routine repeated screening of healthy individuals with previously negative skin tests is not a reasonable use of resources. Local circumstances and risks of exposure vary, so this recommendation should be subject to modification by local or state health authorities.

Since many caregivers lack health benefits and earn minimum wage, the cost of health exams is a problem. For those with health insurance, hepatitis B immunization to meet OSHA requirements may not be covered. For valued workers, child care budgets may have to stretch to cover the cost of health services required such as immunizations and health exams. Otherwise, the adult must be required to pay for these services as a condition for working in child care.

When staff have a disability that affects job performance, administrators should consult with ADA experts through the U.S. Department of Education-funded Disability and Technical Assis-

Figure 8.1. Protect Your Back

Most back pain is not the result of a single injury. Even though pain may be felt suddenly, the problem is almost always due to a combination of several factors, including poor posture, faulty body mechanics, stressful living or work habits, loss of flexibility, and a general decline of physical fitness. Back pain can be prevented by improving posture and body mechanics, organizing the ergonomic set-up of the workplace, and exercising regularly to improve flexibility and general fitness.

POSTURE

Having a firm, flattened abdomen and holding your stomach in when you stand and sit provide needed support for the lower spine.

SITTING

When you sit, maintain a normal spine curve. Sitting produces greater loads on the lower back than either standing or walking. Select a chair with a firm seat and adequate lower back support. Keeping your knees bent and resting your back against the chair prevents back strain. Don't sit too long; occasionally get up, stretch, and walk around.

DRIVING

When driving a car, move the seat forward to keep the knees higher than the hips. A small pillow or towel rolled behind the lower back provides extra support.

STANDING AND BENDING

Standing can be hard on your back. Try not to work for long periods in a bent-over position. Muscles and good posture help keep the spine in a balanced, neutral position. Abdominal muscles pull up in front and buttock muscles pull down in back to maintain the natural curve of the spine, allowing you to hold a balanced standing posture for long periods without tiring. Another technique is to stand with one foot elevated to a comfortable level. Switch feet every so often.

SLEEPING

Sleeping rests the back. When you are lying down, your back doesn't have to support your body weight. It is important to use a firm mattress. Sleep on your side with knees bent or on your back with knees elevated.

LIFTING TECHNIQUES

Everyone has a lifting technique that seems most comfortable. But there are basic rules that apply to all. These rules will help control and prevent back pain.

• Step up close to your work area or to a load. Don't overreach to grasp or lift.

• Get a firm footing. Keep your feet parted: one alongside, one behind the object.

• Grip the object with the whole hand. Get a firm grip with the palms of your hands because the palms are stronger than the fingers alone.

• Draw the object close to you, with arms and elbows tucked into the sides of your body to keep your body weight centered.

• Bend knees, lift with your legs—let your powerful leg muscles do the work of lifting, not your weaker back muscles.

• Avoid lifting above the waist, but if you must, reposition your grip to keep the weight centered. Arching your back during a lift makes nerve roots susceptible to pinching and can cause weak muscles to be strained.

• Twisting during a lift is a common cause of back injury. If you have to turn with a load, change the position of your feet. By simply turning the forward foot out and pointing it in the direction you intend to move, the greatest danger of injury by twisting is avoided.

MOVING

Use the suggestions in Figure 8.2 to avoid injury while doing child care work. For a week or two, think about each move before you make it. Moving to avoid injury soon becomes a habit.

Source: Adapted with permission by the National Safety Council. Click on www.nsc.org/products to order "Back Care."

tance Centers throughout the country. These centers can be reached by calling 800-949-4232.

Adults who work in child care need to notify their supervisor immediately about any injuries or illnesses they experience, especially those that might affect their health or the health and safety of the children. It is the responsibility of the administration, not the ill or injured staff member, to arrange for a substitute provider. Sometimes adults believe it is their responsibility to show up or to stay. No ill employee or volunteer should be required to stay at work; supervisors must insist that an ill employee go home. The supervisor will need to make staff adjustments to cover the duties of an adult whose ability to function is impaired.

If their condition could affect their ability to do their job or require an accommodation to prevent illness or injury to others, staff and volunteers should be required to have a health professional's note indicating their ability to return to work. For example, a pregnant employee, not immune to infections commonly found in child care that could damage the fetus, might be reassigned from an infant-toddler group to other work. Someone with a back injury might hurt himself again if he has to lift children or objects. A caregiver or food handler who had bacterial diarrhea might need to have negative cultures before returning to work.

Accommodating disabilities of staff and volunteers

When an adult who can make a valuable contribution to the program has a disability, supervisors must consider whether any reasonable accommodation would allow performance of the expected tasks. Inclusion of adults with disability in child care is desirable, but it cannot take priority over the primary responsibility of the program to provide competent care for children.

Preservice and inservice training

In addition to personally having up-to-date knowledge about health and safety in child care, a director of a center or a small family child care home network (enrolling 30 or more children) should arrange training for staff to fill any identified gaps in performance or background, and revisit the broad scope of information required for competent child care every 3 years. The topics to be assessed and covered by such training include

- child development knowledge and best practice, including knowledge about the developmental stages of each child in care
- child care as a support to families
- family relations
- ways that communicable diseases are spread and procedures for preventing the spread of disease, including handwashing, sanitation, diaper changing, food handling, health department notification of reportable diseases, equipment, toy selection and proper washing, sanitizing to reduce the risk for disease and injury, and health issues related to having pets in the facility
- immunization requirements for children and staff in child care settings
- common childhood illnesses and their management, including child care exclusion policies
- organization of the facility to reduce the risks for illness and injury
- teaching child care staff and children about infection and injury control
- staff occupational health and safety practices, such as proper lifting of children, handling of blood spills and risks from any chemicals used in the facility, in accordance with Occupational Safety and Health Administration (OSHA) regulations
- emergency procedures
- promotion of health in the child care setting
- management of a blocked airway, rescue breathing, and other first aid procedures required in caring for children
- recognition and reporting of child abuse in compliance with state laws
- nutrition and food service related to expected performance
- medication administration policies and procedures
- caring for children with special needs in compliance with the Americans with Disabilities Act (ADA), Individuals with Disabilities Education Act, and *Caring for Our Children*
- behavior management

Teaching the necessary information and skills involves telling, assigning reading, and orally reviewing what is expected, as well as actually showing what must be done and letting learners practice. The American Academy of Pediatrics (AAP) and the National Association for the Education of Young Children (NAEYC) publish videos, based on *Caring for Our Children,* that illustrate how to meet the

Figure 8.2. Wise Moves to Avoid Injury in Child Care

CHALLENGE	WISE MOVES
Lifting children, toys, supplies	Avoid lifting by having children climb steps with help. Pull child or object to be lifted as close as possible directly in front of you; squat and wrap your arms around whatever you are lifting, then tighten stomach muscles and use thigh muscles to raise yourself and your load. Lower objects and children by sliding them down your body to a level where you can squat or kneel to lower whatever you are putting down to its destination.
Inadequate work heights	Reorganize to store frequently used objects where you can reach them easily. Store heavy objects at waist height so you don't have to lift them. Adjust diapering and similar work surfaces to waist height; use adult-sized chairs whenever you can; squat or kneel on a kneepad if you can't sit down next to children to help. Use step stools to reach high places.
Lifting infants in and out of cribs	Do not use cribs with floor-level mattresses or those that do not have a side you can drop when putting children in or out. Get you and the child as close to the crib side as possible before you lift.
Frequent sitting on the floor without back support	When possible, sit against a wall or furniture that supports your back. Sit with a little pillow in the small of your back when you can. Stretch when you get up.
Carrying heavy objects or children	Use carts and strollers. Let children climb up with a step stool. If possible, divide heavy loads into several smaller loads and use carts that can be slid under the load and then tilt the load onto the cart.
Awkward posture to open windows or adjust objects	Move objects away from the window to get as close as possible to it. Put one foot on a step stool for better leverage. Lubricate the window mechanism to make opening it easier. Ask for help from a co-worker when the job is hard.
Sweeping/picking up crumbs and small toys from the floor	Use a long-handled dustpan and broom. Keep a separate one for toys (clean) and things going into the trash.
Caring for children with special needs	Get specific training from the child's physical therapist about how to move and carry the child.
Caring for children during active play when sudden moves are needed	Avoid twisting. Practice turning and bending to intercept a running or falling child so the move becomes natural. Bend knees when pushing children in swings. Use good body mechanics to help children on and off equipment.

Source: Adapted from "Preventing Work-Related Musculoskeletetal Injuries" by Alicia M. Wortman, in July/August 2001 issue of *Child Care Information Exchange.* Reprinted with permission from Child Care Information Exchange, 800-221-2864, www.ChildCareExchange.com.

standards in centers and family child care homes. These videos can be viewed independently by prospective staff for orientation but are most effectively used as triggers for interactive training sessions. Training may be obtained from qualified personnel of children's and community hospitals, managed care companies, health agencies, public health departments, pediatric emergency room physicians, or other health professionals in the community. For more information about training opportunities, contact the AAP Healthy Child Care America Project, the National Resource Center for Health and Safety in Child Care, or the National Training Institute for Child Care Health Consultants. (See Appendix 1 for contact information.)

Health issues related to turnover of staff and children

Aside from the obvious emotional benefits of low turnover of adults and children involved with the program, there are health benefits too. High turnover constantly introduces new infections. New children and staff may not be immune to the infections already there and may become sick more often. Children who leave the program to go to another facility take their germs with them and can spread disease throughout the community. Risks of injury increase until new staff have learned safety guidelines. By training and working with coworkers as a team over a period of time, child care programs can improve consistency in safety routines.

Preventing turnover of children requires quality programming that satisfies the needs of children and families. When a program does not provide the length of day or number of days when families need child care, parents usually seek supplemental "wraparound" care elsewhere in the community. If children have multiple sources of care over the course of a week or month, these various facilities share infectious diseases.

Staff turnover is widespread and difficult to solve. Much of the problem is due to inadequate compensation and lack of benefits for child care workers. Sometimes the problem is made worse by difficult working conditions. When advocating for worthy wages for caregivers, include the health impact of turnover in your list of arguments for better financing of child care. The fact that turnover poses disease risks may be persuasive to those who do not understand the value of continuous, warm, interactive relationships to quality child care. If your

program experiences an unusual level of turnover despite paying wages comparable to those paid by other child care providers, look for the cause and a solution.

With large numbers of comings and goings, programs with 50 or more children open more than 10 hours a day appear to be at greater risk for spreading infectious diseases. Such centers should be particularly careful about preventive health routines. Grouping children together so that one group does not interact with other groups is a good way to reduce the spread of infection. Frequently, providers mix one group of children with another. Many have early arrivers and later leavers from all the groups stay together to reduce the number of staff needed and yet retain good ratios. While seemingly practical, this mixing of groups ensures spread of disease to everyone. Best practice is to separate groups as much as possible at all times of the day, even if it requires more staff at the beginning and end of the day.

When infectious disease is on the rise, keeping children within their own groups should be even more rigid than usual. Do not admit new children into your program during an outbreak of a serious infectious disease (hepatitis A, for example). With your health consultant, decide on an appropriate waiting period for each infectious disease. At all times, but especially during outbreaks, minimize contact and shared use of facilities by children in diapers with older children. Mixed-age grouping offers developmental learning opportunities but poses special challenges for control of infection. When it is practiced, staff must follow hygiene and surface sanitation procedures vigilantly.

If you can, avoid having staff care for different groups of children during the same day. Moving staff between groups during the day also promotes the spread of disease. If assigning staff to multiple groups during the day is unavoidable, be sure staff wash their hands carefully, and even change their outer clothing, when moving from group to group.

Adult Health

Staff are key in a good program for young children. Most are concerned about personal illness risks, but few recognize specific potential health hazards of their workplace. These hazards include an increased risk of getting illnesses; exposure to toxic chemicals in art supplies, cleaning agents, and pesticides; back problems due to frequent heavy lifting and stooping; poor lighting that increases the risk of injury; high noise levels that affect hearing and stress; clutter that affects cleanliness and safety; and job stress in general.

Committed caregivers may ignore their own health needs because they lack health benefits and time off and because they feel responsible for meeting children's needs first. Programs can alleviate some of these concerns. Each child care program should

- establish an adult health plan
- create a positive, healthful environment for adults
- help adults to look after their own health needs
- provide an adequate benefits package for health care.

Ways to promote good adult health

Staff must care for themselves to be able to provide the best care for children. Take the time to look at your environment and program demands. How can you make staff more comfortable? What policies need to be revised to meet adult needs? Are you encouraging good health for yourself and others? Can sick adults stay home without guilt or loss of pay?

When staff and administration work together, it is possible to adjust a facility and program to the needs of the adults and the children. Here are some examples of solutions to adult health problems:

- Require initial and ongoing health assessments to identify individual susceptibility to the known occupational risks of early childhood programs—infectious diseases, back injuries, rashes, stress, environmental exposures, etc.
- Negotiate flexible benefits packages to meet staff needs, including paid leave (annual, sick, and/or personal), medical insurance, and other options.
- Provide high counters with stools, or an adult-size table and chairs, for staff who do clerical, administrative, or curriculum planning work. Bring in adult-size folding chairs for staff meetings. Place a telephone book on a child-size chair to make it a more comfortable seat.
- Set aside private adult space and provide adequate backup to ensure genuine breaks to alleviate stress.
- Include break and substitute plans in personnel policies.
- Train staff in proper techniques for lifting and bending to prevent leg and back strain (see Figure 8.1)

- Provide gloves to use with cleaning agents to prevent skin irritation.
- Establish preventive health policies that reduce exposure to childhood illnesses, and practice preventive procedures to help keep adults and children healthy.

Infectious Disease Risks for Adults

Infectious diseases are common in groups of young children, but most are not serious and would probably spread at a similar rate in a large family. However, because staff care for a number of young children from different families, many of whom cannot control their body fluids and have not yet learned principles of hygiene, infections can spread to many other employees, children, family members, and—in the case of a pregnant employee or parent—to the fetus. Therefore, it is important that all employees be familiar with common infections and related prevention measures. The two most important barriers to the spread of infection are immunization and hygiene, especially handwashing. See the chapter on infections for details.

OSHA requires that workers in child care whose activities might expose them to blood or body fluids of other individuals should be offered Hepatitis B vaccine within 10 days of starting a job. Alternatively, the employee must be offered gamma globulin and Hepatitis B vaccine immediately following a blood exposure.

All staff should receive training in how to handle blood and other body fluids. OSHA requirements apply to blood spills, but Standard Precautions cover

---

Special Safeguards for Pregnant Women

Female staff of childbearing age should be aware that they can be exposed to infectious diseases that can cause significant health problems for fetuses. These infections include rubella, measles, mumps, varicella (chicken pox), hepatitis B, cytomegalovirus, herpes, parvovirus, and HIV infection. Women of childbearing age should discuss these risks with their health care provider. Some of these infections are a risk to the fetus only if the woman did not have the disease in childhood or receive an immunization.

the exposure that can occur from contact with any body fluid. The specific procedures to follow in these situations are detailed in chapter 2 and in *Caring for Our Children.*

When Not to Come to Work

Children inevitably catch colds and flu. Adults working daily with young children are also likely to become ill. Yet, because of the difficulty of arranging for and keeping dependable substitutes, many programs have inadequate substitute policies. The result is that many staff keep working when they are ill, convincing themselves that they really are not that sick. The guidelines for exclusion of children who have infections that pose a risk to others apply equally to adults who work in child care. Staff and volunteers should not come to work when they cannot participate in the program at the level they would normally or if they have a disease that poses a risk to others in the group care setting.

Substitutes

Even though creating a reliable substitute policy is difficult, substitute coverage is critical to a well-run program. Here are some suggestions for handling the need for substitutes: Consider hiring a flexibly scheduled part-time permanent substitute or joining with other programs to hire rotating substitutes. This allows each program some guaranteed coverage and provides dependable employment for the substitute. Even when nobody is absent, a sub can fill in while regular staff attend parent conferences, planning sessions, or other meetings. Set an appropriate salary for substitutes. Regularly evaluate your substitute procedure to see if it needs to be updated, and keep the sub list active. Call subs periodically to make sure they are still available. Let parents know about the procedure.

Breaks

Because of the cost of hiring additional staff, most programs accommodate breaks by shifting assignments among regular personnel. Remember that whenever staff enter or leave an area occupied by a group of children, they should wash their hands. Here are some suggestions for arranging breaks:

• Nonteaching staff can cover breaks on different days of the week.

• Assign family members, students, and community volunteers as floaters who can work with a regular member of the staff while the usual coworker takes a break. The key to making this plan work is regular scheduling and dependable volunteers. Volunteers should receive a thorough orientation to their duties and have the same monitoring skills and health responsibilities as regular staff. (Be sure to monitor their handwashing.) In a well-staffed program, one volunteer is designated as a floater during break time for a week at a time. This person can become familiar with each classroom and also gain perspective on the program. Again, before moving to a new group, this person must perform careful handwashing and may need to put on a clean smock or some other overgarment.

• Overlap staff shifts. Afternoon shifts, for example, can begin during the last half hour of the morning shift. Although this model is more expensive, it covers breaks and also allows teachers time to communicate.

• Provide a quiet, separate, and relaxing space for staff. Even if space is limited, a comfortable chair placed in front of a window can serve as a place to relax. If at all possible, the program should pay for refreshments for the staff.

Child Care Health Consultants and Trainers

Child care is affected by many technical health and safety issues. Even the most conscientious child care professional cannot be fully informed about all health matters that affect the program, the staff, the children, and their families. *Caring for Our Children* standards specify that infant-toddler programs should have at least a monthly visit from a child care health consultant; all other programs should have at least quarterly visits. In states where regulations require these visits, surveys show that if the requirement were to be eliminated, early childhood professionals find the visits so helpful that they would continue them.

Federal support for states to implement projects under the Healthy Child Care America Campaign have significantly increased community resources for health consultation to child care of all types. Contacts for these state projects can be obtained online through **www.aap.org**, using the Community Pediatrics link to the Healthy Child Care America page.

Few child care staff are trained as health professionals, and few health professionals have training about community child care programs. As a result, relationships between these professionals must be built sensitively. When physical, mental, social, or health concerns are raised about a program, or for a specific child or family, they need to be addressed appropriately, with mutual respect for all concerned.

An overall child care health consultant who can handle most program needs is usually a pediatric nurse, pediatric nurse clinician, community health nurse, pediatrician, or family practice physician. In addition to an overall consultant, programs may need to use other consultants with specialized knowledge in a variety of fields, such as physical and mental health care, nutrition, environmental safety and injury prevention, oral health care, and developmental disabilities.

Knowledge and skills of child care health consultants

In *Caring for Our Children* the standards on child care health consultation define the knowledge base that the child care health consultant must have personally or obtain by involving other health professionals. This knowledge base includes

- use of the reference resource *Caring for Our Children: National Health and Safety Standards: Guidelines for Out-of-Home Child Care Programs*
- how child care facilities conduct their day–to–day operations
- child care licensing requirements
- disease-reporting requirements for child care providers
- immunizations for children
- immunizations for child care providers
- injury prevention for children
- staff health, including occupational health risks for child care providers
- oral health for children
- nutrition for children
- inclusion of children with special health needs
- recognition and reporting requirements for child abuse and neglect
- community health and mental health resources for child and family health.

The health consultant also must have the skills to use the required knowledge base effectively. These skills include the ability to perform or arrange for performance of the following activities:

- teaching child care providers about health and safety issues
- teaching families about health and safety issues
- assessing child care providers' needs for health and safety training
- assessing families' needs for health and safety training
- meeting on-site with child care providers about health and safety
- providing telephone advice to providers about health and safety
- providing referrals to community services
- developing or updating policies and procedures for child care programs
- reviewing health records of children
- reviewing health records of staff
- helping to manage the care of children with special health care needs
- consulting with a child's health professional about medication
- interpreting standards or regulations and providing technical advice separate and apart from the enforcement role of a regulation inspector.

Although the child care health consultant may take on other roles, such as providing direct care to some of the children or serving as a regulation inspector, these roles should not be mixed with the child care health consultation role. To succeed, the child care health consultant must have contact with the facility's administrative authority, the staff, and the children's families. The administration should review, respond to, and implement reasonable recommendations provided by the child care health consultant. Programs with a significant number of non-English-speaking families should seek a consultant who is culturally sensitive and knowledgeable about community health resources serving linguistically and culturally diverse families.

Health professionals who serve as child care health consultants do not always have a public health perspective or the full range of knowledge and skills required for a group program. For example, a pediatrician caring for many of the children in the program may not be able to advise about food safety and sanitation and while a sanitarian may provide excellent health consultation on food safety, hygiene, and infectious disease control, another health professional may need to be consulted about medication administration or playground safety.

Seeking and choosing a child care health consultant

Health consultants should have specific training in the child care setting. Such training is not yet commonly included in health professional curricula but is being provided in special courses offered by health professionals who have become involved in child care health consultation. Trainers of child care health consultants may be graduates of a federally funded program at the University of North Carolina called the National Training Institute for Child Care Health Consultants. In addition to contacting the Healthy Child Care America program in your state, you can ask the child care regulatory agency and your state department of health for help in finding a qualified health consultant.

Child care health consultants may be employed by public or nonprofit agencies such as health departments, resource-and-referral agencies, or other health institutions, or they may work as independent contractors. Graduate students in a discipline related to child health can provide acceptable child care health consultation as long as they are supervised by faculty knowledgeable in child care. Students come and go fairly rapidly and rapid turnover of a consultant may not fit well with the ability of many child care programs to improve operations. By providing continuity of relationship with the child care facility over an extended period of time, the supervising faculty can develop trust, mutual respect, and understanding of the needs of the child care program, essential to an effective child care health consultant's role.

Programs also should not overlook health professionals with pediatric and health consultant experience who are parents of children enrolled in their facility. However, involving parents as health consultants requires caution to avoid crossing boundaries of confidentiality and conflict of interest. Some state regulations limit what roles a parent health professional can fulfill.

Paying a health professional for consultation and training

To foster access to and accountability of health consultants, programs should offer some form of compensation to consultants who do not do this work as part of their regular job. Consider alternative approaches that make the arrangement work best for the program and for the consultant. A yearly retainer entitling the program to unlimited telephone advice and a specified number of on-site visits and training sessions is best for some providers. For others, a contractual arrangement based on a fee-for-service payment is compatible with the uncertain availability of the consultant and the precarious finances of the child care program. In fee-for-service arrangements, it is easier to set a cost per hour of service or a specific fee for each service the program might request rather than negotiating the fee each time.

Public health professionals do not usually charge a fee for their services or they charge only a nominal fee. Even when there is no fee involved, child care facilities should define the expectations with the health consultant in writing so that both parties are clear about each other's expectations.

Specialized consultation for facilities serving children with disabilities

When the program has children with developmental delay or disabilities, the staff or consultants should include health professionals with expertise in the area of the child's disability.

Using a health professional as a consultant or trainer

For both center-based and family child care facilities, the health consultant should review and approve the program's written health policies. The policies and procedures reviewed for approval by child care health consultants should include

- admission and readmission after illness, including inclusion/exclusion criteria
- health evaluation and observation procedures on intake, including physical assessment of the child and other criteria used to determine the appropriateness of attendance
- plans for health care and management of children with communicable diseases
- plans for surveillance and management of illnesses, injuries, and other problems that arise in the care of children
- plans for caregiver training and for communication with families and health care providers
- policies regarding nutrition, nutrition education, and oral health
- plans for the inclusion of children with special health needs
- emergency plans
- policies regarding staff health
- policies for administration of medication.

When their busy schedules permit, many health professionals enjoy doing training sessions for child care providers. Programs can help health professionals be more effective trainers in the following ways:

• Suggest some hands-on demonstrations that would be welcomed by the group, or ask the health professional to plan some.

• Prepare a list of questions that the staff would like to have answered. The questions will help orient the health professional to focus on appropriate concerns and the level of sophistication of the staff and families to receive the training.

• Offer instructional supports such as flip charts and markers, a videotape that orients everyone to the topic, pictures that show where health issues are experienced in the facility. Many health professionals are comfortable talking with slides, and some need to be reminded to spend some time getting to know the audience and letting participants ask questions of concern to them.

All too often, child care programs receive seemingly conflicting recommendations from varied sources. In health-related matters, equally authoritative sources may differ. An issue that affects just one child or one staff member can be decided by that person's physician. But if the issue involves more than one child or adult in the program, the opinion of the program's health consultant should prevail after he or she consults with the sources of the differing opinions. In matters of public policy about health actions, the public health officer in the health department with jurisdiction has the final say. Once an action plan is set, the child care program administrator should inform all others who were consulted about the decision and the rationale for rejecting opinions that are not being followed. This feedback leaves the door open for future input and helps generate support for the action plan.

Suggested Activities

• When was your last health assessment? What was covered that would be an appropriate concern for working in a child care setting? What was not covered that might affect occupational health concerns of child care?

• What health concerns would be issues to address with a volunteer? With a colleague, role-play an interview with a volunteer about health issues. How do you feel about asking these questions? How does your colleague feel about being asked?

• Think about a time when you or someone you know suffered a back injury. What could have prevented the injury? What has been done since to prevent reinjury?

• Look in the community for possible sources of child care health consultation. Call one or two and ask if the agency or individual gives telephone advice, on-site observations, or training of child care staff. If not, ask why not. If service is being provided, ask about arrangements and the service rendered in the past year.

• Use the list of topics on which staff should have training to think about resources for obtaining such training in your community. Who would you ask to do it? How would you prepare the trainer to understand what the child care providers need? What methods of training work best for a group of child care providers?

Chapter 9

Facility Design and Support Services for Safe and Healthy Child Care

Major Concepts

- The physical environment of a child care program influences the behavior of the users.
- Too little or poorly designed free space creates risks for injury and disease.
- Experts in engineering, fire safety, plumbing, heating and cooling, ventilation, and lighting can contribute significantly to the quality of child care.
- Transporting children to and from child care is a universal activity, whether families do it or the program does it.
- Transportation-related injuries are the leading cause of death for young children, about half from passenger injury and the other half as pedestrians. Most of these deaths are preventable.
- Field trips, which usually involve transportation, require special planning for safety.
- Routine cleaning and sanitation schedules and procedures are key elements in a safe and healthy child care setting.

The longest chapter of *Caring for Our Children* addresses specific standards for each aspect of the physical plant of a child care program. Other chapters of *Caring for Our Children* include standards describing the equipment and maintenance routines required for quality child care. In both cases, the standards include references to expert sources of information that child care providers will find helpful when renovating or building a new facility. This chapter of *Healthy Young Children* provides a general overview of facility, transportation, and maintenance issues.

Some of these issues have been identified in other chapters of *Healthy Young Children*. Others are addressed here for the first time. Protecting children from harm requires risk reduction in many areas outside the purview of early education experts. However, a child care program administrator must be aware of these issues and know where to find other experts to help address them when needed.

Space and Structural Design

The design of areas that children and adults use influences how they behave and feel in that space. Open spaces invite gross motor activity, while object-filled spaces focus attention in a smaller frame of things to be seen, touched, or used in some way. Odors, sounds, sights, textures, temperatures, and aesthetic preferences all play a role in the experience that an environment provides.

Many child care facilities are located in buildings never designed for young children. Churches, stores, warehouses and office space are pressed into service as child care facilities. Homes that were intended to care for more than one generation of a single family are being used as community gathering spots for children from multiple families. Such buildings are often available because they have no other economically useful purpose or are not being used for part of the day or part of the week. Usually, the health and safety issues involved in using these buildings rise to top priority when government inspectors call attention to code requirements. Areas with high levels of air pollution, loud noises, heavy traffic, deep excavations, toxic materials in the soil, radiation or radon hazards are undesirable for child care facilities. An environmental audit is essential before choosing a child care site. If one has not been done on at the site of an existing child care facility, it should be arranged so that hazards can be identified and abated.

Child care experts use 35 square feet of free space per child as a guide to meeting the space needs of a group of children younger than school age and 40 square feet per child with special needs. This space does not include space used for kitchen and food preparation areas, toilet rooms, offices, staff rooms, hallways, stairways, storage, laundry, mechanical equipment, rooms for illness care, and furnishings in the child care areas. Lack of space is associated with difficult behavior and increased density of air pollutants, including germs. Usually, in any child care space, measuring 50 square feet wall-to-wall with the usual amount of furniture provides the appropriate space without crowding. In family child care homes, eat-in kitchens and open passages may be used as usable space; children may be able to move more freely from room to room, so a layout is best that ensures that the caregiver can monitor the children from wherever she is at any moment. For school-age child care, space must include a separate area where children have tables and chairs to do their homework.

Child care centers and family child care homes should comply with all applicable building codes. When these codes conflict with one another, each rationale should be examined to see how the intent of the conflicting requirements can be met simultaneously or with the least risk. The entire building should be structurally sound, weather-tight, with finishes that control mold dust and entry of pests. Windows and doors should be suitable for children's environments—fitted with safety glass and guards, views that reach child-eye level, and designed for easy exit in an emergency.

As much as possible, design safety features into the building. Windows in walls deny privacy to adults, thus reducing the potential for child abuse. Vision panels in doors allow adults to see a child who is near the door from the opposite side and allow the child to see someone coming into the room before the door is opened. Doors should have integral finger-pinch protection gaskets and slow-closing devices. Windows should open to ventilate rooms with fresh air or some other system installed to provide the required volume of fresh, outdoor air

to rinse through the room hourly (see ventilation specification below).

Exit routes must lead to a sheltered place if children and staff cannot re-enter the building. Alternate exit routes should be available in case the most convenient way out is blocked. Consideration should be given to how nonambulatory or less cooperative children can be evacuated in an emergency.

The finishes used on room surfaces and the type of furnishings placed in rooms should be chosen based on consideration of where nonporous surfaces are needed for sanitation and where soft elements absorb sound and provide comfort (washable fabrics). Placement of sleep equipment can include areas used at other times for play, but the total area must be sufficient to provide 3 feet of space between sleep equipment of adjacent children who are resting.

The outdoor play area must be ample and well-designed for the intended users. Playgrounds designed for school-age children should not be used by preschoolers and toddlers. Generally, 75 square feet of space per child using the playground is appropriate, with no more than two shifts of children from the facility required. The outdoor space should be designed for play value and safety. Since the greatest number of serious injuries occur during active play, playgrounds deserve special attention. Playground safety has so many technical issues that child care centers should be sure that a Certified Playground Safety Inspector reviews existing playgrounds and any plans for new ones. The same issues apply to indoor areas used for active play; putting a roof over and walls around a space does not change the need for cushioning surfaces under climbing equipment.

Equipment

The interaction between the space and furnishings helps direct people to desired (or undesired) activities. The types of activity centers and tools that are available determine how well children and adults can carry out the program's philosophy. Whatever is chosen should incorporate principles of health and safety. Sinks must be located where handwashing should take place. Food preparation surfaces must be totally separate from surfaces used to change diapers. Diaper-changing tables should have nothing on them that can't be sanitized easily after each diaper change. To avoid injury, equipment used for play should be sized to the developmental abilities of the children. All equipment, materials, furnishings, and toys should be sturdy, safe and in good repair, meeting the recommendations of the Consumer Product Safety Commission (CPSC) for control of known hazards.

More stringent requirements apply to child care than to furnishings in homes. For example, baby walkers that a child can move across the floor should not be used in any type of child care facility. Communal, unsupervised water-play tables should not be used because they have a high probability of spreading infectious disease. Using communal water tables requires considerable attention to detailed arrangements. It is permissible only if the children are supervised, the table is filled with fresh water right before use or supplied with freely flowing water, all surfaces and objects are sanitized before the next group uses the water table, only children free of cuts and runny noses are allowed to play in the water, children wash their hands before water play, and no child is allowed to drink the water from the table.

Equipment should be organized to reduce the risk of back injuries for adults, provided that such measures do not pose hazards for children or interfere with the implementation of the program. Furnishings should enable caregivers to hold and comfort children while minimizing the need for bending, lifting, and carrying heavy children and objects. Caregivers should not routinely be required to use child-size chairs, tables, or desks.

Air Quality, Ventilation, Heating, and Cooling

A draft-free temperature of 65 to 75 degrees F at 30 to 50 percent humidity should be maintained in the winter months, and 68 to 82 degrees F at the same range of humidity in the summer months. Rooms that children use should be heated, cooled, and ventilated to not only achieve the desired temperatures but also prevent accumulation of odors and fumes. Air exchange should be a minimum of 15 cubic feet per minute per person of outdoor air. Heating and air-conditioning equipment should be inspected and maintained by qualified contractors, usually those who follow the guidelines of the national standard setting organizations. Heating devices should not expose children to surfaces hot enough to burn them or expose them to toxic fumes. For details, see the specific standards in *Caring for Our Children* and references to credentialed national organizations.

Lighting

Natural lighting should be provided in rooms in which children work and play for more than two hours at a time. Where possible, install windows at child's eye level so children can see the outdoors while inside. Visual stimulation is developmentally appropriate practice. Natural lighting provided by sky lights exposes children to variations in light during the day that is less perceptually stimulating than eye-level windows but is still preferable to artificial lighting. Studies on school performance suggest that children learn better in classrooms with daylight and the opportunity for natural ventilation. *Caring for Our Children* gives specifics for levels of illumination by type of activity.

Noise Levels

Noise in child care spaces should not exceed 35 to 40 decibels at least 80 percent of the time. In practical terms, this means that it should be easy to hear and understand a conversation spoken without raising one's voice. Use of noise-absorbing materials can help: acoustical tiles on ceiling or walls, carpeting on walls, partitions and other hard surfaces—all located where they are cleanable and installed to meet fire safety requirements.

Electrical Items

Electricity is a potential source of injury. Safety covers and shock protection devices are essential where young children are in care. Water and electricity pose special hazards and must be kept separated. Electric cords must be beyond where children who are mouthing objects can chew or bite into them. Inspect all electrical fixtures and appliances, wiring, and outlets to be sure they do not pose a fire or shock hazard.

Plumbing

We generally take safe water for granted or make assumptions about safe sources of water that are not necessarily correct. For example, many people prefer to drink bottled water even though the bottled water industry is essentially unregulated and the content of water bottles, even from the same company, has been found to vary substantially. Water supplies should be tested by public health authorities to be sure they contain no unhealthy bacterial or chemical contaminants. Water used in child care should be from a source approved by the local public health authorities.

Handwashing sinks are critical to infectious disease control in child care. If plumbing is unavailable to provide a handwashing sink, facilities should use a portable water supply and a sanitary catch system approved by the local public health authority. The water in handwashing sinks should be at a temperature of at least 60 and no hotter than 120 degrees F. The water should flow for at least 30 seconds without having to reactivate the faucet. Hands-free faucets are widely available and provide a significant reduction in hand contamination where they are available. Handwashing sinks should be adjacent to the diaper changing table or, when not possible, within 10 feet. Provide step stools that allow children to use the sinks comfortably. Handwashing sinks should be separate from those used for food preparation or washing out contaminated articles.

Drinking water should be freely available to children indoors and outdoors—preferably in fountains but acceptably with a portable water supply or faucet used with single use drinking cups. Lead content of water should be checked at drinking fountains.

Swimming and wading pools pose special hazards that require not only enclosures to prevent drowning but also monitoring of water quality and equipment for sanitation. Few child care facilities are able to undertake safe maintenance of swimming and wading equipment. Those that choose to do so should check the standards in *Caring for Our Children* for detailed requirements and work with local public health authorities.

Portable sink equipment or camp-type sinks make availability of sinks with running water possible everywhere (for an example, see **www.nuconcepts. com**). Toilets and sinks with running water for handwashing should be located no farther than 40 feet from the perimeter of all areas that children use, and on the same floor as the children unless the children are always escorted to the toilet. The ratio of toilets and hand sinks should be at least 1:10 for toddlers and preschool age children and 1:15 for school-age children. Nonflushing equipment used for toilet learning does not count in these ratios. "Potty chairs" pose a significant sanitation hazard, so their use is strongly discouraged.

Transportation

Transportation is an important aspect of all early childhood programs. Whether you drive the children to and from their homes each day or schedule only an occasional field trip, the cars or buses that you use form part of your environment. Motor vehicle injuries represent the greatest threat to a child's life. You can reduce the chances of injury to children and staff during transport by being alert to potential dangers, eliminating or avoiding these dangers, and knowing what to do when an emergency occurs.

This chapter offers some ideas for setting up and maintaining a safe transportation system. More detailed resources are available from the Healthy Child Care America program of the American Academy of Pediatrics (AAP) at 888-227-5409 or childcare@aap.org and from the Traffic Safety Institute (TSI) at 405-954-3112. TSI also has a training curriculum designed specifically for child care professionals.

Decisions to transport children involve consideration of family needs and legal, regulatory, moral, and ethical concerns. By learning about safe transportation, child care providers can reduce their liability and teach families and children how to avoid injury related to transportation by foot, car, bike, and bus.

The first step is to find out about and follow all state laws and licensing regulations pertaining to your program's transportation. Next, develop a written policy clearly stating the rules, the responsibilities of staff and children, and the emergency procedures to be followed. Written policies and guidelines do not guarantee safety, but if everyone knows and uses them, they reduce the likelihood of injury. See Figure 9.1 for additional safety rules.

Child safety restraints

All states require that children be fastened in a properly adjusted safety seat or seat belt while riding in a vehicle. Properly used child safety restraints are very effective in reducing death and injury. The best ones are those that fit in the vehicle being used, fit the child being transported, are used correctly every time, and have never been in a crash. A child automotive safety device performs three major roles in a crash: (1) it prevents the child from being thrown from the vehicle; (2) it prevents the child from crashing into other passengers and the inside of the vehicle; and (3) it absorbs the crash forces and distributes them over the strong parts of the body.

Figure 9.1. Transportation Safety Rules

1. Make sure all vehicles used to transport children have the most recent federally approved safety seats and/or safety belts. Follow the manufacturer's instructions, then contact local police, state police, or other public safety officials to arrange for a NHTSA-certified car seat technician to check the installation and planned use.

2. Plan travel so no child spends more than one hour in the vehicle.

3. Check staff:child ratios to be sure they are at least what is required for child care spaces indoors (do not count the driver in the ratio.)

4. Secure all children and adults in their own safety seat or safety belt. Never put two or more children in the same safety belt. Always adjust a car seat for the child sitting in it.

5. Daily check vehicles for any problems with seat restraints.

6. Immediately before each trip, the driver should conduct a quick five-minute check to ensure that the vehicle is working well and contains nothing that could harm the children. If the day is warm, the vehicle's air conditioning system must be capable of keeping the temperature below 82 degrees F; if the day is cold, the heating system must keep the temperature above 65 degrees F during the ride.

7. Ask drivers to remain alert to changes in the vehicle while driving. Unusual odors, sounds, or vibrations can be warning signals for a breakdown. No loud radio or other noises should interfere with hearing traffic alerts or mechanical problems.

8. Never transport children or adults in the cargo area of a station wagon or van.

9. Never leave children alone in a vehicle, even briefly.

10. Keep sharp or heavy objects out of the passenger compartment. They can become deadly projectiles in a sudden stop or accident.

11. Load and unload young children only where they will not be exposed to traffic. Pull the vehicle up to the curb, side of the road, or in a driveway, releasing children only to an authorized adult escort.

12. Do not let children put their arms or heads out of the vehicle's windows.

13. There should be no smoking in the vehicle.

14. Drivers should be at least 21 years of age and not use alcohol, drugs, or medications that could impair their judgment within 12 hours of driving.

Only devices having an attached label stating that the device meets Federal Motor Vehicle Safety Standards should be used.

School bus seats are designed for children of school age; they are not designed to provide safe restraint for younger, smaller children unless they have seat belts that can properly anchor child safety restraints. Remember, vehicle injuries are the number one killer of children and half of these are when children are passengers. Properly installed and used child safety seats help prevent death and injury.

Here are the current recommendations.

For infants and toddlers

- Children should face the rear of the vehicle until they weigh at least 20 pounds and are at least 1 year old. Infants who weigh 20 or more pounds before age 1 should ride facing the rear in a convertible seat or infant seat approved for higher weights until they are at least 1 year of age.

- A rear-facing seat restraint must never be placed in the front passenger seat of any vehicle equipped with an air bag. In fact, it is best to never position an infant seat restraint in the front seat. Rear seat, middle position, is the safest place.

- In most rear-facing child safety restraints for infants, harness straps should be at or below the shoulders, and the safety retainer clip should be positioned at the midpoint of the infant's chest, not at the abdomen or the neck.

For children over 1 year of age and less than 4 feet 9 inches tall and 80 pounds in weight

- Convertible seats should be used in the upright and forward-facing position for a child older than 1 year who weighs 20–40 pounds and who fits in the seat well. The strap position should be at or above the shoulders.

- A belt-positioning booster seat should be used when the child has outgrown a convertible safety seat (is over 40 pounds) but is not yet 4 feet 9 inches tall and about 80 pounds. Belt-positioning boosters are used with lap and shoulder belts.

For children over 4 feet 9 inches tall and weighing about 80 pounds

• Use a shoulder-lap belt combination where the shoulder portion lies across the child's shoulder, not the neck or throat. The child should sit against the vehicle's seat back with the lap belt low and flat across the hips, not the stomach. The knees should bend easily over the edge of the vehicle seat. Seat belts are made for adults; if the seat belt does not fit the child correctly, the child should stay in a booster seat until the belt fits.

All new vehicles (except convertibles) made after September 2000 must have a special attachment to secure a top tether strap found on most child seat restraints made after September 1999. This adjustable strap is usually secured to the rear window shelf, rear floor, or back of the rear seat. When adjusted securely, this tether strap keeps the child seat restraint from moving too far forward and reduces the risk of head injuries during a crash. Some seats meet the federal standard without the use of the tether strap.

As of September 2002, new vehicles must have a lower attachment bar located between the seat cushion and seat back, and all child seat restraints have a corresponding hook, buckle, or other connector that snaps onto the vehicle's lower anchor bar. This new system, known as LATCH (Lower Anchors and Tethers for Children) makes child seat installation easier and more secure than using a seat belt to secure the seat.

Incompatibility between the child seat restraint, the vehicle seat, and the seat belt system can be life-threatening. Read the owner's manuals for the vehicle and the child seat restraint carefully. Test the car safety seat for a safe, snug fit, and check with local police to see if they have a trained technician who can check whether the child safety seat is installed correctly and the child who uses it is properly placed and restrained in it. Train all staff and volunteers who will be using safety seats in their proper use. Each person must be able to demonstrate how to properly install and use the seat.

Remember that metal buckles and plastic coverings can get hot and cause serious burns. Cover seats that are not in use with a blanket or towel. Touch all metal pieces to test the temperature before putting a child into a safety seat or safety belt.

Note that some child and infant safety seats have been recalled by the manufacturer due to unsafe features. To obtain information about manufacturer recalls and/or a list of infant, convertible, and booster seats that are certified as meeting the Federal Motor Vehicle Safety Standard, contact the Department of Transportation Auto Safety Hotline at 888-327-4236 or visit the National Highway Transportation Safety Administration online at **www.nhtsa. dot. gov/cars/problems/recalls/index.cfm**.

Legal requirements

Whenever motor vehicles are used to transport children, special safety measures are necessary. The driver must be an experienced licensed driver with an excellent driving record and no history of substance abuse, criminal record, or any medical condition that could impair driving ability. The driver must be mature enough to assume responsibility for the safety of the passengers.

Ratios and supervision during transport

Use, meet, or exceed the facility's staff:child ratios set by state requirements when transporting children. Keep in mind that these ratios are minimum standards. Drivers must be able to focus entirely on driving tasks, leaving supervision of the children to other adults in the vehicle.

The staff of a child care program are responsible for supervising every child all the time. When volunteers assist with transportation, they must follow the program's policies. After each trip be sure that family members and volunteers escort children into the building and stay with them until that responsibility is transferred to another child care provider. Careful counting of children put into and removed from vehicles is essential. A few children inadvertently left asleep in vehicles by staff who moved other children into the building have died.

Carefully assess all pick-up and drop-off locations. Each child care facility is unique in its proximity to local traffic, parking lots, driveways, and pedestrian areas. Drivers of vans and school buses cannot see children who may be walking close to the vehicle; some children have died as a result. The danger zone is 10 feet in front and beside the vehicle. Teach children to take the number of giant steps required to move them 10 feet from the vehicle as soon as they exit from it.

All drivers and staff must familiar with emergency plans, how to use safety restraints, supervision requirements, and pediatric first aid in the event of an injury.

Transporting children with special needs

There are automotive safety devices designed to protect children with special physical and behavioral needs when they are riding in motor vehicles. Devices are available for children of various weights and heights with conditions such as prematurity, muscular and skeletal problems, head and spinal cord injuries, temporary orthopedic conditions (such as a fracture), neurological diseases, developmental disabilities, recent surgery, and emotional/behavioral problems that might distract a driver.

The principles of passenger safety apply to all children, including children with special needs. Keep certain practical considerations in mind when choosing a safety device or when advising someone who plans to buy a device for a child with special needs. Soft padding adds to comfort but *not* to safety. Firm, energy-absorbing materials that cushion in a controlled way are best. The head and neck should be protected from whiplash. Wheelchairs should face forward, not sideways, during transport. Crash-tested wheelchair tie-downs, *not* homemade devices, should be used to secure wheelchairs in a van.

Devices must be easy to use or they will not be used correctly, if at all. Special devices tend to be expensive so it is best to choose one that can be used for a number of years and adjusted as a child grows or for different sized children. All restraint systems must be crash tested according to federal safety standards and retested even if only a small modification is made. Other equipment, such as an oxygen tank, should be secured so that it does not become a missile in a collision. The child's physician, the public health department, or organizations such as Easter Seals may be helpful resources in locating appropriate safety devices.

Additional recommendations for safe transportation of children with special needs include special training for drivers and, when appropriate, pediatric CPR, and equipping vehicles with a two-way radio or mobile phone.

Emergency procedures

Always expect the unexpected, no matter how efficient and safe your transportation system may be. Prepare by taking the following steps:

- Be sure that children, families, driver(s), and other staff all know what to do in an emergency. Develop a procedure using suggestions from older children, families, and staff for each of the following issues. Use discussion groups and/or handouts to inform everyone of these procedures. Transportation emergency issues include
  —how to evacuate the vehicle
  —how to assess injuries and provide first aid
  —how to explain the situation to the children and reassure them of their safety
  —what staff still in the building are to do
  —when and who to call for emergency support
  —what to do in bad weather
  —what to do when a child becomes ill or injured during transport
- Train drivers in the specific steps to follow under various emergency conditions.
- Make sure that staff who remain at the facility know what to do when they are notified of any emergency on the road (for example, contact parents or provide alternate transportation).
- Annually remind families of emergency procedures and collect accurate contact information from them.
- If you use a bus, practice emergency evacuation drills so the children will be familiar with what they may be asked to do.

Emergency situations must be handled calmly, efficiently, and with constant attention to the children's fears, concerns, and safety.

What to have in the vehicle

A well-organized transportation system is important even if you do not transport children regularly. Special trips mean special circumstances. First of all, drivers may be traveling an unfamiliar route or transporting children who may not ordinarily ride with them. Drivers may be sharing responsibility with volunteers who are themselves in a new situation. Finally, the children may be overly excited or overly tired or even may be frightened.

Certain information and equipment kept in vehicles are helpful in various circumstances.

Information. Specific information about the children and the route should be kept in a three-ring notebook in the vehicle. Make sure the information is up-to-date and the driver and other staff can find it easily. In the notebook include

- a map of the route with estimated mileages and travel times and the names and addresses of children on the route
- an information/emergency card for each child that describes how to reach parents and emergency contacts and special medical or health information
- information on children with special needs, including descriptions of the condition and medications, behavior patterns, and warning signs for medical attention
- telephone numbers of emergency services such as local police, fire station, hospital, and ambulance service, and name and telephone number of the program and a contact person there
- pen and paper to record information from the families at pickup so this information can be passed on to caregivers

Equipment. Also keep these in the vehicle:

- First aid kit—Use the list of suggested items in Figure 4.3 to assemble your kit.
- Emergency toy chest—Songs, books, and toys help keep children occupied during an unscheduled wait.
- Travel rope—Use for children to hold onto for easy evacuation or for walks from the vehicle to a safe place.
- Fire extinguisher, extra water, and tools for minor repairs—These may be indispensable in case of a breakdown.

Field trips/car pools

The following suggestions can help staff safely transport children during special trips. Refer also to page 32 for other information about pedestrian safety and field trips.

- When the destination is known in advance, review the route mentally or with a map if the distance is great. Practice the route if you have time and the vehicle is available.
- Make sure you have a signed authorization for every child and a list of all adults who will be traveling. Check your insurance coverage for car pools.
- Make sure both the driver and other adults (for example, volunteers, staff, or bus driver) know who is responsible for responding to discipline issues with the children. Tell children who is in charge and what the rules are.

- Make sure that all children and adults use age- and size-appropriate safety restraints (child car seats and safety belts).
- Never have more passengers than seat restraints.
- Help the driver concentrate by providing soft books or toys, songs, and conversation for the children.
- Use travel time to talk about rules for safe riding or other important concepts.
- If children become unruly or remove their safety restraints, stop and pull off the road to calm them down. *Do not drive and discipline at the same time.*
- Make sure all passengers know when and where they are supposed to return to the vehicle.
- If more than one vehicle is used for the trip, make sure all passengers know which vehicle they are to ride in on the return trip.
- On field trips, make sure that no child enters the vehicle alone or plays on the vehicle while the others are visiting the site. *Never leave children alone in the vehicle.*
- Use a trip sheet to record destination, mileage, times of departure and return, and a list of passen-

gers. For large field trips, the latter is particularly important.

- Be sure that all participants in the car pools understand and agree to follow the established guidelines.
- Provide enough staff assistance to be sure every child is buckled up, unbuckled, and removed from all vehicles. People who are in a hurry may make unsafe "just this time" decisions.

Passenger safety education

For children. Preschoolers are old enough to understand simple concepts of passenger and pedestrian safety. Consistent use of safe behaviors helps children continue to practice them in later years. There are four major messages to emphasize with children and parent passengers:

1. Everyone in the car must buckle up—including drivers and passengers in the front and back seats—no matter how short the trip.
2. Safety belts go across the hips, not the stomach.
3. The back seat is the safest place for child passengers.
4. Good passengers ride quietly.

The Risk Watch™ curriculum available from the National Fire Prevention Program includes child passenger safety activities. It also includes materials for use with parents. You might make pretend cars with cardboard boxes, chairs, or seats, and safety belts from fabric scraps. Play games such as Simon Says for using safety belts and entering/leaving vehicles correctly. Practice taking giant steps after exiting the vehicle, counting out how many are needed to reach 10 feet, the distance that allows the driver to see where you are. These games are also fun for role-playing and dramatic-play activities. Invite the safety officer from your community to come to the program and talk about traffic safety.

Teach pedestrian safety to children from infancy onward. Adults who discuss and practice these rules consistently can teach children basic rules to walk safely. The messages are detailed in chapter 3.

Pedicycle safety should be taught for riding wheeled vehicles that have a wheel base over 20 inches in diameter. Start teaching these rules when children first learn to ride any vehicle with pedals (big wheels, tricycles, bicycles):

- Always wear a properly fitted helmet.
- Ride only on something that is the right size for you.
- Ride on the right side of the road.
- Learn hand signals to let others know what you will do (right and left turning, stopping).
- Stop before crossing any street to look left-right-left, scanning for cars.

For families. It is important to involve families in all educational activities; they can promote concepts presented in the classroom. Keep them informed with letters, parent education meetings, and personal contacts. With transportation topics, send home suggestions and activities that parents and children can work on together (for example, counting the number of seat belts in the car). Focus on three main issues:

- the importance of always using child safety seats and safety belts
- selecting a suitable child safety seat
- using child safety seats and seat belts correctly.

The American Academy of Pediatrics regularly updates materials on family transportation safety. Materials can be ordered online at **www.aap.org**.

Maintenance of the Facility

Early childhood programs should have written policies and procedures for the routine cleaning and maintenance of the facility. Such written policies and procedures should specify the type of cleaning and chemicals used and the method and schedule for cleaning and sanitizing. They should also name the person responsible for supervising and monitoring cleaning and other maintenance activities.

Use a cleaning and sanitation schedule

The routine frequency of cleaning and sanitation in the facility should follow the timeline in Figure 9.2. Increase the frequency of cleaning and sanitation whenever there are outbreaks of illness, there is known contamination, visible soil, or when recommended by the health department to control certain infectious diseases. By having some barrier that can easily be installed, arrange to take out of service any surfaces, furnishings, and equipment not in good repair or that have been contaminated by body fluids until they are repaired, cleaned, and, if contaminated, sanitized effectively.

Figure 9.2. Routine Frequency of Cleaning and Sanitation

AREA	CLEAN	SANITIZE	FREQUENCY
Classrooms/Child Care/Food Areas			
Countertops/tabletops, Floors, Door and cabinet handles	X	X	Daily and when soiled.
Food preparation & service surfaces	X	X	Before and after contact with food activity; between preparation of raw and cooked foods.
Carpets and large area rugs	X		Vacuum daily when children are not present. Clean with a carpet cleaning method approved by the local health authority. Clean carpets only when children will not be present until the carpet is dry. Clean carpets at least monthly in infant areas, at least every 3 months in other areas and when soiled.
Small rugs	X		Shake outdoors or vacuum daily. Launder weekly.
Utensils, surfaces and toys that go into the mouth or have been in contact with saliva or other body fluids	X	X	After each child's use, or use disposable, one-time utensils or toys.
Toys that are not contaminated with body fluids. Dress-up clothes not worn on the head. Sheets and pillowcases, individual cloth towels (if used), combs and hairbrushes, wash cloth and machine-washable cloth toys. (None of these items should be shared among children.)	X		Weekly and when visibly soiled.
Blankets, sleeping bags, Cubbies	X		Monthly and when soiled.
Hats	X		After each child's use or use disposable hats that only one child wears.
Cribs and crib mattresses	X		Weekly, before use by a different child, and whenever soiled or wet.
Phone receivers	X	X	Weekly.
Toilet and Diapering Areas			
Handwashing sinks, faucets, surrounding counters, soap dispensers, door knobs	X	X	Daily and when soiled.
Toilet seats, toilet handles, door knobs or cubicle handles, floors	X	X	Daily, or immediately if visibly soiled.
Toilet bowls	X	X	Daily.
Changing tables, potty chairs (Use of potty chairs in child care is discouraged because of high risk of contamination).	X	X	After each child's use.
General Facility			
Mops and cleaning rags	X	X	Before and after a day of use, wash mops and rags in detergent and water, rinse in water, immerse in sanitizing solution, and wring as dry as possible. After cleaning and sanitizing, hang mops and rags to dry.
Waste and diaper containers	X		Daily.
Any surface contaminated with body fluids: saliva, mucus, vomit, urine, stool, or blood	X	X	Immediately, as specified in STANDARD 3.026.

Source: *Keeping Healthy*, NAEYC brochure, 1999.

Keep the facility neat, clean, and free of rubbish.

- Clean the facility in a way that avoids contamination of food and food-contact surfaces.
- Keep soiled linens or aprons in laundry bags or other suitable containers.
- Wash all windows inside and outside at least twice a year.
- Do not use deodorizers to cover up odors caused by unsanitary conditions or poor housekeeping. Ventilate and clean bad smells away.
- Keep storage areas, attics, and cellars free from refuse, furniture, old newspapers, and other paper goods.
- Keep flammable cleaning rags or solutions in closed metal containers in locked cabinets.
- Wash surfaces with detergent and water until you cannot see any soil. Rinse with water.
- Use a standard bleach solution consisting of a ¼ cup bleach to 1 gallon of water (1 tablespoon of bleach to 1 quart of water) to sanitize clean and rinsed surfaces. Dispense the solution, made up fresh daily, from a spray bottle, and leave solution in contact with surface for at least 2 minutes. Dry with a paper towel or allow to air dry. You can use hospital-grade sanitizers or disinfectants instead of the bleach water solution, but be sure to read the Manufacturer's Data Sheet to find out how toxic these solutions are and how to safely use them. Many disinfectants and sanitizers other than bleach must be rinsed off before the surface can be used. Surfaces treated with bleach and allowed to dry have no bleach on them, since the chlorine evaporates into the air.

Keep equipment and cleaning supplies clean, in good working condition, and stored safely.

- Keep on hand wet and dry mops, mop pails, brooms, cleaning cloths, and at least one vacuum cleaner.
- Store housekeeping equipment in a separate, locked space such as a closet or cabinet—not in bathrooms, halls, on stairs, or near food.
- When possible, use a separate sink (not used for food preparation) with hot and cold running water only for cleaning equipment.
- Use disposable rags rather than reusable sponges. Sponges allow germs to grow in trapped organic material. If you must use sponges, store them in bleach solution between uses.

- If potty chairs are used, use a separate sink to wash, rinse, and disinfect the potty-chair bowl and chair surfaces. This sink should not be used for handwashing or any other purpose. Because potty chairs pose a significant sanitation hazard, their use is strongly discouraged.

Have a pest control program for the facility.

- Provide screens for exterior windows and doors.
- Store pesticides only in original containers away from child activity areas and in nonfood service and storage areas. Lock all storage areas.
- Post instructions on the safe and proper use of these chemicals in a highly visible location.
- All extermination using chemicals and pesticides should be provided *only* by a certified/licensed pest control operator and in a manner approved by the EPA. Have a qualified staff member accompany the pest control operator to be sure no chemical is applied to surfaces that children can touch. Most insects are much less harmful than pesticides. Ventilate treated areas for the recommended time before using again.
- Do not use over-the-counter products for crawling insects such as roaches, ants, and spiders. Over-the-counter products may be used for flying insects such as bees, wasps, and hornets. Read directions carefully, wash your hands after use, and store the product safely out of the reach of children.
- Be sure that bait for catching pests is kept out of children's reach and in tamperproof boxes.
- Do not use no-pest strips in food service or sleeping areas. Fly paper is acceptable if it is changed regularly.
- Fly swatters are the best way to get rid of individual insects indoors.

Choose, house, feed, and clean pets to avoid disease.

- Do not allow any animals in areas used for preparing, eating, or storing food.
- Do not allow turtles, birds of parrot family, ferrets, or any wild or dangerous animals.
- Be certain that no child is allergic to the animals in your program. Since it may be traumatic to remove an animal after an allergy is discovered, think about whether you truly need an animal likely to cause such problems (rabbits, guinea pigs, and other furry animals).

- Be sure that animals are friendly and have an appropriate temperament to be around children.
- Use only cages that are of an approved type with false bottoms.
- Clean animal areas frequently. Do not use food service facilities to clean anything involved with a pet. Wash hands afterward.
- Animals must be healthy and appropriately immunized and licensed. Dogs and cats should be maintained on a flea, tick, and worm control program. Check pet health and care requirements with a veterinarian before bringing the pet into child care.
- Be sure children and staff always wash their hands after handling or feeding animals. To protect young children from contamination, do not let them assist with pet cleaning or maintenance.
- Separate animal food and cleaning supplies from food service supplies.
- Keep all animal litter boxes out of children's reach.
- Teach children safe practices around animals (for example, do not provoke or startle animals, remove their food, etc.). Do not allow children to abuse animals.

Remember, handwashing must follow any maintenance task to remove germs and chemicals from the skin.

Use special procedures in the kitchen

Make sure food is handled and used properly by doing the following:

- Limit contamination of food by using utensils such as forks, knives, trays, spoons, and scoops.
- Wash raw fruits and vegetables before use.
- Cover foods that are stored in the refrigerator and on shelves.
- Throw away handled leftovers and food left in serving bowls.
- Pay close attention to expiration dates, especially on foods that spoil easily (dairy products, mayonnaise, processed meats, all dated products, etc.).
- Take special care when handling raw meat, chicken, and eggs. These foods have small amounts of bacteria that can cause disease if allowed to grow. After contact with these raw foods, food preparers should wash their hands well and clean and sanitize contaminated cutting boards, dishes, bowls, and utensils.

- Do not use the kitchen area as a traffic way or meeting room while food is being prepared.

See chapter 5 for more information about food preparation and service.

Require staff preparing food to follow these hygiene procedures:

- Wear clean clothes, maintain a high standard of personal cleanliness, and carry out strict hygiene procedures during working hours.
- Wash hands according to prescribed handwashing procedures before preparing and serving food and as necessary to remove soil contamination.
- Keep hands clean while handling food-contact surfaces, dishes, and utensils.
- Do not prepare or serve food while ill with a communicable disease or with uncovered hand or skin lesions. A staff person with lesions on the hands should use gloves while preparing food.
- Do not diaper children or assist with toileting on the same day you prepare food.
- Keep hair covered with a hairnet or cap while preparing food.

Provide easy-to-clean equipment and utensils.

- Use food contact surfaces and utensils that are nontoxic, corrosion resistant, nonporous, and nonabsorbent (for example, do not use wood utensils or cutting boards).
- If you use disposable articles, be sure they are made of nontoxic materials. Do not reuse disposable articles or utensils, even if you wash them carefully
- Install appliances so that they, and areas around them, can be cleaned easily.
- Be sure food contact surfaces are free of cracks and crevices, pots and pans are free of pits and dents, and plates are free of chips and cracks. Cracks in any surface can harbor germs.

Make sure that food contact surfaces and utensils are kept clean.

- Clean and disinfect all eating and drinking utensils, tableware, kitchenware, and food contact surfaces after use.
- Do not use cloths for wiping food contact surfaces for anything else. These cloths must be sanitized after they are used.

- Wash a used spoon or other utensil before using again.
- Wash food contact surfaces with detergent and water, rinse, sanitize with bleach solution, and air dry.
- Clean kitchenware and food contact surfaces that have come in contact with spoiled food or raw meat, chicken, or eggs; sanitize with the bleach solution; and let them air dry.
- Scrape and presoak dishes, pots and pans, and utensils, if necessary, to remove food particles before washing.
- Wash high chair trays, bottles, and nipples in a dishwasher, if available. If the trays do not fit in dishwasher, wash with detergent, rinse, spray with bleach solution, and air dry.
- Use the proper concentration of suitable detergent for hand and machine dishwashing, according to package directions.

Procedure for washing dishes and mouthed toys

The easiest way to wash dishes and mouthed toys is with a dishwashing machine. Commercial dishwashers should meet the requirements of the National Sanitation Foundation and be used according to the manufacturer's instructions. The dishwashing machine must incorporate a chemical or heat sanitizing process.

Three types of household dishwashers are capable of producing the cumulative heat factor to meet the NSF time-temperature standard for commercial, spray–type dishwashing machines. Two of the three are capable of doing so only if the temperature of inlet water is 155 degrees F or higher, but this temperature exceeds what is considered a safe temperature to prevent scalding. One way to manage this conflict is to install a separate small hot water heater for the dishwasher. The water in the dishwasher must be 170 degrees F. Because this temperature is higher than that allowed for most hot water heaters, you may have to adjust the heater for the water in the dishwasher so that the water reaches this temperature. Periodically check the temperature of the water by using special test strips or a thermometer made for this purpose that is held by a rubber band to a glass or cup during a dishwasher cycle.

Washing dishes by hand requires more diligence in child care than doing dishes at home because of the risk of sharing germs across multiple families. First, you need a three-compartment dishwashing arrangement. This can be a combination of dishpans and sink compartments to wash, rinse, and sanitize dishes. (If this is not possible, paper cups and plates and plastic utensils must be used and disposed of after every use.)

Using the three-compartment set-up to prepare reusable food service equipment and eating utensils requires the following procedure:

1. Scrape off any leftover food.
2. Use the first compartment to wash all surfaces thoroughly in hot water containing a detergent solution.
3. Rinse all surfaces in the second compartment.
4. Sanitize all surfaces by one of these methods:
    - immersion for at least two minutes in a luke-warm (not less than 75 degrees F) chemical-sanitizing solution (bleach solution of a least 100 parts per million made by mixing one and a half teaspoons of domestic bleach per gallon of water) and then air-drying the sanitized items, or
    - complete immersion in hot water and maintenance at a temperature of 170 degrees F for not less than 30 seconds, followed by air-drying

These procedures provide for proper sanitizing and control of viruses and bacteria. To manually sanitize dishes and utensils in hot water at 170 degrees F, a hot water booster is usually required. To avoid burning the skin while immersing dishes and utensils in this hot water bath, use special racks designed for this purpose. If dishes and utensils are being washed by hand, the chemical sanitizer method using household bleach is usually a safer choice.

Instead of a sponge, use a cloth that can be laundered. The structure of natural and artificial sponges provides an environment in which microorganisms thrive. The concentration of bleach used for sanitizing dishes is much more diluted than the concentration recommended for sanitizing surfaces. After washing and rinsing the dishes, the amount of infectious material on the dishes should be small.

Handling clean dishes and utensils

Pick up and touch clean spoons, knives, and forks only by handles, not by any part that will be in contact with food. When children help set the table, be sure they have washed their hands thoroughly and remind them not to touch the parts of the tableware that will have contact with food and go into the mouth. Handle clean cups, glasses, and bowls so that fingers and thumbs do not touch the inside or the lip contact surfaces.

Storage and disposal of garbage

Keep the facility free of accumulated garbage. Containers for garbage attract animals and insects. When trash contains organic material, decomposition creates unpleasant odors. Therefore, child care facilities must choose and use garbage containers that control sanitation risks, pests, and offensive odors. Lining the containers with plastic bags reduces the contamination of the container itself and the need to wash the containers, which itself can spread the contamination into the environment. Trash and garbage should be removed from all occupied spaces of the facility every day, and from the premises at least twice a week. Use durable metal or plastic containers that keep out pests, do not leak, and do not absorb odors. There should be enough containers to hold all waste properly until it is removed. Using plastic bags as overflow waste storage without a rigid metal or plastic container is not acceptable; it invites pest infestations. Store toxic wastes and infectious wastes separately from other refuse, in clearly labeled containers. Disposal of these materials should be done according to instructions from the local department of health.

Each waste and diaper container should be labeled to show its intended contents. Clean these containers daily to keep them free from build-up of soil and odor. The cleaning wastewater should be disposed of by pouring it down a toilet or floor drain. Wastewater should not be poured onto the ground, into handwashing sinks, laundry sinks, kitchen sinks, or bathtubs.

Containment of soiled diapers

Caring for Our Children offers specific guidance on handling soiled diapers. Since feces and urine in the diapers are likely to contain infectious material, caregivers and volunteers who change children in child care must be careful about where soiled diapers are placed. The approach is quite different from what people do at home, where contamination of the members of only one family is possible.

Soiled diapers must be stored inside the facility in containers separate from other waste. Fecal material and urine should not be mixed with regular trash and garbage. Where possible, dispose of soiled disposable diapers as biological waste rather than in the local landfill. In some areas, recycling depots for disposable diapers are available.

Washable, plastic-lined, tightly covered receptacles, with a firmly fitting cover that does not require touching with contaminated hands or objects, should be within arm's reach of diaper-changing tables. The container design for soiled diapers should prevent the user from contaminating any exterior surfaces of the container or the user when inserting the soiled diaper. Do not individually bag soiled diapers before placing them in the container; increased handling increases the risk of contamination, and a lidded plastic-lined container should contain odor. However, do bag soiled cloth diapers and soiled clothing that are to be sent home with a parent.

Some types of diaper containers should not be used in child care settings. Those that require the user's hand to push the diaper through a narrow opening increase the risk of contamination of the user's hand and may squeeze out onto other surfaces. Those with exterior surfaces or handles that must be touched and are likely to be in contact with the soiled diaper also are not acceptable.

Separate containers should be used for disposable diapers, cloth diapers (if used), and soiled clothes and linens. All containers should be placed away from where children usually go by themselves and should be tall enough to prevent children from reaching into the receptacle or from falling headfirst into them. Child care providers should not use the short, poorly made domestic stepcans because when the foot pedals don't work, caregivers must use their hands to open the lids. Invest in commercial-grade stepcans big enough to hold all the of soiled diapers collected before taken out to a trash receptacle. These cans are used by doctor's offices, hospitals, and restaurants; a variety of sizes and types are available from restaurants and medical wholesale suppliers. Other types of hands-free containers can be used as long as the user can place diapers into the receptacle without increasing contact of the user's hands and the exterior of the container with the soiled diaper.

Laundry

Many articles of differing fabrics are used in child care facilities. Sheets, pillowcases, cot covers, dress-up clothes, furniture covers, and other soft articles accumulate soil and become contaminated by drooling children or those with small sores. Young children have toileting accidents and sometimes vomit when they are ill. Child care centers should have a mechanical washing machine and dryer on site or a contract with a laundry service. Family child care homes that do laundry for children must keep the laundry equipment separate from the kitchen and child care areas. The laundry equipment must either wash or dry at above 140 degrees F or an approved sanitizer must be used in the rinse cycle. Dryers must be vented to the outside. Store soaps, bleaches, and other laundry supplies in locked cabinets.

Suggested Activities

- Visit a child care facility and check how well the building meets the guidelines in this chapter. Where there are differences, could modifications be made at reasonable cost and with time and personnel resources that are available?

- What compromises that increase health and safety risks have you seen made in facilities? Why were these compromises made? Were better alternatives possible?

- Make an observational inspection of passenger safety restraint use by standing at the curb outside a child care facility during an hour when the largest number of children in the program are arriving or leaving. What proportion of the adults are wearing seat belts? What proportion of the children are in seat restraints? Are infants rearward seated?

- Ask a child care center director about the cleaning routines for the facility. Use the table in this chapter to check how each item is cleaned and how often, and whether and how it is sanitized.

- Contact the licensing agency in your area to see if you can accompany a licensing inspector to see what maintenance issues get checked and how they are observed. Are any problems overlooked?

Chapter 10

Managing Illness

Major Concepts

- Children with chronic illness have varying severity of health problems that require planning by child care providers, but most of these conditions cause only mild or intermittent problems.
- Caring for children with chronic illness requires closer coordination among the child's clinicians, family members, and the child care staff than for typically developing children.
- Since all children inevitably become ill, mostly with mild infectious disease, all child care programs must be prepared to recognize and respond appropriately to minor illness.
- Specialized programs that take care of children who are excluded from typical program care require specific staff training, facilities, procedures, and access to consultants so that they can provide such care safely.

Almost every early childhood program includes several children with chronic health problems or medical conditions. More than 1 in every 10 preschool children has some type of allergy. Asthma occurs in around 7 percent of all children. Skin problems such as eczema are fairly common. Other less common conditions are heart problems, epilepsy, and diabetes. Chronic health conditions of children enrolled in child care programs generally are mild, and most of the time the children are able to participate in the normal routines. With sound planning, children with short-term mild illness and even children with more severe conditions, or with less common chronic illnesses, can be in child care.

Get detailed information from families about their children's health problems. Ask specific questions about how the illness will affect the child's ability to participate and the expectations of staff to provide services that differ from those required for typically developing children.

Families of children with chronic illnesses need child care to carry on family life and adult responsibilities just like families with typically developing children. In addition, the day-by-day work of caring for a child with a chronic illness puts increased stress on families.

Caring for Children with Chronic Illness

Caring for children with chronic illness involves opportunities for the caregiver to be on a professional team. Inclusive care is a legal requirement, but meeting the child's and family's needs while caring for the other children may seem overwhelming to already short-staffed and inadequately financed programs. Even when few adaptations are required to accommodate children with special needs, many programs are reluctant to enroll them—or indicate to families that children may not be able to receive adequate care. Not only is such rejection illegal under the Americans with Disabilities Act (ADA), it denies typically developing children the opportunity to experience the reality of children with differences with whom they live in their communities.

Children with special needs spend more hours outside the family in child care than in clinics or special treatment programs. As with typically developing children, the child care provider gives day-by-day support to these children's families. Caregivers have opportunities to implement therapies and make observations that can be instrumental in meeting medical and rehabilitative service needs.

The federal Individuals with Disabilities Education Act (IDEA), discussed in the next chapter, recognizes children with chronic illness as well as those with developmental disabilities as eligible for funded services if the condition would affect education of the child. For practice purposes, children who are not developmentally delayed but have chronic medical problems do not receive services via the process specified in the law to develop Individual Family Service Plans and Individual Education Plans. Child care providers should seek services for such children who cannot receive service under IDEA from the child's usual source of medical care and health insurance.

For children with special needs, the health record should include an additional section that describes the chronic illness, what child care providers need to watch for, and what to do for the child routinely and when the child has a problem. (See Special Care Plan and Special Care Plan for a Child with Asthma, Figures 10.1 and 10.2.) Since each child has a unique expression of a particular chronic illness, caregivers should not only use credentialed sources of information about the illness but also the information provided by the child's clinicians and family.

General information about specific chronic conditions can be obtained by contacting an organization or agency associated with the disease (see Figure 11.2). The National Information Center for Children and Youth with Disabilities (**www.nichcy.org**) provides online access to state resource sheets that list state agencies, state chapters of disability organizations, and related parent groups.

NAEYC distributes *Child Care and Children with Special Needs,* an excellent two-part video series with a training manual, that can help prepare child care staff and parents for inclusion of children with special needs. The manual includes specific information about different types of special needs and many excellent references to organizations that have additional detailed information. All child care providers should plan for practice of inclusive child care, and using the video series with the manual is a good place to start. *Caring for Our Children* has separate standards for including children with special medical conditions, such as epilepsy, asthma, and those who

require medical technical support. Since allergy, asthma, and febrile seizures frequently occur among the child care population, directors and caregivers should review both the material in this manual and the standards in *Caring for Our Children* to plan care for children with these conditions.

Planning Care for Children with Special Medical Conditions

Seizures

A child who has a seizure may not have epilepsy or even a history of seizures. Seeing a child have a seizure involving large muscle movements can be frightening. Child care providers should be trained to care for any child who has a seizure. The classification system currently used for seizures replaces earlier terminology:

- Grand mal seizures (large muscle movements of most of the body) are now called *generalized seizures.*
- Petit mal seizures (brief periods when the child is unaware of surroundings, usually happening hundreds of times a day) are now called *partial seizures.*

Seizures that occur in children under 4 only when the child has a fever are still called *febrile seizures.* Children with febrile seizures (who are not diagnosed with any form of epilepsy) do not receive anticonvulsant medication. These children usually outgrow this condition.

First aid training should address how to handle a child who has never had a seizure before, and has a seizure in child care. The usual procedure includes proper positioning, keeping the airway open, and calling for medical assistance. As in any medical emergency, caregivers also need to have a plan for managing the other children in the group when a child has a seizure.

Seizures are usually self-limited events. Prolonged seizures, sequential seizures without recovery to a normal status, or unresponsiveness for 20 minutes after a seizure are danger signs. Child care staff must respond appropriately both to self-limited seizures and seizures that are more serious.

For a child with epilepsy, the staff need detailed information and skills to understand the specific health needs and how to meet these needs in the child care setting. Many children who have a problem with seizures will have have a seizure from time to time. Although they may be sleepy for a period after a generalized seizure, caregivers should be aware that sending a child home who is known to recover easily after a seizure is unnecessary. Unless it is specified in the child's health plan, or ulness it is the child's first seizure, a seizure does not warrant sending the child home.

The appropriate response varies and should be dictated by that child's physician. Staff members need training on how to follow the specific procedure prescribed. All staff also need to know about the relevant side effects of anticonvulsant medications that children take and how to observe and report them.

Epilepsy can be overwhelming for the child and family. The child care staff should offer support in understanding the condition and contribute positively to management of the child. The child's physician needs reliable information on the number and type of seizures as well as symptoms of the medication's side effects so appropriate adjustments can be made in the child's therapy. With family consent, child care providers should establish a close and continuing liaison with the child's clinician, especially if the seizures are not well controlled. Sometimes the child's clinicians will monitor the medication by blood samples and sometimes through observations by caregivers and parents. In either case, dosage may have to be adjusted to reduce side effects or provide better control.

If a child has epilepsy or a history of febrile seizures that are not a form of epilepsy, the child's seizure care plan needs to include the following:

- types of seizures the child has (such as partial, generalized, or unclassified) as well as a description of what the seizure looks like when it occurs
- the child's current treatment regimen, including medications, doses, schedule of administration, guidelines, route of administration, and potential side effects for routine and as-needed medications
- any restrictions from activities that could be dangerous during a seizure or that could precipitate a seizure
- recognizing a seizure and providing first aid
- guidelines on when emergency medical help should be sought
  —when a major convulsive seizure lasts more than 5 minutes

  —when the child has one seizure after another without waking up between seizures
  —when the child is completely unresponsive for 20 minutes after a seizure
- documentation in the child's health report that indicates
  —whether there is a history of any type of seizures
  —whether the child is taking medication to control the seizures
  —what observations caregivers should make to help the child's clinician
  —the type and frequency of reported seizures as well as seizures observed in the facility
- how the child and his or her family can be supported.

Asthma

Asthma affects at least 7 to 10 percent of all preschool and school-aged children. It is a major cause of illness in childhood, resulting in sleep disturbance, limitations in exercise, absenteeism from child care and school, hospitalization, and occasional death. Because respiratory infections and asthma are common in early childhood, child care providers should expect to serve children with asthma.

Asthma is a chronic lung disease caused by overly sensitive bronchial tubes to various stimuli or *triggers*. Allergies are common among children with asthma. Not all children with asthma have allergies, but all have one or more situations that trigger their symptoms. Because sensitivity fluctuates over time, exposure to one or more triggers may not always precipitate an asthma episode. Triggers also tend to be cumulative; the more a child is exposed to at one time, the more likely she is to have symptoms. When triggered, the body reacts by developing swelling and inflammation of the lining of the air tubes that carry air from the windpipe into the lung tissue. The linings of the tubes produce extra mucus, plugging the opening where the air needs to flow. Muscles surrounding the airways tighten so that the air passages become narrower still.

Despite increased awareness and knowledge of the problem, asthma remains underdiagnosed and undertreated. Proper diagnosis, treatment, and prevention of exposure to environmental triggers can help children live more normal lives. Reducing exposure to potential triggers is important to control symptoms and prevent attacks and also to

Figure 10.1. Special Care Plan

Facility Name:_____

Facility Address:_____

Child's Name:_____

Date of Birth:_____ Times and Days in Child Care:_____

1. Describe the child's special need during group care:_____
_____

2. Child's present functional level and skills:_____
_____

3. What emergency or unusual episode might arise while the child is in care? How should the situation be handled?_____

(Prepare and maintain information on the "Emergency Form for Children with Special Needs" available from the American Academy of Pediatrics, www.aap.org)

4. Accommodation which the facility must provide for this child:_____

_____

 a) Are there particular instructions for sleeping, toileting, diapering, or feeding?_____
_____

 b) Will the child require medication while in care? If so, attach the physician's instructions for use of the child's medication._____

_____

 c) Are special emergency and/or medical procedures required? If so, what procedures are required?_____
_____

 d) What special training, if any, must staff have to provide that care?_____
_____

 e) Are special materials/equipment needed?_____

_____

5. Other specialists working with the child (e.g., occupational therapist, physical therapist):_____

_____
(usually the doctor in charge)
Primary Case Manager:_____ Phone:_____

Address:_____

On-site child care facility case manager:_____ Phone:_____

Authorization for Release of Information

I, _____give permission for
(parent or legal guardian)

_____
(professional/facility)

to release to _____the following information
(child care program)

_____
(screenings, tests, diagnoses and treatment, or recommendations)

The information will be used solely to plan and coordinate the care of my child and will be kept confidential and may only be shared with_____
(staff title/name)

Name of Child:_____

Address:_____

City: _____State:_____ Zip Code:_____

Date of Birth:_____

_____
Parent/Legal Guardian Signature   Date

_____
Witness Signature   Date

_____
Staff member to be contacted for additional information

Figure 10.2. Special Care Plan for a Child with Asthma

Child's Name: _____ Date of Birth: _____
Parent(s) or Guardian(s) Name: _____
Emergency phone numbers: Mother _____Father_____
 (see emergency contact information for alternate contacts if parents are unavailable)
Primary health provider's name: _____ Emergency Phone: _____
Asthma specialist's name (if any): _____Emergency Phone:_____

Known triggers for this child's asthma (circle all that apply):

colds	mold	exercise	tree pollens
house dust	strong odors	grass	flowers
excitement	weather changes	animals	smoke
foods (specify):_____			room deodorizers
other (specify):_____			

Activities for which this child has needed special attention in the past (circle all that apply):

outdoors	*indoors*
field trip to see animals	kerosene/wood stove heated rooms
running hard	art projects with chalk, glues, fumes
gardening	sitting on carpets
jumping in leaves	pet care
outdoors on cold or windy days	recent pesticides application in facility
playing in freshly cut grass	painting or renovation in facility

other (specify):_____

Can this child use a **flowmeter** to monitor need for medication in child care?   NO   YES
personal best reading:_____ reading to give extra dose of medicine:_____
                                          reading to get medical help:_____
How often has this child needed urgent care from a doctor for an attack of asthma:
in the past 12 months?_____ in the past 3 months? _____

Typical signs and symptoms of the child's asthma episodes (circle all that apply):

fatigue	face red, pale or swollen	grunting
breathing faster	wheezing	sucking in chest/neck
restlessness, agitation	dark circles under eyes	persistent coughing
complaints of chest pain/tightness	gray or blue lips or fingernails	
flaring nostrils, mouth open (panting)	difficulty playing, eating, drinking, talking	

Reminders:
1. *Notify parents immediately if emergency medication is required.*
2. *Get emergency medical help if:*
– the child does not improve 15 minutes after treatment and family cannot be reached
– after receiving a treatment for wheezing, the child:

• is working hard to breathe or grunting	• won't play
• is breathing fast at rest (>50/min)	• has gray or blue lips or fingernails
• has trouble walking or talking	• cries more softly and briefly
• has nostrils open wider than usual	• is hunched over to breathe
• has sucking in of skin (chest or neck) with breathing	• is extremely agitated or sleepy

3. *Child's doctor & child care facility should keep a current copy of this form in child's record.*

Adapted from: American Academy of Pediatrics.

Source: *Child Care and Children with Special Needs: A Training Manual for Early Childhood Professionals.*
Wilmington, DE, Video Active Productions.

improve the long-term outlook for children with asthma.

Respiratory infections are the primary trigger of asthma (especially of severe episodes) in the young child. Children with asthma also should be protected from respiratory irritants such as secondhand cigarette smoke, fumes, odors, chemicals, excess humidity, and very hot or cold air that may also trigger asthma. In older preschoolers and school-age children, allergens (including pets, mold, cockroaches, and dust mites) may contribute as well.

Medications to keep asthma symptoms from occurring are called *controller* medications. Prompt and appropriate intervention during an acute episode of asthma is essential to prevent severe or prolonged effects. The medicines used for an acute worsening of asthma symptoms are called *rescue* medications.

Many hospitalizations and most deaths from asthma are the result of delayed recognition of the symptoms or delayed and inadequate treatment. In general, when a child has symptoms suggesting an acute asthma episode, treatment should begin promptly, according to instructions. In most instances, a delay in treatment has more negative effects than overtreatment. Children should not have to wait for treatment until a parent arrives.

Child care providers should try to reduce exposure of asthmatic children to common asthma triggers by

- using allergen impermeable nap mats or crib/ mattress covers
- prohibiting pets (particularly furred or feathered pets) in the spaces used by children with asthma
- prohibiting smoking inside the facility or on the playground
- discouraging the use of perfumes, scented cleaning products, and other fumes
- promptly fixing leaky plumbing or other sources of excess water to prevent mold growth
- frequently vacuuming carpet and upholstered furniture (when the children are not present) and using hepa-filters that contain the vacuumed material inside the machine
- storing all food in airtight containers, cleaning up all food crumbs or spilled liquids, and properly disposing of garbage and trash to reduce cockroach and other pest infestations
- using integrated pest management techniques to get rid of pests (using the least hazardous treatments first and progressing to more toxic treatments only as necessary)

- keeping children indoors when local weather forecasts predict unhealthy ozone levels or high pollen counts.

Typical symptoms of asthma include coughing, wheezing, tightness in chest, and shortness of breath. Symptoms can occur together or alone; they vary from very mild to severe and life threatening and can be occasional or continuous. Often the only symptom is chronic or recurrent cough, particularly while sleeping, during activity, or with colds. Asthma is not the only condition that can cause these symptoms but is certainly the most common. Specific symptoms and warning signs vary from child to child, so specific recommendations for treatment also may vary. Appropriate treatment depends on the frequency and severity of the symptoms. Accurate assessment by caregivers helps clinicians determine what is happening and what should be done about it.

By 4 or 5 years of age, many children with asthma can learn to use a peak flow meter, a tool that measures how much air a child can blow when blowing out as hard and fast as possible. Although peak flow meters can only be used with children who are old enough to understand directions for use and able to cooperate, they are very helpful. Peak flow readings change before the asthmatic child feels or shows any symptoms. They allow early treatment with controller medicines and help reduce the amount of rescue medicines children need. Measurements show when treatment is helping, and when additional treatment or medical advice is needed. However, peak flow readings do not replace observations of how the child is doing.

Caregivers can manage asthma symptoms in child care so that children can fully participate in the program. However, the following red flags signal the need to notify parents or have emergency medical services (EMS) come to the facility:

- Symptoms persist despite one dose of prescribed rescue medication (especially if symptoms are bad enough to interfere with sleep, eating, or activity).
- Two or more doses of rescue medication have been needed during the course of a single day for recurrent symptoms.
- Peak flow remains 50 to 80 percent of normal despite one dose of the prescribed rescue medication.
- Peak flow is less than 50 percent of normal.
- Child is struggling to breathe, hunches over, or sucks in chest and neck muscles in an attempt to breathe.

Figure 10.3 Instructions for Daily Health Check

1. Be at the child's level so you can interact with the child even if talking with the parent.

2. Check:

- behavior typical or atypical for time of day and circumstances
- appearance

  skin: pale, flushed, rash (feel the child's skin by touching affectionately)

  eyes, nose, mouth: Note color; are they dry or is there discharge? Is child rubbing eye, nose, or mouth?

  hair: in a lice outbreak, look for nits

  breathing: normal or different; cough

- report of parent on how child seemed to feel or act at home
- sleeping normally?
- eating/drinking normally? When was last time child ate or drank?
- any unusual events?
- Bowels and urine normal? When was last time child used toilet or was changed?
- any evidence of illness or injury since the child was last participating in child care?

Source: Appendix G, *Model Child Care Health Policies*

- Child is having difficulty walking or talking because of shortness of breath.
- Lips or fingernails turn gray or blue.

Additional resources on caring for children with asthma such as the *How Asthma-Friendly Is Your Child-Care Setting? Checklist* can be obtained from the National Heart, Lung, and Blood Institute. Other useful materials designed to address asthma in child care settings are available from the Asthma and Allergy Foundation of America (see Appendix 1).

Staff members must receive training about how to reduce asthma triggers, as well as how to know when to give medications, the purpose, expected response, and possible side effects of medications they are expected to administer. They need hands-on training on how to use equipment such as inhalers, nebulizers, and peak flow meters. To make such training specific to the needs of the children in care, each child with a diagnosis of asthma should have a special asthma care plan prepared and kept up-to-date by the child's health provider at each check-up or treatment visit (see Figure 10.2). The plan should include the following specific information:

- written instructions about how to avoid the conditions that are known to trigger asthma symptoms for the child
- indications for treatment in the child care facility

- names, doses, and method of administration of medications that the child should receive for an acute episode (rescue medications) and for ongoing prevention (controller medications)
- when the next update of the special care plan is due.

Medical procedures

In *Caring for Our Children,* Standard 3.063 provides guidance for accommodating the growing number of children who are considered "medically fragile"—that is, need medical technical procedures during their usual day. Some children require tube feedings, endotrachial suctioning, oxygen, postural drainage, catheterization to release their urine, or other special medical procedures to be performed routinely. Some children, especially school-age children, know how to do certain procedures (such as catheterization, blood testing, or injections) on their own. Some conditions require special procedures on an urgent basis.

For all children who require medical procedures while in child care, providers should obtain a written report from the health care provider who prescribed the special treatment (such as a urologist for catheterization). The report should include any special preparation needed to perform urgent procedures other than those that might be required for a typical child (because typical children do not need cardiac resuscitation, caregivers are not expected to know CPR). The clinician's report should include instructions for performing the procedure, how to receive training in performing the procedure, and what to do and who to notify if complications occur.

The specialized skills required to implement special medical procedures are not traditionally taught to educators or educational assistants as part of their academic or practical experience. Very few children's needs are so complex that they require specialized facilities with health personnel as caregivers. Since inclusion is best for children with and without disabilities, and for the community as a whole, reasonable accommodation is legally required by the Americans for Disability Act. Few parents feel comfortable with child care providers who are not confident about managing their child's medical technology needs. When families want their child included, caregivers must do their best to make the accommodations required to enroll and ensure the safe care of the child with medical technology.

Training for the child care staff should be provided by a qualified health care professional. Arranging for such training is the responsibility of all concerned—families, clinicians, and child care providers. Training for these procedures is sometimes paid for by the child's health insurance or is included in the Individual Family Service Plan or Individual Education Plan for a child who has developmental disabilities as well. Creative arrangements may be required, such as having the durable medical equipment company deliver the equipment to the child care facility so that caregiver and parent can receive instruction at the same time.

Families are responsible for supplying the required equipment. The facility should offer staff training and allow sufficient staff time to carry out the necessary procedures. Caring for children who require intermittent catheterization or supplemental oxygen is not as demanding as it first sounds, but staff must be able to practice what to do with competent health professional consultation.

Before enrolling a child who will need medical technical procedures, child care providers can request and review fact sheets and instructions and training that includes a demonstration of competence of caregivers for handling specific procedures. Often the child's parents or clinicians have these materials and know where training is available. When the specifics are known, caregivers can make a more responsible decision about what would be required to serve the child.

Emergency Planning Considerations for Children with Special Needs

To prepare for emergency episodes with a child with a chronic illness, ask the family to describe a situation that required such action in the past. Find out what may cause a crisis and how often it may occur. Ask how the child may behave before a crisis, behaviors likely during and after a crisis, and how long the episode usually lasts. Ask the child's parent and doctor to describe, demonstrate, and teach what to do during and following the crisis. Can you do it alone or will you need help?

Since few health professionals have firsthand knowledge about the operation of the child care setting, prepare a list of typical classroom activities for them. Ask the child's doctor to check off activities that must be avoided and to describe modifications so the child can participate. For more complex conditions, ask the physician to arrange for a knowledgeable health professional to visit the facility and work with the staff to prepare for competent care of the child.

Figure 10.4. Situations that Require Medical Attention Right Away

In the two boxes below, you will find lists of common medical emergencies or **urgent** situations you may encounter as a child care provider. To prepare for such situations:

1) Know how to access Emergency Medical Services (EMS) in your area.
2) Educate Staff on the recognition of an emergency.
3) Know the phone number for each child's guardian and primary health care provider.
4) Develop plans for children with special medical needs with their family and physician.

At any time you believe the child's life may be at risk, or you believe there is a risk of permanent injury, seek immediate medical treatment.

Call Emergency Medical Services (EMS) immediately if:

- You believe the child's life is at risk or there is a risk of permanent injury.
- The child is acting strangely, much less alert, or much more withdrawn than usual.
- The child has difficulty breathing or is unable to speak.
- The child's skin or lips look blue, purple, or gray.
- The child has rhythmic jerking of arms and legs and a loss of consciousness (seizure).
- The child is unconscious.
- The child is less and less responsive.
- The child has any of the following after a head injury: decrease in level of alertness, confusion, headache, vomiting, irritability, or difficulty walking.
- The child has increasing or severe pain anywhere.
- The child has a cut or burn that is large, deep, and/or won't stop bleeding.
- The child is vomiting blood.
- The child has a severe stiff neck, headache, and fever.
- The child is significantly dehydrated: sunken eyes, lethargic, not making tears, not urinating.

After you have called EMS, remember to call the child's legal guardian.

Some children may have urgent situations that do not necessarily require ambulance transport but still need medical attention. The box below lists some of these more common situations. The legal guardian should be informed of the following conditions. If you or the guardian cannot reach the physician within one hour, the child should be brought to a hospital.

Get medical attention within one hour for:
- Fever in any age child who looks more than mildly ill.
- Fever in a child less than 2 months (8 weeks) of age.
- A quickly spreading purple or red rash.
- A large volume of blood in the stools.
- A cut that may require stitches.
- Any medical condition specifically outlined in a child's care plan requiring parental notification.

Source: Appendix N, *Caring for Our Children.*

In conjunction with the federal Maternal and Child Health Bureau of the Health Resources and Services Administration, the American College of Emergency Physicians and the American Academy of Pediatrics disseminate the "Emergency Information Form for Children with Special Needs," a form to be kept up-to-date and always physically with children who have special medical needs that might require emergency medical service personnel. This form provides the key information that EMS and emergency room personnel need, including current medications and doses, usual baseline findings on physical examination, and rapid treatment options that may be appropriate for the child. This form is available online from both organizations at **www.aap.org** or **www.acep.org**.

Prepare other children in the group for possible health crises by giving them a simple explanation as part of discussing other types of emergencies. Assure children that the staff can handle all such situations. If an event occurs, matter-of-factly review with the children what happened, allow them to play out what they experienced, draw pictures, and tell stories related to the event until their interest wanes, indicating they have become comfortable with it.

For fact sheets on the following issues related to serving children with special health needs in child care, visit the ECELS page online at the Pennsylvania Chapter of the American Academy of Pediatrics (**www.paaap.org**)

- asthma
- asthma and tobacco smoke
- children with diabetes
- children with seizures
- intermittent catheterization cleaning
- pediatric gastroesophageal reflux
- spina bifida
- tube feeding

Care of the Mildly Ill Child

The care of ill children in group programs can be viewed from many perspectives: the child's needs, the family needs, the caregiver's needs, and the employer's needs. The parent's need to prepare for inevitable illness is addressed in the NAEYC brochure *Preparing for Illness*. Parents often are unaware of a child's illness when they drop off their children at child care. When children do show some symptoms, parents often wish for the best. Many illnesses have mild, transient symptoms. However, sometimes children's symptoms worsen during the day. Children sometimes regress and want additional attention and care from those they know and trust.

Caregivers know that ill children are sometimes more demanding and need special attention. They worry about spreading illness within the group and to them and their families as well. Employers put both overt and implied pressure on workers to come to the job every day and want their employees to find ways to manage illness without affecting work performance.

The most common—and usually best—alternative care arrangement is for a parent of the ill child to stay home from work and care for the child. For children who are excluded from their usual care arrangements, some communities have one or more of the following alternative care arrangements available:

- care in the child's own home by a nonfamily caregiver
- care in a small family child care home
- care in the child's own center if there are special provisions designed for the care of ill children (sometimes called the infirmary model)
- care in a separate center serving only children with illness or temporary conditions.

In *Caring for Our Children* the standards specify exclusion and inclusion criteria for child care in facilities that care for children who are well and at different levels of illness. (Exclusion/inclusion issues are also included in chapter 2 of this manual.) In addition, the CFOC standards specify the types of services that a child care program must be prepared to offer for each level of illness.

Setting Policies on Levels of Illness

Each child care program needs to specify in its policies what severity level(s) of illness the facility can manage and how much and what types of illness to address. The plan of care should be consistent with state regulations and approved by the facility's health consultant. *Caring for Our Children* defines three levels:

Severity Level 1. Care for children whose health condition is accompanied by high interest and complete involvement in activity and an absence of symptoms of illness (such as recovery from pink eye, rash, or chickenpox) but who need further recuperation time. Appropriate activities include most of the normal activities for the child's age and developmental level, including both indoor and outdoor play. For full recovery, children at this level need no special care other than medication administration as offered at the facility.

Severity Level 2. Care for children whose health condition is accompanied by a medium activity level because of symptoms (such as children with low-grade fever, children at the beginning of an illness, and children in the early recovery period of an illness). Appropriate activities for this level include crafts, puzzles, table games, fantasy play, and opportunities to move about the room freely.

Severity Level 3. Care for children whose health condition is accompanied by a low activity level because of symptoms that preclude much involvement. Appropriate activities for this level are sleep and rest; light meals and liquids; passive activities such as stories and music; and, for children who need physical comforting (especially under 3 years of age), being held and rocked.

For a more detailed discussion about the staffing and facility adjustments required to care for children at Severity Levels 2 and 3, refer to "Specific standards for facilities that care for ill children" on page 156 of this manual.

When children become ill during the hours they are in child care, the family should be notified. To keep the child comfortable until parents can come, the facility should have quiet space separate from the rest of the children where the sick child can be supervised and receive care from someone who is familiar and competent to provide care. Personnel must have sufficient training to recognize the child requiring prompt medical attention. Most states have laws requiring reporting of specific communicable diseases when they occur in a public facility. Child care staff should be familiar with these requirements and promptly report the designated diseases.

Basic issues for decision making about caring for ill children

Many health policies concerning the care of ill children have been based upon common misunderstandings about contagion, risks to ill children, and risks to other children and staff. Research clearly shows that certain ill children *do not* pose a health threat. Also, the research shows that keeping certain mildly ill children at home or isolated at the program *will not* prevent other children from becoming ill. Many children shed viruses before they are obviously sick and, for gastrointestinal infections, even after they seem perfectly well. Respiratory and gastrointestinal infections can spread before children develop symptoms.

Children with common colds who feel well enough to participate in the program do not need to be excluded from child care. Children receiving antibiotics for a specific bacterial infection usually are not contagious after a day's treatment and can return. Refer to the tables in *Preparing for Illness* for when to exclude children with specific symptoms and conditions and when children who have been excluded can return.

The essential question is, can the child participate with *reasonable comfort* and receive adequate, appropriate care without interfering with the care of the other children? One child with a low fever and cough may still have a high-energy level, good appetite, and good mood; but another child may be droopy, whiny, uninterested in any activity, and very unhappy. *Every case is different and should be decided individually by staff and family together using guidelines and procedures developed in consultation with health professionals.* The focus of policies for all children should be on what conditions and symptoms the program can include and manage.

Issues for programs. When you need to decide whether to keep a mildly ill child at your facility, ask these questions:
• Are there sufficient staff (including volunteers) to change the program for a child who needs some modifications, such as quiet activities, staying inside, or extra liquids?
• Are staff willing and able to care for a sick child (wiping a runny nose, checking a fever, providing extra loving care) without neglecting the care of other children in the group?
• Is there a space where the mildly ill child can rest? Is there a space that might be used as a get-well room so several children could be cared for at once? Is the child familiar with the staff?
• Is the family able or willing to pay extra staff costs for sick care if other resources are not available?

Issues for families. When families need to decide whether to send a child to the group program, they

Figure 10.5. Medication Consent and Log

Child's Name _____

PARENT COMPLETE THIS SECTION

I give permission to administer medication to my child as stated below:

Date	Parent's Signature	Name of Medication/ Any Side Effects to Watch For	To Be Given		Amount Each Dose/ By Route , e.g., Mouth, Nose, Ear	Refrigeration?	Safety Check	Time Given	Staff Initials	Date Given	Reaction/Notes
			Date	Time							

STAFF COMPLETE THIS SECTION

Safety Check:
1. Child resistant container
2. Original prescription or manufacturer's label with the name and strength of the medication and physician's directions for use (phone or written)
3. Name of child on container is correct for both first and last names
4. Current date on prescription/expiration label covers period when medication is to be given
5. Name and phone number of licensed health professional who ordered medication on container or on file
6. Instructions are clear for dose, route, and time to give medication

must weigh many facts, such as how the child feels (physically and emotionally), the program's ability to serve the needs of the mildly ill child, and income/work lost by staying home. Lost work in many cases means lost income, but sometimes it may mean the loss of a job.

Although many families may honestly try to consider all the facts and to decide what is best for the child, this is hard to do when the facts are fuzzy. A child may awaken cranky but show no signs of illness. Or the child may have vomited after dinner the night before but slept well and awakened cheerful. Or the child may have an unexplained low-grade fever but seem absolutely fine. In these situations families need to use their best judgment.

It is important to establish health policies that are reasonable and discussed with families in advance. Keep the daily lines of communication open. When an illness arises, communication is key—discuss the issue with the family sensitively, demonstrate concern about the health of the child and the situation for the parent, refer to the health policies, and demonstrate flexibility to make the situation best for all involved.

Keep the communication lines open

A child's parent or guardian should always talk with staff at drop-off about any mild illness that occurred the night before. If there is no opportunity for personal contact, the family should write a note or complete the Symptom Record (see Figure 7.3). When the child leaves, staff must let the family know what happened during that day—preferably also in written form. Simple information about activity level, appetite and food intake, naptime, and bowel movements can be invaluable to the family and to the doctor who may be called for advice later in the evening. Written reports (see Figure 7.3) from the staff about a child's illness help overcome the natural tendency to miss some of the details when the child is picked up at the end of the day.

Conduct a daily health check

When you greet the children in the morning (preferably before parent or guardian has left), give each child a quick health checkup (see Figure 10.3). This does not have to be a big deal! Just as you would notice a new haircut or a new pair of sneakers, you can be attuned to

• general mood (happy, sad, cranky)

• activity level (sluggish, sleepy, or whatever)

• breathing difficulties, severe coughing

• discharge from nose, ears, or eyes

• skin color, itching, rashes, swelling, bruises, sores.

If you have concerns about how a particular child looks or feels, discuss them with the parent right then. Perhaps the child needs to be taken home if you feel strongly that the child should not stay. If you decide the child can remain, be sure to discuss how you will manage the child and at what point you will call the parent. Note that it is the program's decision, not the family's, whether the program will accept responsibility for the ill child. If the child stays all day, make sure you let the family know what happened during the day.

Know what to do when a child appears ill

When you have a seriously ill or injured child, have procedures that tell you what to do. Some conditions require calling the emergency medical services number (usually 911). Other situations require bringing the child to a source of medical care within an hour. Still others require consulting a health professional about what to do; this advice could be provided in a telephone conversation or the recommendation might involve having the family take the child to an appointment at a clinical facility. For a list of conditions that require medical care right away, see Figure 10.4.

If a child appears *mildly* ill, take the him aside, encourage rest, and assess the situation. *Remember, you are not expected to diagnose illness.* Report the symptoms you have observed to the proper person(s)—the family, the director, the health staff person (if any) or health consultant, and/or the child's health provider.

Take these general steps when a child becomes ill:

• keep the child comfortable

• observe, report, and document the symptoms

• call the family (or emergency contact)

• decide if the program can care for the child

Each child's family should identify at least two emergency contact people who are usually available to take the child home if the parent cannot be reached or is not available. Be sure these two contacts are in the child's record, and test their telephone numbers occasionally to be sure they are current. Testing telephone numbers is most easily incorporated into the office routine if you divide the number of children in the program by the number of working days in six months (approximately 120) and test that number of telephone contacts every day.

Common minor Illnesses

Most programs need to provide at least *temporary* care of ill children even if their general policy is to send sick children home. If children become ill during the day, have a set of guidelines to help you manage their illnesses and keep them comfortable. Start by reviewing and modifying the following guidelines with your program's child care health consultant so you have a set adapted for your setting.

Guidelines for fevers

Fever is a common symptom in young children; it is not a disease. Many families (and the public in general, including teachers) have unrealistic fears about fevers, but in fact, fevers are rarely harmful and treatment is not always necessary. An above-average body temperature can be caused by many things, including strenuous exercise, time of day (temperature rises in late afternoon), infection, environment (a hot room, a hot day, or being bundled up), or individual variations.

Fever is generally defined as a temperature of 100 degrees F or more whether taken orally, rectally, or axillary (in the armpit). (See Figure 10.6 for details on how to take a child's temperature.) A fever of 105 degrees F is considered high, although in general the height of the fever does not correlate to the seriousness of the illness. How sick a child acts and the cause and potential complications of the illness are the most important issues.

Fever is often the child's body's response to infection. Fever between 100 and 102 degrees F may help children fight off infections, and experts believe that fever should not be treated unless the child seems uncomfortable or the temperature is high enough to cause excessive fluid loss (over 102 degrees F for more than a few hours). The fever itself does no harm unless it is at or above 106 degrees F— a temperature that does not occur except when children are in very hot environments. The most significant sign of serious illness is a child who looks and acts very ill.

Guidelines for colds

- Try to keep room temperature at or lower than 70 degrees F.

- Use a cool mist humidifier (properly cleaned/disinfected) to keep the air moist during winter. Do not add anything to it. Do *not* use steam vaporizers. Ultrasonic humidifiers are better.
- Sit the child up so mucus will drain away from the ears.
- Raise the mattress or cot under the head and chest for sleeping. Do not use pillows because they tend to flex the head on the chest, making breathing more difficult. Put something under the mattress instead.
- Offer lots of clear liquids.
- Assist the child by helping to blow/wipe nose. *Wash your hands afterward.*
- Remove mucus from babies' noses before they eat. Use a soft, rubber bulb with a soft, narrow tip to suck out (aspirate) mucus for children who cannot blow their noses. Ask parents to send an individual aspirator, and use it only for that baby. (A 3-oz. ear syringe works very well for this purpose.)
- Let the child rest whenever she seems tired.
- Let the child eat as much or as little as she seems to want.
- Don't give cold medicine without parental consent *and* physician's order.

Guidelines for vomiting and nausea

- Stop solid food.
- Offer clear liquids—water, flat cola or ginger ale (shake bottle or stir in glass to remove the bubbles), gelatin, broth. *Do not force child to drink,* but offer liquids often.
- Offer liquids in *very* small amounts: one half to one ounce (1 to 2 tablespoons) every 5 to 15 minutes for 30 to 60 minutes. If a tablespoon of fluid is vomited, reduce the amount given each time to a teaspoon.
- Offer frozen juice or ice chips to help soothe the child.
- If the child asks for food and has not vomited for an hour or more, give plain crackers, plain cookies or toast, or rice cereal.
- Ask the family to call the doctor when a baby younger than 6 months is vomiting.
- If a child vomits on clothing, remove the clothing and sponge the child with soap and water, if necessary. Dress him in clean clothing or wrap in a blanket or towel. Place the soiled clothing in a leak-proof plastic bag, label, and send home for the family to wash.

Figure 10.6 How to Take a Child's Temperature

Preparation

- Oral temperatures should not be taken on children younger than 4 years of age unless a digital thermometer can be used successfully.
- Rectal temperature or aural (ear) equivalent to rectal temperature should be taken only by people with specific training in this technique.
- Wash your hands and be sure the thermometer is clean before your start.

Taking axillary (armpit) temperature

- Use an oral thermometer, if possible.
- Place the tip of the thermometer in a dry armpit
- Close the armpit by holding the elbow against the chest for 5 minutes
- If you're uncertain about the result, recheck it with a rectal temperature.

After the newborn period, axillary temperatures are not reliable. Use this method for screening purposes only.

Taking rectal temperatures

- Use for children 6 months to 2 years old
- Have the child lie stomach down.
- Lubricate the end of the thermometer and the child's anal opening with petroleum jelly.
- Carefully insert the thermometer about ¾" but never force it.
- Hold the child still while the thermometer is in and press the buttocks together.
- Leave the thermometer inside the rectum for 2 to 3 minutes. Never leave the child alone when a thermometer is in place.
- Never use an oral thermometer in the rectum.

Taking oral temperatures

- Be sure the child did not recently drink a very cold or warm drink, or wait 15 minutes.
- Place the thermometer tip under the right side of the tongue.
- Have the child hold the thermometer in place with the lips and finger (not the teeth).
- Have the child breathe through the nose with the mouth closed.
- Leave the thermometer inside the mouth for 3 minutes.
- If the child can't keep the mouth closed because the nose is blocked, take an axillary temperature. If the child cannot keep the bulb of the thermometer between the bottom of the tongue and the floor of the mouth, the reading will not be accurate.

Taking aural (ear canal) temperatures

- Follow the manufacturer's instructions.

Cleaning the thermometer

- Wash the thermometer with cold water and soap.
- Rinse the thermometer with cold water
- Wipe it with rubbing alcohol or immerse it in the sanitizing bleach solution. Then let air dry.
- Wash hands thoroughly afterward.

Guidelines for diarrhea

Diarrhea is a change in stool pattern that is not explained by a change in diet or medication and is observed as

- an increase in the number of stools over what is normal for that person *and*
- stools that are unformed—loose/watery, taking the shape of the container they are in. (Exceptions: Breast-fed babies and exclusively formula-fed babies have stools that are *normally* loose. Children who have recovered from a bout of diarrhea and are acting normally may have a persistent pattern of looser stools for weeks afterward that test negative for diarrhea-causing bacteria and parasites.)

Some children get diarrhea when they take antibiotics. Others may have loose stools for a long time after recovering from an infectious gastrointestinal disease. However, carefully watch a child with even one loose stool and take precautions. Children with diarrhea that is not contained by the use of the toilet (children in diapers and children who know how to use the toilet but whose diarrhea keeps them from getting to the toilet on time) must be excluded until the diarrhea resolves. Children who wear diapers and develop diarrhea must be excluded because diaper-changing poses a high risk of contamination of the child care environment.

While the child with diarrhea is waiting to be picked up by family, the following guidelines for care should be followed.

- Offer clear, dilute liquids (see vomiting section). Liquids high in sugar (colas, apple juice, grape juice) should be diluted.
- Avoid any milk except breast milk. (The sugar in full-strength juice and milk can make diarrhea worse.)
- If the child acts hungry, offer bland foods (for example, rice, noodles, oatmeal, dry cereal, crackers, low-sugar gelatin, mashed banana, applesauce).

Although vomiting and diarrhea are generally considered mild illnesses, they can sometimes lead to *dehydration*. Dehydration—an excessive loss of water and nutrients from the body—is a special concern in infants. Watch for these *symptoms* of dehydration:

- decreased frequency and amount of urinating
- concentrated (dark) urine
- few or no tears
- sunken eyes
- a sticky or dry mouth, and/or thirst
- loss of skin elasticity (that is, skin does not spring back when pressed gently).

Call your health consultant or local public health agency if more than one child in the same group has diarrhea.

Guidelines for constipation

Constipation is present when a child has excessively hard bowel movements that cause pain or are accompanied by mucus or blood. A child who has infrequent bowel movements is not constipated if the stool appears normal when passed. Normal bowel patterns vary from twice a day to once or twice a week. When the stool is hard it usually means the child is not drinking enough fluid to keep up with the body's needs or does not have enough roughage (fiber) in the diet. If a child is constipated, be sure to discuss the problem with the family so that together you can decide what to do.

To help reduce the hardness of stools, begin by increasing fluid intake. Temporarily increase juices. Have the child drink at least 32 ounces (four medium glasses) of fluid each day, divided into frequent, small amounts. Try to have the child eat fruits such as apricots, pears, peaches, and prunes—fresh, dried, or canned in their own juice—twice a day. High-fiber (for example, bran) cereals hold fluid in the intestine to keep stools soft; and leafy, green vegetables such as lettuce, spinach, greens, and green and yellow beans provide roughage. Limit binding foods such as bananas, apples, and high-fat dairy products. If these measures do not work, ask the family to consult a doctor.

Guidelines for rashes

Although rashes are usually not symptoms of serious illness, people tend to worry about them because unusual skin conditions are so easily seen. While you will not diagnose or decide on treatment for rashes, you should supply families with detailed information. Their child's physician will want to know the following:

- Is the rash itchy to the child?
- Is the rash red (blood colored) or pink?
- Is the skin warm to the touch?
- Is the rash raised or flat? pinprick size or blotchy? dry or blistery?

• Where on the body was the rash first noted? How has it changed since then?
• Has the child had a recent injury or exposure to infection, drugs, or chemicals?
• Does the child look or act sick in any other way?
• Has the child had this rash before?
• Has the child been in contact with someone who has this rash?

Solid red, warm areas that are spreading may be caused by infection. Many infections that affect the whole body are associated with rashes. Many rashes look alike; sometimes even a doctor cannot make a definite diagnosis. The best clues are provided by any other symptoms accompanying the rash and by knowing what's going around.

Although most rashes are more troublesome than dangerous, there is a group of them associated with severe and life-threatening illness. These rashes look like little blood spots or bruises under the skin. Children may develop little blood spots around their faces and necks from crying hard or vomiting, but when this type of rash appears elsewhere on the body, without being explained by trauma, a health professional should be called *immediately*. The rashes from spontaneous bleeding into the skin signal serious disturbances in the body's bleeding control systems. *Spontaneous blood-red or purple spots or bruises without trauma should be addressed as a medical emergency. Also, a rash of hives or welts that appears quickly should be evaluated immediately by a health professional.* Fortunately, these illnesses occur infrequently.

Use cold soaks with plain water to relieve itchy rashes. Do *not* use ointments, creams, powders, or lotions or give medicine unless you have both the doctor's instructions and parent consent.

• *For diaper rash*—the result of a combination of irritation, from rubbing of moist surfaces on the skin, chemical action of stool and urine on the skin, and wetness for prolonged periods. The ammonia odor in the diaper area comes when bacteria on the skin break down urine. To care for diaper rash take the following steps:

—Treat the irritated skin. Keep the baby as dry as possible. Pat the skin dry after you clean it and before you close the clean diaper. If the child's doctor recommends it, apply a diaper cream.
—Keep stool away from the child's skin since feces contains broken-down bile that is like a detergent and irritating. Change the child right away and

---

Standard 3.081—Permissible Administration of Medication

The administration of medicines at the facility shall be limited to:
a) Prescribed medications ordered by a health care provider for a specific child, with written permission of the parent or legal guardian;
b) Nonprescription (over-the-counter) medications recommended by a health care provider for a specific child or for a specific circumstance for any child in the facility, with written permission of the parent or legal guardian.

RATIONALE: Before assuming responsibility for administration of medicine, facilities must have clear, accurate instruction and medical confirmation of the child's need for medication while in the facility. Caregivers should not be involved in inappropriate use of drugs based solely on a parent's desire to give the child medication. Parents are victims of their own desire to do something for self-limited illnesses and the vigorous advertisement for many over-the-counter medications, including acetaminophen and combinations of antihistamines and decongestants as cold remedies. Overuse of medications has been confirmed by results of the National Center for Health Statistics' survey of the incidence of medicated respiratory tract infection, which showed that 29.5 percent of children under 5 years of age in the survey were reported by their parents to have received a medication for a respiratory tract illness in the 2 weeks before the interview. Decongestants and antihistamines have been shown to prolong the retention of secretions in the middle ear rather than helping children get well. No existing evidence reports that decongestants or antihistamines, alone or in combination, prevent middle ear infections; therefore, the use of such medications for common colds is not recommended.

COMMENTS: A health care provider can write a standing order for a commonly used non-prescription medication (such as acetaminophen or sunscreen) that defines when the medication should be used for any child in the facility. For example: "With parental consent, children who are older than 4 months of age may receive acetaminophen when their body temperature exceeds 101 degrees F, according to the dose schedule and instructions provided by the manufacturer of the acetaminophen," or "With parental consent, children may have sunscreen applied to exposed skin, except eyelids, 30 minutes before exposure to the sun and every 2 hours while in the sun. Sunscreen preparations shall be applied according to the instructions provided by the manufacturer." Parents should always be notified in every instance when medication is used. Telephone instructions from a health care provider are acceptable if the caregiver fully documents them and if the parent initiates the request for health care provider instruction. Advance notification of the parent (before medication is given) is ideal but may not be appropriate if a child needs medication urgently (such as to stop an allergic reaction) or when contacting the parent will unreasonably delay appropriate care. Safeguards against liability for accepting telephone instructions for medication administration should be checked with an attorney. Nonprescription medications should be given according to the manufacturers' instructions unless a health care provider provides written instructions otherwise.

Source: *Caring for Our Children.*

---

clean the child's bottom well.
—*Avoid talcum or baby powder. It can be inhaled into the lungs.*

• *For heat rash* (also known as prickly heat)—small red bumps usually occuring on the neck, upper chest, and back of the head. To help manage heat rash,
—Do not overdress child
—Wash and dry the child's skin, especially between skin creases
—Frequently sponge and dry the area with cool tap water
—*Do not use baby powder.*

Guidelines for teething

Teething can cause irritability, drooling, rubbing at the mouth, pulling at the ears, and slightly looser stools. Teething, however, does not cause fever in a child. If a child has a significant fever while teething, it is likely a sign of another illness, and medical evaluation may be recommended. Give the child something hard and/or cold to bite on. Families may want their children to receive some pain medication for comfort.

Guidelines for sunburn

Young children are more likely to get sunburned than adults (although everyone should avoid prolonged skin exposure to the sun). Sun causes aging of the skin and changes that can lead to skin cancer in later life. Certain areas such as the face, shoulders, and back of knees are more likely to burn than other areas. Protect these areas by wearing hats, long-sleeve shirts, and sunscreeen or sunblock. Have a "standing order" for the use of sunscreen or sunblock on the skin of all children whose families give consent to use it. The number on the sunscreen or sunblock indicates how many times the normal exposure time the product will provide protection. Use products with number 15 or more. Do not apply sunscreen or sunblock to broken skin.

Because it takes several hours for a sunburn to show, watching for reddening of the skin is not a dependable way to tell when a child has been in the sun too long. By the time you notice any change, it is too late. The sun's rays are most intense between 10 A.M. and 2 P.M. Reflections of the sun's rays from water and sand increase sunburn dangers. Cloudy days can fool you; clouds don't stop the sun from burning. It is a good idea on most summer days to plan for playtime in the shade, frequent fluid intake, and skin cooling.

When a child has a sunburn, do not apply medications to the skin without a doctor's recommendation. There is no *cure* for sunburn, but the pain and itching that accompany a burn can be treated with a cool bath or cold compresses applied three or four times a day for 10 to 15 minutes at a time. Severe burns may be accompanied by intense pain, blistering of the skin, nausea, chills, and fever. If a child has these symptoms, ask the families to consult their physician.

Guidelines for heat-related illness and dehydration

After prolonged exposure to high temperatures and high humidity, children may have one or more of these symptoms of heat exhaustion:

• pale and clammy skin
• heavy sweating
• fatigue
• weakness
• dizziness
• headache
• nausea
• muscle cramps
• vomiting
• fainting.

Avoid heat-related illness and dehydration by encouraging children to drink liquids and cool off frequently. Children should not play outside when the heat index is greater than 90 degrees F. Provide small amounts of clear liquids at least every 2 hours to help restore fluids that the body loses through evaporation. Achieve quick and sanitary cooling by having children play under a sprinkler or by using cool water on paper towels to remove perspiration and oil from their skin.

Thirst is *not* a good indicator of dehydration because a child can become dehydrated before becoming thirsty. Check the child's frequency of urination and urine color (concentration) to determine fluid needs. Normally, urine should be pale yellow or colorless, and urination should occur every 2 or 3 hours. Dark yellow (concentrated) urine is a sign the body is not well enough hydrated. A child's temperature can rise dangerously with overheating.

When a child (or adult) has symptoms of heat exhaustion, the first thing to do is to move him to a cool and shaded area. Then contact the family and ask that the child's health care provider be called immediately.

Giving Medication in Child Care

Almost all children, at one time or another, need medication. Families probably will ask you to give medication either for a chronic problem, for a mild illness, or as needed for temporary discomfort. The Americans with Disabilities Act (ADA) may require providers to administer medications to children with chronic conditions or special health needs. Check state regulations on administering medication to children in your care. The American Academy of Pediatrics recommends that all child care providers be trained in how to safely administer medication.

Enlist families' help when children require medication. This might include setting up a schedule for giving medications only at home or consulting with the health care provider about prescribing medication in a different form (liquid, pill, capsule) and/or varying the number of times a day a medication is required (for example, morning and bedtime versus three times a day). You might ask a parent to come during the day to give the medication, but it is burdensome to require families to do this unless a parent works near the facility.

In *Caring for Our Children* the standards define when medication administration is permissible in child care. Note that child care providers may give only medications that have both the recommendation of a health professional and the family's consent. Use the standard to write the facility's medication administration health policy (see page 152). To be sure everyone abides by the policy, share the rationale and comments that accompany the standard with staff and parents.

Labeling and storing medications

Prescribed medication brought into a child care facility should be in the original child-resistant container labeled and dated by the pharmacist with the following information:

- the child's first and last name
- the date the prescription was filled and the medication's expiration date
- the name of the health care provider who wrote the prescription
- the manufacturer's instructions or prescription label with specific, legible instructions for administration, storage, and disposal
- the name and strength of the medication.

Over-the-counter medications should be in the original container, as sold by the manufacturer; labeled by the parent with the child's name; and accompanied by specific instructions given by the child's health professional for administration.

All medications, (refrigerated or stored at room temperature, prescribed or over-the-counter) should have child-resistant caps. Although not child-proof, child-resistant safety packaging decreases poisonings among children ages 0–4. Note: All prescribed medications must, by law, be dispensed in child-resistive packaging unless the purchaser specifically requests otherwise. Those who work with children should monitor compliance at the pharmacy so all medications are safely packaged.

The child care facility should keep medications organized by group or alphabetically by child's name, by the time that medicines need to be given, or some other logical fashion. They should be kept where they are inaccessible to children, at room temperature or refrigerated as the label says is necessary, and where a tip-over and spill can not contaminate food. A small lock box can be kept in the refrigerator and another in a cabinet to hold medications. No medication should be given beyond the date of expiration.

Training staff for administration of medication

Any caregiver who administers medication should receive training to

- check that the name of the child on the medication and the child receiving the medication are the same
- read and understand the label/prescription directions in relation to the measured dose, frequency, and other circumstances relative to administration (such as in relation to meals)
- administer the medication according to the prescribed methods and the prescribed dose
- observe and report any side effects from medications
- document the administration of each dose by the time and the amount given.

A child's reaction to medication occasionally is extreme enough to initiate the protocol developed for emergencies. The medication record is especially important if medications are frequently prescribed or if long-term medications are being used. The facility should have a written policy for the use of any medication ordered for a particular child by that child's primary health care provider. The facility also should have a written policy for the use of any nonprescription oral or topical medication that the facility keeps on hand to use with parental consent.

The medication record

A medication record should include the following:

- specific, signed parental consent for the caregiver to administer medication
- prescription by a health care provider, if required
- administration log
- checklist information, including possible side effects, brought to the facility by the parents.

See Figure 10.5 for a sample Medication Consent and Log form.

Any unused medication should be disposed of or returned to the parent(s).

Practical guidelines for medication administration

- Only staff who have training on medication administration should give medicine. Ask a physician or nurse to describe/demonstrate the specific procedures to be used.
- Have the family ask the pharmacist to give them an extra *labeled* bottle to bring to your program so that one can be kept at home.
- Post a medicine log sheet at the spot (for example, on refrigerator) where you give medication to the child so you won't forget to write down the exact time and date. Put this log sheet in the child's folder after the course of medication ends.
- Be sure you receive very specific instructions about how the medicine should be given (for example, before or after meals, with a full glass of water, by tilting the head). Most prescription labels do not have this information.
- Learn the possible side effects of the medication and inform the family immediately if you observe any. Do not give more medication without the approval of the parent or child's physician.
- Always read what the label says about storage. Avoid storing medication in warm, wet, or lighted places.
- *Always read the label carefully before you give any medicine; bottles often look the same. Give the right medication to the right child; give the right dose, by the right method at the right time.* Be sure that the child's name is on the bottle (several children may

be taking the same medicine). As an extra precaution, put medication in a bag labeled with the child's name in large letters. Double-check the name of the child, dose, time, and method of administration.

- Never leave medicine out where a child can get to it. When you answer the telephone or leave the room, put away the medication or take it with you. A child can take an overdose in seconds.
- Never refer to medicine as candy or something else children like. They may try to get more of it than they should have.

Special Considerations for Programs That Care for Mildly Ill Children

When young children become ill they need adequate rest, appropriate diet, medications as ordered, and appropriate physical and emotional support. Alternatives for care can include a variety of arrangements in centers or home-based facilities, including care by a child care worker in the child's own home.

Working parents should be entitled to family sick leave days to care for their ill children. Professionals and the public generally agree that when a child is seriously ill, or when it is not yet clear that the illness is a mild one, the parent should be able to stay home with the child. At a minimum, working parents should be able to use their own sick or personal days to care for their ill children. However, because children are ill frequently, some families need help in making alternative arrangements for the days when the child is not very ill and the parents need to be at work.

Facilities unable to care for ill children should be supportive and helpful to families, giving them ideas for alternative arrangements. However, the responsibility for care cannot be transferred from family to child care provider unless the caregiver is willing to accept this responsibility. The decision to accept responsibility for the care of ill children should rest with a designated person at the facility; she must weigh all staffing and programmatic considerations. Although considerations may vary from one instance to another, families must know who will make the decision.

Sometimes, with modified activities, a child can be included in the facility's regular group of children. A center can set up a "get-well room" where ill children not able to participate with the regular group can receive care. Some centers set up satellite small family child care homes for their enrolled children. Ideally, the children know the caregiver because she regularly works at the center. Similarly, a child's regular small or large family child care home provider could include the child in the regular group if appropriate or set up a get-well room, if adequate supervision can be provided. Other alternative care arrangements include a worker sent by a home health agency or from a pool of caregivers to the child's home; or in a pediatric unit of a hospital, pediatric office, or other similar setting. Special facilities caring only for ill children should meet more specialized requirements.

Requirements for facilities that care for mildly ill children include specific qualifications and training of staff, child:staff ratios, space and equipment requirements, special services from health consultants, as well as administrative procedures that differ from those used by facilities that care for well children only. In some states, facilities that care for ill children must be separately licensed. These standards are detailed in chapter 3 of *Caring for Our Children*. Those who would like to consider providing care for children excluded from routine care should study these standards carefully.

Specific standards for facilities that care for ill children

The following information is adapted from Chapter 3 of *Caring for Our Children*.

Space. The standards specify that environmental space for the care of children who are ill with infectious diseases and cannot receive care in their usual child care group must meet all requirements for well children and some additional requirements. If the program is in the same facility as the well-child program, well children shouldn't use or share furniture, fixtures, equipment, or supplies designated for use with ill children unless they have been cleaned and sanitized before use. Indoor space, including hallways, bathrooms, and kitchens, must be separate from indoor space used with well children. This reduces the likelihood of mixing supplies, toys, and equipment. However, the facility may use a single kitchen for ill and well children if the kitchen is staffed by a cook who has no child care responsibilities other than food preparation and who does not handle soiled dishes and utensils until after food preparation and food service are completed for any meal.

Children whose symptoms indicate infections of the gastrointestinal tract (often with diarrhea) or liver, who receive care in special facilities for ill children, need to be in a space separate from other children with other illnesses. The likelihood of disease being transmitted between children is reduced by limiting child-to-child interaction, separating staff responsibilities, and not mixing supplies, toys, and equipment.

If the facility cares for children with chickenpox, these children must receive care in a separate room that is ventilated externally (the chickenpox virus travels very easily through the air). This illness should disappear with the implementation of universal immunization with chickenpox vaccine. However, because some families choose to expose their children to the complications of natural chickenpox, programs should consider carefully whether illness care should be provided to families who have made this choice. Children who develop a rash after chickenpox vaccine do not need separate care as long as their spots can be covered until they scab.

Each child care room where sick children are in care must have a handwashing sink that can provide a steady stream of water, no less than 60 degrees F and no more than 120 degrees F, at least for 10 seconds. Supply these sinks with soap and disposable paper towels at all times. Sinks must be handy to be used frequently. A room in which children in diapers receive care needs its own diaper-changing area adjacent to the handwashing sink. There can be no compromises in diaper-changing sanitation when ill children are in care.

Qualifications of directors. The director of a facility that cares for ill children needs some additional qualifications over what would normally be required. The director should have at least 40 hours of training in prevention and control of communicable diseases and care of ill children, including all aspects of care for the types of illnesses children in care might have. The director should also have at least 2 prior years of satisfactory performance as a director of a regular facility and at least 12 credit hours of college–level training in child development or early childhood education.

Program requirements. Any facility that offers care for ill children of any age must provide

- a caregiver who is familiar to the child
- care in a place with which the child is familiar and comfortable

- a caregiver who has time to give individual care and emotional support, who knows the child's interests as well as activities that appeal to the age group and to a sick child
- a program planned in consultation with qualified health care personnel and with ongoing medical direction.

Caregiver qualifications. Meeting the physical and psychological needs of ill children requires a higher level of skill and understanding than does caring for well children. Staff caring for ill children in special facilities or in a get-well room in a regular center should meet the staff qualifications that are applied to child care facilities generally, plus have additional training. Training and work experience help the caregiver develop the necessary skills. States that have developed rules regulating facilities recognize the need for training in illness prevention and control and management of medical emergencies.

Child care providers have to be prepared for handling illness and must understand their scope of work. Each caregiver should have training to decrease the risk of transmitting disease. The potential for medical emergencies is greater in facilities for ill children than in regular well-child facilities, so these facilities have to be prepared for such events. Health departments or hospital pediatric and nursing departments may be resources for providing the necessary training.

Each caregiver in a facility that cares for ill children with severity level 2 or level 3 illness (as defined earlier) should have at least 2 years of successful work experience as a caregiver in a regular well-child facility. In addition, a level 1 or level 2 facility should document, for each caregiver, 20 hours of preservice orientation training on care of ill children beyond orientation training. This training should include

- pediatric first aid, including management of a blocked airway, rescue breathing, and first aid for choking
- general infection–control procedures, including
  —handwashing
  —handling of contaminated items
  —use of sanitizing chemicals
  —food handling
  —washing and sanitizing of toys
  —education about methods of disease transmission
- care of children with common mild childhood illnesses, including

  —recognition and documentation of signs and symptoms of illness
  —administration and recording of medications
  —temperature taking
  —nutrition of ill children
  —communication with families of ill children
  —knowledge of immunization requirements
  —when and how to call for medical assistance or notify the health department of communicable diseases
  —emergency procedures
- child development activities for children who are ill
- orientation to the facility and its policies.

This training should be documented in the staff personnel files, and compliance with the content of training routinely evaluated. Based on these evaluations, the training should be updated annually with a minimum of six hours for individuals who continue to provide care to ill children.

Child:staff ratios. No studies are available to substantiate appropriate staffing levels for care of ill children. Most staffing requirements developed by state licensing authorities are stated in terms of number of staff members required to remove children from a building quickly in the event of fire or other emergency. The expert consensus is that ill children require more intensive and personalized care; therefore, these ratios seem appropriate.

Age of Children	Child to Staff Ratio
2–24 months	3 children to 1 staff member
25–71 months	4 children to 1 staff member
72 months or older	6 children to 1 staff member

Health consultants. Appropriate involvement of health consultants is especially important for facilities that care for ill children. Programs should use the expertise of health professionals to design and provide a child care environment with sufficient staff and facilities to meet the needs of ill children. Caregivers should seek the services of a health consultant through state and local professional organizations, such as American Academy of Pediatrics (AAP), American Nurses Association (ANA), Visiting Nurse Association (VNA), American Academy of Family Physicians, National Association of Pediatric Nurse Associates and Practitioners (NAPNAP), National Association for the Education of Young Children (NAEYC), National Association for Family Child Care (NAFCC), Emergency Medical

Services for Children (EMSC) National Resource Center, National Training Institute (NTI) for Child Care Health Consultants, and or state or local health department (especially public health nursing, communicable disease, and epidemiology departments).

Caregivers also should not overlook health professionals with appropriate pediatric experience who are parents of children enrolled in their facility. A health professional (community health nurse, for example) may provide consultation as a volunteer or be paid via a stipend, hourly rate, or honorarium. If a parent provides health consultation, address possible conflicts of interest in advance.

While making such arrangements may be difficult and an additional expense of operation, each special facility that provides care for ill children should use the services of a health consultant for ongoing consultation on overall operation and development of written policies relating to health care. The health consultant should be a health professional with training and experience with pediatric health issues. The facility should involve the consultant in development and/or implementation, review, and sign-off of the written policies and procedures for managing specific illnesses. The program staff and the consultant need to review and update the written policies annually. The facility should arrange for the health consultant to take responsibility for reviewing written policies and procedures for the following areas:

- admission and readmission after illness, including inclusion/exclusion criteria
- health evaluation procedures on intake, including physical assessment of the child and other criteria used to determine the appropriateness of attendance
- plans for health care and for managing children with communicable diseases
- plans for surveillance of illnesses that are admissible and problems that arise in the care of children with illness
- plans for staff training and communication with families and health care providers
- plans for injury prevention
- situations that require medical care within an hour.

Information required. The caregiver must have child-specific information to provide optimum care for each ill child and to make appropriate decisions regarding whether to include or exclude a given child. The caregiver needs to have contact information for the child's primary source of health care to assist with the management of any situation that arises. Too often, parents contact the child's source of health care to seek advice while the child is actually with the caregiver. This results in the parent relaying secondhand information and often being unable to answer questions that could be addressed by the caregiver who is with the child at the time. These discontinuous three-way conversations are frustrating and can lead to inappropriate advice.

For school-age children, a facility should document care of the child during the illness for the family to deliver to the school health program upon the child's return to school. Coordination with the child's source of health care and school health program facilitates the overall care of the child.

Facilities that care for ill children with conditions requiring additional attention beyond what is usually provided for in the program plan need to arrange for or ask the health consultant to arrange for a clinical health evaluation for each child who is admitted to the facility by a licensed health care professional. These programs may include children with conditions that would otherwise be excluded if the policies and plans address the management of these conditions. There are limits for inclusion of sick children in child care, however. Certain conditions require exclusion from all types of child care facilities because they require care in medical care institutions such as hospitals or skilled nursing facilities. As specified in *Caring for Our Children,* these conditions are:

- fever and a stiff neck, lethargy, irritability, or persistent crying
- diarrhea (three or more loose stools in an 8-hour period or more stools compared to the child's normal pattern, with more stool water or less form) and one or more of the following:
  —signs of dehydration
  —blood or mucus in the stool, unless at least one stool culture demonstrates absence of shigella, salmonella, campylobacter, and E. coli 0157:H7
  —diarrhea attributable to salmonella, campylobacter, or giardia except that a child with diarrhea attributable to campylobacter or giardia may be readmitted 24 hours after treatment if cleared by the child's physician
  —diarrhea attributable to shigella and E. coli 0157:H7 until diarrhea resolves and two stool cultures taken 48 hours apart are negative

- vomiting three or more times, or signs of dehydration
- contagious stages of pertussis, measles, mumps, chickenpox, rubella, or diphtheria, unless the child is appropriately isolated from children with other illnesses and cared for only with children having the same illness
- untreated infestation of scabies or head lice
- untreated tuberculosis
- undiagnosed rash
- abdominal pain that is intermittent or persistent
- difficulty in breathing
- lethargy such that the child does not play
- undiagnosed jaundice (yellow skin and whites of eyes)
- other conditions as may be determined by the director or health consultant.

For each day of care in a special facility providing care for ill children, the caregiver should have the following information on each child:

- the specific diagnosis and the individual providing the diagnosis (physician, parent, or legal guardian)
- current status of the illness, including potential for contagion, diet, activity level, and duration
- health care, diet, allergies (particularly to foods or medication), and medication plan, including appropriate release forms to obtain emergency health care and administer medication
- communication with the parent or guardian on the child's progress
- name, address, and telephone number of the child's source of primary health care
- communication with the child's primary health care provider.

Suggested Activities

- Think about people you know who have a chronic illness. What type of illness do they have? How do you know when they are not feeling well? What happens when they have a flare-up? How does their illness affect them and the people around them? What would happen if these individuals were denied the opportunity to do what brings them in contact with the others?
- Recall the illnesses you have had over the past 12 months. For how many days did these illnesses restrict your activities to staying at home? How many days did you go to work or school with some symptoms? How did you decide whether to limit your activity? What measures did you take to hasten recovery?
- Recall a childhood illness that kept you home from school. What do you remember about it? What gave you comfort? Why do you remember particular aspects of the illness experience?
- Recall a childhood illness that kept you home from school. What do you remember about it? What gave you comfort? Why do you remember particular aspects of the illness experience?

Chapter 11

Special Issues

After the discussion in preceding chapters of many of the facility and performance issues required to operate a safe and healthy child care program, some special issues remain to be addressed. These are inclusion of children with special needs, child abuse, and the administration of the health component in a child care program.

Federal law requires inclusion of children with special needs. Nevertheless, compliance with the law is not the only reason for fostering inclusion. When programs serve children with special needs, the quality of care for all children improves. In addition to children who have special needs because of medical or developmental health problems, some children have special needs because their families or other caregivers are under unusual stress and cannot provide appropriate care, or the characteristics of the child may exceed the ability of parents or other caregivers to meet the child's needs. These and other contributing factors of the child or his caregivers can combine to lead to child abuse or neglect.

These special issues, as well as all other aspects of the health component discussed in this manual, require competent administrative management. The responsibilities and facility health policies recommended for providing such ongoing program administration are outlined in the close of this chapter.

Major Concepts

- Inclusion of children with special needs enriches the program for typically developing children by the addition of specialists who broaden understanding about how to foster optimum development for all children.
- Federal programs for children with developmental disabilities provide substantial resources and impose specific duties on caregivers to ensure appropriate services reach these children.
- Most child abuse and neglect is perpetrated by family members or individuals living with the family, not by child care workers.
- Child care providers are mandated to report child abuse and neglect.
- Child care is a therapeutic environment for families under stress, and thus plays a key role in prevention of child abuse and neglect.
- Denial of privacy to children and adults in child care settings can prevent child abuse and the suspicion of abuse.
- Implementing safe and healthy child care requires competent administration and evaluation of the health component.

Inclusion of Children with Special Needs

Children with a wide range of special needs or disabilities—those with speech and language delays, problems getting along with other children, chronic illnesses, family difficulties, abusive or neglectful parents, developmental delays or physical impairments—can benefit from being in group situations with children who do not have special needs. The lives of other children and staff can also be greatly enriched by including children with special needs in early childhood programs.

Some children with special needs require extensive individual program planning, and some need extra services. Others need staff to help them in minor ways or for limited times. Whatever the special need, staff must be attentive to reactions of the child, family, other children and families in the program, and other staff members, and they must be flexible in planning. Each program needs to be realistic about what it can and should do to safely and appropriately meet the special needs of a child. In many instances, representatives of other programs providing special services to the child can assist staff in the child care setting.

Child care programs cannot deny care simply because a child has a disability. The Americans with Disabilities Act (ADA), which went into effect in 1992, states that people with disabilities are entitled to equal rights and protections in employment, state and local public services, and public accommodations such as preschools, child care centers, and family child care homes. Section 504 of the 1975 Rehabilitation Act includes very similar requirements for any program that receives federal assistance, including those programs administered by religious institutions.

Each child's needs must be *evaluated on an individual basis* to determine whether a program can *reasonably accommodate* the child's needs. Extensive study of the implications of ADA by the Child Care Law Center helps clarify the issues for child care programs. Consult Figure 11.1 or go online to **www.childcarelaw.org**, to help determine whether your program can reasonably accommodate the needs of a particular child. Several other chapters in this manual provide helpful information to guide a program's thinking about inclusion. The sections on specific types of special needs, chronic illnesses, transportation and emergency preparedness should be particularly useful when thinking about inclusive care.

Benefits of inclusion

Inclusion, as a value, supports the right of all children, regardless of their diverse abilities, to participate actively in natural settings with their peers within their communities. A natural setting is one in which children would spend time had they not had a disability. Such settings include but are not limited to home and family, play groups, child care, nursery schools, Head Start programs, kindergartens, and neighborhood school classrooms. Support for inclusion requires help for young children and their families to access and provide health, social service, education, and other supports and services that promote full participation in community life.

Research has shown repeatedly that the early years of life are critical for learning and growth. This is the period of maximum opportunity to promote children's cognitive, speech and language, physical, social, and emotional development. If their special needs are recognized and met during these years, children with disabilities will have a much better chance of succeeding and becoming independent adults. Children with special needs who are given the opportunity to play and learn with other children in the classroom learn more about themselves, how to cope with the give-and-take of everyday life, and have opportunities to model and practice new skills every day. This is one of the first steps toward developing independence.

Inclusion helps all children. When children with special needs participate in inclusive early childhood settings that provide for their special needs and have teachers who know how to adapt teaching techniques and activities, they *and* their typically developing peers do better. The development-promoting techniques used for children with disabilities fosters richer programming for typically developing children as well. Inclusion can help children without disabilities to accept and be comfortable with individual differences. Some studies show that children's attitudes toward children with special needs become more positive when they have the opportunity to play together regularly. They learn that children with special needs share with them the ability to do some things better than others. Inclusion allows all children the opportunity to make friends with many different individuals.

Inclusion helps families. Inclusion also helps the families of children with special needs. Such parents may feel less isolated when child care providers and specialists share the responsibility for teaching their child. They can learn new ways to help their own child. As they watch their child progress and interact with other children, parents can think about their child realistically. They will see that some of the behaviors that concern them are probably typical of all young children, not just children with special needs. For children with developmental disabilities, parents in some cases can see that their children are progressing along a path modeled by other children, albeit more slowly.

Inclusion helps teachers. Inclusion has advantages for teachers. Many of the most effective teaching techniques were first developed for children with disabilities. Working with children with special needs is a chance to broaden both teaching and personal experience. Teachers who have helped young children learn how to hold their cups by themselves or to modulate their behavior appropriately have accommodated to the developmental level of the child. This type of accommodation is generally what is needed for children with developmental delay as well.

How Is Inclusion Carried Out?

Inclusion can be carried out in a variety of ways. The decisions about the best ways to include a particular child with special needs will depend upon the child's strengths and needs. Every child is an individual with different abilities and characteristics. All children display a broad range of behavior and abilities.

Children with special needs generally have some abilities and behaviors within the range of typical development, and some that are outside of it. Planning should involve maximum use of family and staff resources and services within the community. The most inclusive setting should be *individually* determined for a *particular* child at a *particular* time and reassessed *regularly.*

Inclusion involves the efforts of many people working as a team. This team includes teachers, the child's family, other specialists providing consultant services on a full- or part-time basis, agencies serving young children with special needs, and the public schools. Coordination of efforts is both a challenge and a critical requirement for meeting the needs of a child with special needs.

Staff's feelings about and attitudes toward children with special needs

Most child care providers did not choose special education as a career and may feel unprepared to work with children with various special needs. Each staff member brings different attitudes and experiences different feelings, usually both positive and negative, when including a child with special needs in the program. Different needs may evoke different emotions and responses. Staff may feel sympathy for the family, acceptance of the child's needs, concern about their ability to meet this child's needs, frustration in not getting needed support, and/or enthusiasm for new challenges and opportunities. Each of these feelings may affect responses to a child with a special need.

Feeling sorry for the child often leads to an overly protective attitude; caregivers may try to shelter the child from experiences that are part of daily life. This may prevent seeing the child's strengths and expecting the most from him. Anger may flare when the extra responsibility or work required to deal with a child with special needs is apparent. Fear and insecurity are natural responses to inadequate information about the condition. Feelings of acceptance and caring may surface immediately or may develop over time.

Sharing feelings may help. Teachers often find that working on a daily basis with children who have special needs helps to ease their anxiety and fear. These teachers have taken steps to see the children as children first and learn about the specific special need. They place emphasis on the whole child rather than on the child's limitations.

Resources and support

Caregivers are not expected to be experts in special education; however, there are many ways to prepare to work with a child with special needs. NAEYC resources include several related publications: *Widening the Circle: Including Children with Disabilities in Preschool Programs; Natural Environments and Inclusion;* and *A Place for Me: Including Children with Special Needs in Early Care and Education Settings.* The child's parents have a wealth of information to share. Caregivers can visit other classrooms where children with similar special needs are being taught.

Specialists, particularly those who have evaluated or worked with the child, may have valuable suggestions and resources to contribute. If the child is under 3 and eligible for early intervention under Part C of IDEA, early intervention staff will be a valuable resource. For preschoolers with disabilities eligible under IDEA, staff from other preschool programs can assist. In either case, it is ideal for the child care provider to be an ongoing member of the team that plans for the child. Seek permission from the family to contact the child's health care provider and others working with the child so program goals, activities, and evaluations can be coordinated among all the members of the child's team. Training sessions, conferences, or workshops provide excellent background material. National associations and professional organizations can provide information describing a specific disability and may serve as an important resource for parents. A list of some national associations is provided in Figure 11.2. Local hospitals, colleges, clinics, or other community agencies may be able to provide additional information and assistance.

Inclusive Education: The Individuals with Disabilities Education Act

State or local school systems are responsible for providing services to preschool children with special needs under the Individual with Disabilities Education Act (IDEA). State agencies are responsible for providing services to infants and toddlers with disabilities under IDEA. IDEA is a federal law that affords caregivers a unique opportunity to support children whose special needs might affect their educational success as well as impact upon both the children and families in other ways in the child care

setting. The purpose of Part B of the law is to provide "free appropriate public education" regardless of disability or chronic illness to all eligible children, ages 3 through 21, in the least restrictive environment appropriate to the child. Part C of IDEA provides for a collaborative system to serve the needs of eligible infants and toddlers between the ages of birth and 3 years through early intervention. Child care programs can play a significant role in maximizing children's development by supporting the services required.

Part C of IDEA

Part C makes federal funds available for states to implement an interagency system of early intervention services for eligible infants and toddlers and their families. The state governor selects the lead agency that is responsible for the administration of the program. The intent of Part C is to enhance the development of, and to provide other needed services for, infants and toddlers who have developmental delays or have diagnosed conditions. A further intent is to support the capacity of families to enhance the development of their children in the home and community and to transition children to effective and appropriate preschool services.

The focus of services to the child and family under Part C is the achievement of two related goals:

- to enhance and support the development of young children with disabilities and minimize their need for special education and related services when they enter the public school system.

- to maximize the potential for infants and toddlers with disabilities to enjoy the benefits of their communities and grow into adults capable of living independently, pursuing vocations, and participating in the benefits their communities offer all citizens.

Although a lead agency is responsible for implementation, the program is designed to be a coordinated, collaborative effort among a variety of state agencies for screening of children, assessment, service coordination, and development of an Individualized Family Service Plan (IFSP) for every eligible infant or toddler and his or her family. The IFSP describes early intervention services for the child and the family, including family support and the child's developmental, therapeutic, and health needs. Among the more important aspects of this interagency model is the belief that children and their families should be viewed from the perspective of an ability model rather than a deficit model, that is, emphasizing the strengths and capabilities of the family and child rather than the family's or child's perceived weaknesses. This means that the IFSP approach should be that of enhancing and supporting already-existing resources, priorities, and concerns of the child and family rather than assuming that services can correct "deficiencies."

Serving children in natural environments

Part C of the IDEA requires delivery of services in natural environments to the maximum extent appropriate to the child. These are defined as settings that are "natural or normal for the child's peers who have no disabilities." Natural environments reflect those places routinely used by families and typically developing children and represent a wide variety of options such as the child's home, the neighborhood, community programs, and services such as child care centers, parks, recreation centers, stores, malls, museums, and so on. By incorporating elements of the child's regular environment—such as furniture, toys, schedule, siblings, care providers, extended family—in the planning and delivery of services and supports, the family and providers can best discover the child's talents and gifts and enhance these in the normal course of play, relationships, and caregiving. Learning about and understanding the child's routines and using real-life opportunities and activities, such as eating, playing, interacting with others, and working on developmental skills, greatly enhance a child's ability to achieve the functional outcomes identified in the IFSP.

For these reasons, it is critical to have a representative from the child care at the table when the IFSP is developed or revised. Written informed consent must be obtained from the family before confidential information (written or verbal) is shared among providers. The child care provider must become familiar with a child's IFSP and understand both the role the provider is to play and the resources available through the IFSP to support the child's family and provider.

Part B and the Individualized Education Program

Three through five-year olds eligible for services under Part B of the IDEA are generally served through a written Individualized Education Program (IEP). (In some states and communities the IFSP is still used for preschoolers.) The IEP is developed by a team with the local education agency (LEA) assuming responsibility for its implementation in either a public preschool program or a private preschool setting. Services can be provided in a LEA preschool. Local education agencies may also contract with private providers for preschool services or provide educationally related services identified in the IEP, such as speech and language therapy, in a private preschool or child care setting. Child care providers should become familiar with a preschooler's special needs as identified in the IEP. The provider may wish to send a representative, with prior informed written parental consent, to the IEP review meetings to share valuable insight and information regarding the child's special needs in both the educational and child care settings.

The standards in chapter 7 of *Caring for Our Children* articulate those opportunities and responsibilities that child care agencies share with other agencies in serving a child with special needs, whether the child is served through an IFSP or IEP. (For an overview of federal laws and related information for early childhood educators and families working to meet the needs of children with disabilities in inclusive programs, see *Including All Children: Children with Disabilities in Early Childhood Programs,* a brochure published jointly by NAEYC and the Division of Early Childhood of the Council for Exceptional Children.)

Modifying a Child Care Program to Accommodate Children with Special Needs

When children with special needs are enrolled, modifications or adaptations in the policies, equipment, practices, or routine may be needed to facilitate these children's active participation in the child care program. The primary goal of inclusion is to enable all children to participate actively in the activities of the program to maximize their development and to allow them to operate as independently as possible. For this reason, a program that enrolls children with special needs should meet these objectives:

- adapt the program to ensure successful participation
- develop all children's feelings of competence
- promote peer acceptance
- avoid overprotection

Figure 11.1. Understanding the Americans with Disabilities Act

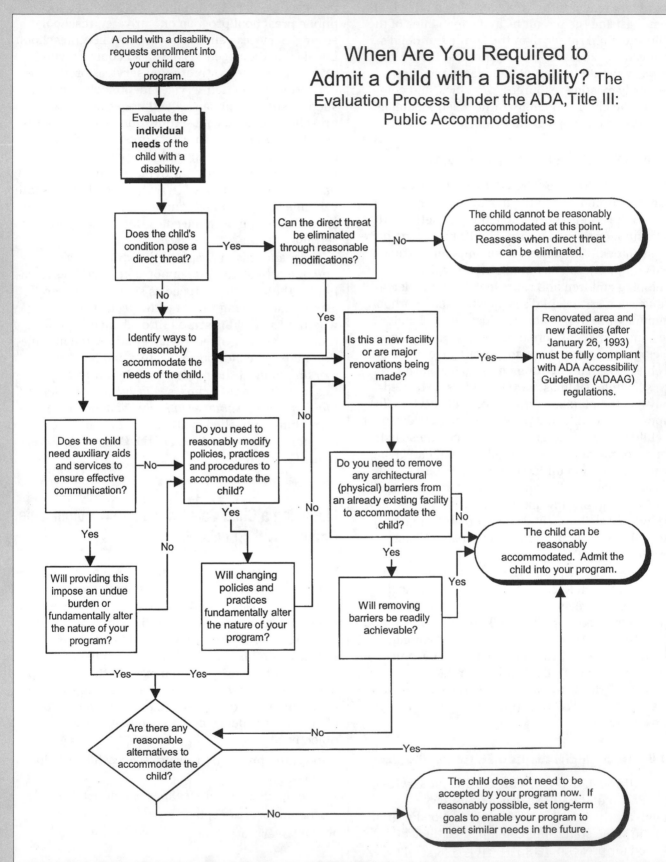

When Are You Required to Admit a Child with a Disability? The Evaluation Process Under the ADA, Title III: Public Accommodations

A child with a disability requests enrollment into your child care program.

Evaluate the **individual needs** of the child with a disability.

Does the child's condition pose a direct threat? —Yes→ Can the direct threat be eliminated through reasonable modifications? —No→ The child cannot be reasonably accommodated at this point. Reassess when direct threat can be eliminated.

No (from direct threat) and Yes (from modifications) → Identify ways to reasonably accommodate the needs of the child.

Is this a new facility or are major renovations being made? —Yes→ Renovated area and new facilities (after January 26, 1993) must be fully compliant with ADA Accessibility Guidelines (ADAAG) regulations.

Does the child need auxiliary aids and services to ensure effective communication? —No→ Do you need to reasonably modify policies, practices and procedures to accommodate the child?

Do you need to remove any architectural (physical) barriers from an already existing facility to accommodate the child? —No→ The child can be reasonably accommodated. Admit the child into your program.

Yes → Will providing this impose an undue burden or fundamentally alter the nature of your program?

Yes → Will changing policies and practices fundamentally alter the nature of your program?

Yes → Will removing barriers be readily achievable? —Yes→ The child can be reasonably accommodated. Admit the child into your program.

Will providing this impose an undue burden... —Yes— and Will changing policies... —Yes→ Are there any reasonable alternatives to accommodate the child?

Will removing barriers be readily achievable? —No→ Are there any reasonable alternatives to accommodate the child?

Are there any reasonable alternatives to accommodate the child? —Yes→ The child can be reasonably accommodated. Admit the child into your program.

—No→ The child does not need to be accepted by your program now. If reasonably possible, set long-term goals to enable your program to meet similar needs in the future.

THE AMERICANS WITH DISABILITIES ACT (ADA)
A NEW WAY OF THINKING: TITLE III

ADA GOAL:

> To *make reasonable accomodations for* individuals with disabilities in order to *integrate* them into the program to the extent feasible, given *each individual*'s limitations.

ADA PRINCIPLES:

- INDIVIDUALITY
    the limitations and needs of *each* individual;

- REASONABLENESS
    of the modification to the *program* and to the *individual;*

- INTEGRATION
    of the individual *with others* in the program.

TYPES OF MODIFICATIONS:

- AUXILIARY AIDS AND SERVICES
    special equipment and services to ensure effective communication;

- CHANGES IN POLICIES, PRACTICES AND PROCEDURES;

- REMOVAL OF BARRIERS
    architectural, arrangement of furniture and equipment, vehicular.

REASONS TO DENY CARE:

- ACCOMMODATION IS UNREASONABLE, and there are no reasonable alternatives.

    □ For **auxiliary aids and services**, if accommodations pose an *UNDUE BURDEN* (will result in a significant difficulty or expense to the program);

    □ For **auxiliary aids and services**, or **changes in policies, practices or procedures**, if accommodations *FUNDAMENTALLY ALTER* the nature of the program;

    □ For **removal of barriers for existing facilities**, if accommodations are *NOT READILY ACHIEVABLE* (cannot be done without much difficulty or expense to the program). Child care facilities built after January 26, 1993 must comply with ADA Accessibility Guidelines (ADAAG)

- DIRECT THREAT

    The individual's condition will pose or does pose a significant threat to the health or safety of other children or staff in the program, and there are no reasonable means of removing the threat.

Source: Both charts reprinted with permission from the Child Care Law Center.

Figure 11.2. Some National Resources for Children with Special Needs

Alexander Graham Bell Association for the Deaf and Hard of Hearing, 3417 Volta Place, NW, Washington, DC 20007. 202-337-5220; 202-337-5221 (TTY). E-mail: info@agbell.org. Online: www.agbell.org.

American Academy of Pediatrics, 141 Northwest Point Boulevard, Elk Grove Village, IL 60007-1098. 847-434-4000. Online: http://www.aap.org.

American Diabetes Association, National Service Center, 1701 N. Beauregard Street, Alexandria, VA 22311. 703-549-1500 or 800-342-2383. E-mail: customerservice@diabetes.org. Online: www.diabetes.org.

American Foundation for the Blind, 11 Penn Plaza, Suite 300, New York, NY 10001. 212-502-7600. E-mail: afbinfo@afb.net. Online: www.afb.org.

American Heart Association, National Center, 7272 Greenville Avenue, Dallas, TX 75231. 214-373-6300 or 800-242-8721. E-mail: inquire@amhrt.org. Online: www.americanheart.org.

American Lung Association, 61 Broadway, 6th Floor, New York, NY 10006. 212-315-8700 or 800-586-4872. E-mail: info@lungusa.org. Online: www.lungusa.org.

American Speech-Language-Hearing Association, 10801 Rockville Pike, Rockville, MD 20852. 301-897-5700 or 800-638-8255 (Voice/TDD). Online: www.asha.org.

The Arc, Headquarters, 1010 Wayne Avenue, Suite 650, Silver Spring, MD 20910. 301-565-3842. Online: www.thearc.org.

Asthma and Allergy Foundation of America, 1233 20th Street, NW, Suite 402, Washington, DC 20036. 202-466-7643 or 800-727-8462. E-mail: info@aafa.org. Online: www.aafa.org.

Autism Society of America, 7910 Woodmont Avenue, Suite 300, Bethesda, MD 20814. 301-657-0881 or 800-328-8476. Online: www.autism-society.org.

Blind Children's Center, 4120 Marathon Street, Los Angeles, CA 90029-3584. 323-664-2153 or 800-222-3566. Online: www.blindchtr.org.

Child Care Law Center, 221 Pine Street, 3d Floor, San Francisco, CA 94104. 415-394-7144. Online: www.childcarelaw.org.

Council for Exceptional Children, 1110 N. Glebe Road, Suite 300, Arlington, VA 22201. 703-620-3660 (Voice) or 703-264-9446 (TTY). E-mail: cec@cec.sped.org. Online: www.cec.sped.org.

Division for Early Childhood of the Council for Exceptional Children, 634 Eddy, Missoula, MT 59812-6696. 406-243-5898 E-mail: dec@selway.umt.edu. Online: www.dec-sped.org.

Easter Seals, 230 West Monroe Street, Suite 1800, Chicago, IL 60606. 312-726-6200 or 800-221-6827. Online: www.easter-seals.org.

Epilepsy Foundation of America, 4351 Garden City Drive, Landover, MD 20785. 301-459-700 or 800-332-1000. Online: www.efa.org.

Head Start Bureau, U.S. Department of Health and Human Services, Administration for Children,Youth and Families, Head Start Bureau, 330 C Street, SW, Suite 2018, Washington, DC 20201. 202-205-8572. Online: www2.acf.dhhs.gov/programs/hsb/.

IDEA Infant and Toddler Coordinators Association. Go online: www.IDEAinfanttoddler.org for further information and to contact directors at-large.

IDEA Partnerships, ASPIIRE and ILIAD Projects, 1110 N. Glebe Road, Suite 300, Arlington, VA 22201. 877-232-4332 or 866-915-5000 (TTY, toll free). Online: www.ideapractices.org.

International Dyslexia Association, Chester Building #382, 8600 LaSalle Road, Baltimore, MD 21286-2044. 410-296-0232 or 800-222-3123. E-mail: info@interdys.org. Online: www.interdys.org.

Learning Disabilities Association of America, 4156 Library Road, Pittsburgh, PA 15234. 412-341-1515 or 888-300-6710. Online: www.ldanatl.org.

March of Dimes Birth Defects Foundation, 1275 Mamaroneck Avenue, White Plains, NY 10605. 914-428-7100 or 888-663-4637. Online: www.modimes.org.

National Association for the Visually Handicapped, 22 West 21st Street, 6th Floor, New York, NY 10010. 212-255-2804. Online: www.navh.org.

National Attention Deficit Disorder Association, 1788 Second Street, Suite 200, Highland Park, IL 60035. 847-432-2332 (leave a message). E-mail: mail@add.org. Online: www.add.org.

National Center for Learning Disabilities, 381 Park Avenue South, Suite 1401, New York, NY 10016. 212-545-7510 or 888-575-7373. Online: www.ld.org.

National Down Syndrome Society, 666 Broadway, 8th Floor, New York, NY 10012-2317. 800-221-4602 or 212-460-9330. E-mail: info@ndss.org. Online: www.ndss.org.

National Early Childhood Technical Assistance System (NECTAS), 137 East Franklin Street, Suite 500, Chapel Hill, NC 27514-3628. 919-962-2001 or 919-843-3269 (TDD). E-mail: nectas@unc.edu. Online: www.nectas.unc.edu.

National Information Center for Children and Youth with Disabilities (NICHCY), P.O. Box 1492, Washington, DC 20013. 202-884-8200 or 800-695-0285 (V/TTY). Online: www.nichcy.org.

National Information Clearinghouse for Infants with Disabilities and Life-Threatening Conditions, Center for Developmental Disabilities, University of South Carolina, School of Medicine, Columbia, SC 29208. 803-777-4435 or 800-922-9234.

National Mental Health Association, 2001 N. Beauregard Street, 12th Floor, Alexandria, VA 22311. 703-684-7722 or 800-969-6642 or 800-433-5959 (TTY). E-mail: nmhainfo@aol.com. Online: www.nmha.org.

National Organization on Fetal Alcohol Syndrome (NOFAS), 216 G Street, NE, Washington, DC 20002. 202-785-4585 or 800-666-6327. E-mail: information@nofas.org. Online: www.nofas.org.

National Pediatric and Family HIV Resource Center, University of Medicine & Dentistry of New Jersey, 30 Bergen Street, ADMC #4, Newark, NJ 07103. 973-972-0410 or 800-362-0071. Online: www.pedhivaids.org.

Office of Special Education Programs, U.S. Department of Education's Office of Special Education and Rehabilitative Services, 400 Maryland Avenue, SW, Room 3086, Switzer Building, Washington, DC 20202-3511. 202-205-5507. Online: www.ed.gov/offices/OSERS/OSEP.

Sickle Cell Disease Association of America, Inc, 200 Corporate Point, Suite 495, Culver City, CA 90230. 800-421-8453. Online: www.sicklecelldisease.org.

Spina Bifida Association of America, 4590 MacArthur Boulevard, NW, Suite 250, Washington, DC 20007-4226. 202-944-3285 or 800-621-3141. E-mail: sbaa@sbaa.org. Online: www.sbaa.org.

United Cerebral Palsy Association, Inc, 1660 L Street, NW, Suite 700, Washington, DC 20036. 202-776-0406 or 800-872-5827 or 202-973-7197 (TTY). E-mail: ucpnatl@ucpa.org. Online: www.ucpa.org.

• strengthen the teamwork between family, teachers, and other specialists.

The selection and adaptation of materials and activities for children with special needs sometimes requires problem solving and creativity. Special materials may be required and have to be purchased. Examples of such materials are

• eating utensils with special grips or edges

• puzzles with large pieces and/or knobs for children with fine-motor problems

• books with large pictures for children with visual impairments

• hypoallergenic art materials

• foods that do not have ingredients that are a problem for children with allergies, food intolerance, or other nutrition problems

In many cases, staff can adapt materials already available. For example, they can

• apply masking tape to thicken brush handles and crayons so children can get a firmer grip

• slit a small rubber ball and slide the paintbrush or crayon through it so the children can grab it better

• cut out fabric to paste on a storybook to make it more tactile

• lower an easel or coat hooks

• use more visuals to accompany classroom discussions for children with impaired hearing or more listening activities for those with visual difficulties

• use a wedge, standing table, bolster, or adapt other equipment

• eliminate pets or plants in the room if they aggravate a child's asthma or allergies

Necessary adaptations depend on the type and severity of a child's needs. For example, if a classroom is to accommodate a child in a wheelchair, staff can

• measure traffic lanes to ensure that the child can maneuver from one area to another

• check the height of tables to ensure that the arms of the wheelchair fit under them, add blocks to slightly increase the height, or find an alternate seating arrangement

• explore the use of a scooter board instead of a wheelchair, if appropriate, for mobility around the classroom

• ensure ready access to and from the building, adding ramps instead of, or in addition to, steps

• position a water tray or a table so the child can reach it.

Developing feelings of competency in children

All children need to feel a sense of competence. For some children, learning and relating take more time and effort. To ensure successful experiences for all children, staff should

- observe children closely to see what interests them
- talk with children about themselves, their families, pets, and experiences
- break tasks into a sequence of smaller units
- allow sufficient time to learn and use new skills before moving on to something else
- offer a variety of materials and activities suited to different levels of ability
- provide an emotionally safe classroom by respecting all children

---

Figure 11.3. Medical Home for Children with Special Health Care Needs: Activity Checklist for Child Care Providers

To ensure that health care is

ACCESSIBLE

- Provide literature on community agencies that offer services to children with special health care needs (CSHCN), such as Title V, Department of Public Health, Respite, Mental Health.
- Assist families, who may be eligible, to enroll in either Medicaid or the state Children's Health Insurance Program.
- Provide a directory of pediatricians who care for CSHCN.

COMPREHENSIVE

- Ensure that all children with special needs have a primary health care professional.
- Develop a transportation policy and procedure for transporting CSHCN. Identify a local child passenger safety technician to provide up-to-date transportation safety information, education, and technical assistance support.
- Develop an emergency plan for each CSHCN with the child's family and primary health care professional.

COMPASSIONATE

- Become an advocate for the child by communicating observations and concerns to the family.
- Be aware of applicable laws and regulations concerning CSHCN. Distribute information about the requirements of the Americans with Disabilities Act that relate to quality child care.

CONTINUOUS

- Train all caregivers on signs and symptoms of distress and emergency procedures.
- Keep updated emergency contact information as part of each child's record.

- Coordinate educational inservices for parents related to immunizations, developmental screenings, or other health-related topics presented by a local pediatrician or primary pediatric health care professional.
- Transmit information about observations and concerns to the child's primary health care professional, with appropriately obtained consent from the family.
- Create a file with a CSHCN's information so that all caregivers are knowledgeable of each child's condition(s).

COORDINATED

- If applicable, participate in each child's Individualized Family Service Plan or Individualized Education Plan.
- Ensure that CSHCN receive their individual services in the least restrictive and most natural environment. Include caregivers in the provision of special services, including speech, physical, and occupational therapies.

CULTURALLY COMPETENT

- Provide information to parents in their primary language.
- Incorporate family customs, beliefs, or rituals into the everyday care of the child when possible.

FAMILY CENTERED

- Involve parents of CSHCN in advisory roles for the child care setting.
- Ask families for guidance regarding accessibility and developmentally appropriate practices (e.g., floor plans, playground equipment, transportation, activities, and toys).

Source: Adapted from American Academy of Pediatrics, Policy Statement, "The Medical Home," online at www.aap.org.

- focus on the *process* of learning rather than the end result
- accept different answers from different children
- set clear and realistic goals for each child.

Promote peer acceptance. Children must be provided with positive role models so they can learn to interact with others in a kind, accepting way. When given opportunities to watch adults relating comfortably to children with special needs, they take the first step toward learning peer acceptance. Children should be given factual information about disabilities to dispel misunderstandings and diminish fear. Staff can encourage the acceptance of a child with special needs in the following ways:

- Always answer children's questions accurately, using language that is easily understood.
- Reassure children that disabilities are not catching (contagious).
- Provide simulation activities so that children can have some idea what it is like to have a special need. For example, whisper or put cotton in children's ears to demonstrate hearing loss; lead children on a blindfold walk so that they can experience the loss of vision; have children wear gloves while doing a task to experience fine motor coordination difficulty.
- Plan activities that allow the other children to see the child with a special need in a successful role.
- Have materials that reflect diversity routinely available. For example, include books about children with special needs in the reading corner, and include dolls or puppets with disabilities.
- Invite adults with disabilities into the classroom and have them participate in activities.
- Focus on similarities as well as differences among people.
- Use a model showing competence and adaptation rather than a deficit model emphasizing weakness.

Avoid overprotection. Overprotection limits a child's opportunities to grow to full potential. Pity and fear limit a teacher's ability to allow a child with a special need to take risks, to respond to limits, to engage in conflict, and to experience *real* success and failure. Staff can avoid overprotection by remembering to do the following:

- Set limits for *all* children (a child with a special need also must wait for a turn on the slide).

- Provide many classroom options and activities so that children do not become overly dependent on adult direction.
- Encourage all children to try new activities they wouldn't naturally choose.
- Communicate a positive attitude and real feelings to the children, who see their caregivers as important role models.

Strengthening teamwork

Including a child with special needs makes the necessity for teamwork even greater. To ensure that the special needs of a child and family are met, parents/guardians, teachers, and administrators must communicate closely and regularly. With family consent, periodic communications with the child's source of health care and any specialists who provide special care or services during child care hours is essential too. Collaboration on the following tasks is especially important:

- Identify the special needs of the child.
- Plan and implement a program responsive to the child's needs, including transitional activities when the child moves on to the next source of care.
- Note any changes in the child's condition.
- Talk or meet with other specialists providing therapeutic services.
- Share information, observations, concerns, and the progress of the child.
- Obtain special materials and resources to help work with the child.
- Promote and track the connection of the child to a medical home (see chapter 7 for the definition of a medical home and the role of child care as a safety net in finding children who are not receiving needed services). Figure 11.3 helps child care providers ensure that each component of the medical home concept is achieved for children in their care.

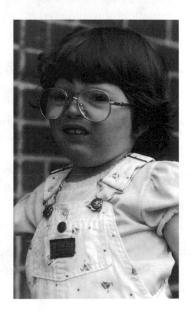

When team members focus on providing a child and family with a supportive, caring environment, feelings of role possessiveness, inferiority, or superiority can often be eliminated. Focusing helps a team see each member's contribution as essential to achieving the goals for the child.

Child Abuse and Neglect

Many factors contribute to the maltreatment of children, making the identification, treatment, and prevention of child abuse and neglect complex. There are several types of child abuse and neglect and each leaves a permanent (physical and/or psychological) mark on the victim.

No standard definition is used by all professionals who deal with child abuse and neglect. Every state has one or more legal definitions that are used to establish official reporting procedures. Various agencies also develop their own definitions for reporting and accepting cases of abuse and neglect. However, most definitions have common elements. Prevent Child Abuse America (see Appendix 1) identifies child abuse as including intentional physical injury, neglect, sexual molestation, or emotional abuse.

Caring for Our Children further defines each of these common elements:

- *Emotional abuse:* Acts that damage a child in psychological ways but do not fall into other categories of abuse. For prosecution, most states require that psychological damage is well defined and clearly diagnosed by a psychologist or psychiatrist.
- *Neglect:* Divided into two categories:
  —general neglect, failure to provide the common necessities, including food, shelter, a safe environment, education, and health care, but without resultant or likely harm to the child
  —severe neglect, neglect that results or is likely to result in harm to the child
- *Physical abuse:* An intentional (nonaccidental) act affecting a child that produces tangible physical harm
- *Sexual abuse:* Any sexual act performed with a child by an adult who exerts control over the victim. (Many state laws provide considerable detail about the specific acts that constitute sexual abuse.)

Identification of children who have been abused or neglected

It is impossible to know how many children are abused each year because the definitions of abuse and neglect, as well as reporting practices, vary from state to state. Nevertheless, the estimates are large; annually, about a million cases of child abuse and neglect are substantiated and about a thousand children die as a result of abuse. Abuse occurs in all communities—urban, suburban, and rural—regardless of ethnicity, race, religion, or income level.

Educators are required to report all suspected cases of abuse and neglect. Teachers and caregivers may feel that they lack the skills required for accurate identification of those cases, or they may be concerned about how a report will affect their relationship with the family and other staff. However, many families are grateful when support and assistance are offered to them.

Some indicators help identify suspected cases of abuse and neglect in children. Many are signals that the child is *possibly* being abused; however, some indicate other physical, environmental, or emotional problems. Poor growth can be a sign of any type of abuse or neglect in a child.

Physical abuse. Physical abuse includes injury from shaking, beating, striking, burning, or other similar acts. *Suspect* physical abuse if a child has repeated, unexplained injuries or injuries that are inconsistent with the story told about how they happened. Be alert for burns, fractures, bruises, bites, eye or head injuries, bilateral clustered injuries beyond the usual bumps and bruises of active children. Here are some clues:

- Bruises and welts
  —bruises on any infant, especially bruises on the face
  —bruises on the backside of a child's body
  —bruises in unusual patterns that might be made by an instrument (for example, belt buckle or strap) or human bite marks
  —clustered bruises that might indicate repeated contact with a hand or object
  —bruises in various stages of healing
- Burns
  —immersion burns indicating dunking in a hot liquid ("sock" or "glove" burns on the arms or legs or "doughnut" shaped burns of the buttocks or genitalia)

—cigarette burns

—rope burns

—dry burns indicating that the child has been forced to sit on a hot surface or has had a hot instrument applied to the skin

• Cuts, tears, or scrapes

—cuts of the lip, eye, or any portion of an infant's face

—any cut or scrape on external genitalia

• Head injuries

—absence of hair or bleeding beneath the scalp due to hair pulling

—black eyes

—bruised, bloody, swollen eyes

—swollen mouth or jaw

—loose or missing teeth

Children who are physically abused may appear to have "minor" physical injuries, yet medical examination may indicate evidence of serious injuries, including retinal (eye) hemorrhages (shaken-baby syndrome), multiple healing fractures, and sexually transmitted diseases.

Other conditions that may indicate physical abuse include

• frequent complaints of pain

• wearing clothing to hide injuries, such as clothing inappropriate for weather conditions

• reports of harsh treatment

• frequent lateness or absenteeism (parents arriving too early or leaving child after closing)

• unusual fear of adults, especially parents or guardians

• malnourished or dehydrated appearance

• lack of logical explanations for injuries

• withdrawn, anxious, or uncommunicative behavior; outspoken or disruptive behavior, especially if this is a change from the child's usual behavior

• lack of seeking and/or giving affection

• evidence that the child was given inappropriate food, beverage, or drugs.

Emotional abuse. A child who has been emotionally or psychologically abused child is one who has been verbally abused by parent(s) or guardians or who has had excessive or inappropriate demands placed on her or his emotional, social, or physiological capabilities. A family member may emotionally abuse a child by rejecting, ignoring, terrorizing, isolating, or corrupting a child. *Suspect* emotional abuse has occurred when a child displays any of the following:

• is generally unhappy and seldom smiles or laughs

• is aggressive and disruptive or unusually shy and withdrawn

• reacts without emotion to unpleasant statements and actions

• displays behaviors that are unusually adult or childlike

• exhibits delayed growth and/or delayed emotional and intellectual development

• has low self-esteem

• receives belittling or degrading comments from parents or guardians

• fears adults.

Note, however, that some of these characteristics may be present due to a developmental or behavioral disorder. Remember, you need only suspect—you do not need proof.

Sexual abuse. A child who has been sexually abused is one who has been exploited for any sexual gratification such as rape, incest, fondling of the genitals, exhibitionism, and/or voyeurism. S*uspect* sexual abuse has occurred when a child exhibits any of the following:

• Physical indicators

—difficulty in walking or sitting

—torn, stained, or bloody underclothing

—complaints of pain, itching, or swelling in genital area

—pain when urinating

—bruises or bleeding in external genitalia, vaginal or anal areas, mouth, or throat

—vaginal discharge

—venereal disease or vaginal infections

• Behavioral indicators

—unwilling to have clothes changed or to be assisted with toileting

—holds self, wants to be changed although not wet

—unwilling to participate in physical activities

—extreme changes in behavior such as loss of appetite

—withdrawn or infantile behaviors; may go back to earlier behaviors (bed-wetting, thumb sucking)

—extremely aggressive or disruptive behavior

—unusual interest in or knowledge of sexual matters (normally, 3-year-olds may masturbate frequently and show great interest in body parts, especially the genitalia); expressing affection in

ways inappropriate for a child of that age, such as wanting to kiss sexual parts of someone else's body
—poor peer relationships
—fear of a person or a strong dislike of being left somewhere or with someone
—child reports sexual assault

Physical and emotional neglect. A child who is a victim of physical or emotional neglect is one who has not received sufficient physical, emotional, intellectual, or social support from her or his caretaker(s). Neglect is not necessarily related to poverty; it reflects a breakdown in household management as well as a breakdown of concern in caring for the child. The level of neglect may range from beginning stages to truly gross proportions. *Suspect* neglect when a child lacks

• supervision
—left unattended at a young age
—left in the care of other children too young to protect them
—inadequately supervised for long periods or when engaged in dangerous activities
• adequate clothing and good hygiene
—children dressed inadequately for the weather
—persistent skin disorders resulting from improper hygiene
—children chronically dirty and unbathed
• medical or dental care
—needs for medical or dental care or medication and health aids are not met
• adequate education
—chronically absent
• adequate nutrition
—lacking sufficient quantity or quality of food
—consistently complaining of hunger or rummaging for food
—suffering severe developmental lags
• adequate shelter
—structurally unsafe housing or exposed wiring
—inadequate heating
—unsanitary housing conditions

In identifying neglect, be sensitive to different cultural expectations and values as well as different childrearing practices

Risk factors related to child abuse or neglect

All adults have the capacity to strike out in anger, fear, pain, or frustration; theoretically, we all have the potential to be child abusers. Yet most people have the ability to control these violent impulses. There are numerous complex risk factors for child abuse or neglect. They can be related to the child, the adult, social stresses, and can be triggered by certain situations. By being familiar with these risk factors, teachers and caregivers can more accurately identify child abuse and potentially abusive situations.

Child abuse often happens when adults

• are isolated, without support
• have unmet needs for nurturance and dependence

Figure 11.4. Risk Factors for Abuse and/or Neglect

1. Child Risk Factors
• Premature birth
• Colic
• Physical disabilities
• Developmental disabilities
• Chronic illness
• Emotional/behavioral difficulties
• Unwanted child

2. Abuser's Risk Factors
• Low self esteem
• Depression
• Poor impulse control
• Substance abuse
• Abused as a child
• Teenage parent
• Unrealistic expectations of child's behavior
• Negative view of themselves and children in care
• Punitive child-rearing style

3. Social/Situational Stresses
• Isolation
• Family/domestic violence
• Non-biologically-related male in the home
• Unemployment/financial problems
• Single parenthood

4. Triggering Situations
• Crying baby
• Child's misbehavior
• Discipline gone awry
• Argument, adult-adult conflict
• Overly zealous toilet learning/training

Source: Appendix L, *Caring for Our Children;* reprinted with permission from Pennsylvania Chapter, American Academy of Pediatrics.

- feel that their failures outnumber their successes
- were abused themselves and lack nurturing childrearing experiences
- are under stress
- keep their frustrations inside until they finally boil over or cannot control their emotions
- are under the influence of alcohol or other drugs that reduce their ability to control impulses
- have mental health problems.

Many of the causes of child abuse also can be traced to societal or personal problems such as family difficulties, domestic violence, economic problems, unemployment, the loss of a way of dealing with problems. Figure 11.4 summarizes some characteristics and risk factors related to child abuse and/or neglect.

How Programs Can Help Abused Children and Stressed Families

Early childhood programs are the only places where young children are seen on a daily basis for an extended time by professionals trained to observe their appearance, behavior, and development. A child care provider may be the first person to suspect (and to report) abuse and neglect. Every program should have a written child abuse and neglect policy and procedure. When caregivers suspect that something is amiss, they should follow the program's child abuse policy and procedure without delay.

Children who are abused or neglected are not able to learn or participate to their potential. They may carry physical and emotional scars throughout life. Depending on the kind and/or severity of abuse and neglect, long-term effects can include motor impairment, loss of hearing or vision, mental retardation, and/or learning and emotional problems. Thus it is essential that caregivers take action to interrupt the cycle of abuse and neglect by helping children and parents receive needed treatment. The caregiver's trusting relationship with children is a major factor in helping children and families cope with and resolve such difficult situations.

Legal and ethical issues

All states have mandatory reporting laws for child abuse. Most states require—and no state forbids—the reporting by educators of suspected child abuse and neglect. Many states provide penalties for those who are mandated to report suspected child abuse but who fail to do so. On the other hand, *every* state provides immunity from civil or criminal liability for persons who in good faith report suspected child abuse or neglect.

The Code of Ethical Conduct: Guidelines for Responsible Behavior in Early Childhood Education (NAEYC 1998) states that, above all, we shall not harm children. Several related principles specify that early childhood professionals shall

- be familiar with symptoms of child abuse
- know and follow state laws and community procedures that protect children against abuse and neglect
- report to the appropriate community agency when there is reasonable cause to suspect child abuse or neglect
- inform parents or guardians, when appropriate, when a report has been made
- assist another person who reveals a suspicion that a child is being abused or neglected to take appropriate action.

Common problems with reporting child abuse or neglect

Caregivers may have mixed feelings about reporting suspected abuse. They may not want to become involved, or they may feel that families have the right to discipline their child in their own way. Caregivers also may be reluctant to face the fact that someone known to them may be a possible abuser. These are natural feelings, but ones that must be overcome for the sake of the child.

Some caregivers have had previous negative experiences in reporting suspected abuse and neglect and are reluctant to become involved again. Maybe a social worker discouraged reporting, was unresponsive, or did not adequately handle the case. Perhaps someone knows of cases where nothing was done and the abuse continued or escalated. Although these concerns may be valid, a previous bad experience does not mean that the next case will not be handled better. In most states, the law requires filing a report regardless of previous experiences, with no exemptions. Children cannot be protected from abuse and neglect unless they are first identified and reported.

Caregivers may worry about endangering their relationship with the child's family by reporting a suspicion. Although the identity of the reporter of child abuse is supposed to remain anonymous, families will suspect who reported them by the nature of the information contained on the report. Abusive adults need help and some are grateful when they receive it. In other situations, parents are unaware that their child is being abused by another adult. Each case requires individual handling, but in general it is best to advise the parent that an abuse/neglect report is being filed, as required by law, and that help is available for the family. Even if the person adamantly denies any abuse or neglect, or knowledge of abuse by others, filing of suspected abuse or neglect is required so child protective services can investigate and initiate action if appropriate.

It is sometimes difficult to tell a parent beforehand about making a report. If a child is in imminent danger and the parent may disappear with the child, call the appropriate agency immediately and do not tell the parent. However, most often, caregivers will know and care about the parent, and the child will not be in imminent danger. In addition, caregivers may worry that telling the parent will evoke hostility and anger that may result in removal of the child from the program. However, failure to inform families about making a report may lead them to feel betrayed or deceived. As a general rule, it is probably better to inform the family of a decision to make a report. Start by explaining that educators are *required* by law to report all instances of suspected child abuse. It is the job of the investigators to determine whether there is actual abuse. Although parents may be very angry, showing concern for the child may help them see that there was no choice in the matter.

Obtain a copy of the state's child abuse reporting statute. Check with a local department of social services, law enforcement agency, district attorney's office, or the Department of Health and Human Services' regional office of child development. Ask what will happen after a report is made to explain the procedure when the family is informed about the responsibility to report a suspicion. Every program has a responsibility to inform staff of appropriate federal, state, local, and program regulations regarding child abuse and neglect.

Preventing abuse or accusations of abuse in child care settings

Directors of centers and caregivers in large and small family child care homes should check references and examine employment history and criminal and other appropriate records (including fingerprint-ing and checks with state child abuse registries) before employing any staff member (including substitutes, volunteers, administrative and maintenance staff, cooks, and transportation staff). In family child care homes, older children and other adults present should also be screened.

Such checks should be part of licensing in states where there is licensing of caregivers. Do not hire anyone with a record of prior child abuse of any type. Check all records before allowing an adult to have contact with children; until then, have another adult present to observe and intercede at all times.

Many abusive adults have not been reported and entered into child abuse registries. While these adults are unlikely to admit their past or current abuse to another person, employment applications should include the question about previous experience with hitting, shouting, losing control, or sexual misconduct. These questions may discourage some potentially abusive individuals from seeking work in child care. They also alert potential child care staff about what behaviors are unacceptable. Failure of a prospective employee to disclose previous convictions of child abuse is grounds for dismissal.

Other ways to learn about an individual include observation of the candidate performing the job for which she or he is applying and a probation (trial) period for new employees and volunteers. During the probation period, observe and discuss the performance of the worker with coworkers and families who should be encouraged to drop in and observe too. Each adult who works in child care must receive preservice training on accepted methods of discipline and prevention of child abuse as well as a copy of the program's written policies on staff conduct and on reporting procedures for suspected child abuse.

The most important measure program directors can take to prevent child abuse and neglect is to ensure that there is adequate daily supervision of all staff. Children should not be taken to any area of the child care program where they cannot be easily viewed by other adults. The physical layout of the facility should reduce the likelihood of isolation or privacy of individual caregivers with children, especially where children may be undressed or have their private parts exposed. Provide windows, mirrors, or video cameras, and remove doors on toilet stalls and toileting rooms where children need assistance, so that all adult-child interactions can be seen.

Denial of privacy and the increased possibility of observation by another adult are strong deterrents to abuse or accusations of abuse. This is more likely to be the case in programs with multiple caregivers than at child care sites with only one caregiver. Where caregivers work in isolation, such as in family child care homes, screening the caregiver and adult family members who will be in the house with the children is especially important, and families should be encouraged to make drop-in visits.

Elements to include in a child abuse and neglect policy

Every child care program's written policy on child abuse and neglect should include

- requirements for staff to receive training about and report suspected child abuse and neglect
- procedures for reporting suspected abuse and neglect (who must be informed, who makes the report, who communicates with the other families, the staff, and the press)
- a code of conduct for staff relating to their behavior with children, including permissible methods of discipline and prohibition of unobservable interaction of adults with children in the facility—especially in situations in which caregivers assist with dressing, undressing, and toileting
- program commitment to stress management breaks for caregivers of no less than 15 minutes every 4 hours and at least a 30-minute break for lunch
- a method for caregivers to signal and receive relief from caregiving tasks immediately if they feel overwhelmed and unable to appropriately care for children
- procedures for investigating job applicants and volunteers prior to hiring and whenever suspicion is raised concerning a staff member in the employ of the program
- approaches to management of children who have been abused or neglected including special training for staff by experts in behavior management of victims of child abuse and neglect.

Reporting procedures

What and when to report. Consult state statutes to determine what constitutes child abuse and neglect. *No state requires that the reporter have proof that abuse or neglect has occurred.* The law may specify that you need only to have a suspicion or a "reason to believe." Child abuse and neglect must be re-

ported *as soon as it is suspected* because delay may expose the child to significant harm.

Where to report. Each state specifies one or more agencies to receive reports of suspected child abuse and neglect. Usually this agency is the department of social services, human resources, or public welfare. Know which agency receives reports of suspected child abuse and neglect and how to make contact. The Childhelp USA National Child Abuse Hotline at 800-422-4453 provides 24-hour-a-day, 7-day-a-week access to where and how to file a report. Childhelp USA also lists reporting numbers online at **www. childhelpusa.org/child/report.htm**.

How to report. Reporting forms and the contents of reports of suspected child abuse and neglect vary from state to state. All states require that a verbal or written report (or both) be made to the specified agency. Obtain copies of your state's reporting form so you can be prepared to give all the information during a telephone report.

Preventing Abuse and Neglect in Programs for Young Children

Sensitive, perceptive teachers and directors should know the risk factors associated with child abuse and neglect. Early attention and intervention by providers can save a child from harm and maintain a family's integrity. Build a trusting, sharing relationship with families. Become aware of, and let parents know about, community agencies that provide needed support services such as respite care, counseling, temporary shelter, drug treatment, and food stamps. Share child development and child-rearing techniques. Let families know when the staff recognize signs of stress in their children. Share concerns with families and listen as they share their concerns.

Another part of prevention is educating young children, particularly in the area of sexual abuse. Children can learn about their right to say no and how to tell a trusted adult about the experience. Be aware that the concept of teaching children about "good touches" and "bad touches" is controversial. Care must be taken not to teach children that genital touching or fondling is *bad,* since touching is a normal and good part of mature sexual practice, and because masturbation is commonplace among preschoolers. Children can be taught that doctors must check "private parts," but that otherwise, if someone wants to check or touch their private parts, they should say no and find another grownup they trust to tell about it.

For additional information on how child care providers can address issues related to child abuse, as well as to access a large library of resource materials on the topic, visit the National Clearinghouse on Child Abuse and Neglect Information online at **www.calib.com/nccanch** or send a request by email to nccanch@calib.com.

Discipline

All child care programs should have a philosophy and policy that provide guidelines for disciplining children. *Corporal punishment should not be used under any circumstances.* Children should not be punished in any way that interferes with their daily functions of living, such as eating, sleeping, and toileting. Expectations should be developmentally appropriate for children, and limits should be realistic. Children should be taught positive and appropriate words, actions, and ways of relating to other children and adults. Adults should model positive patterns of interaction and communication with all children and families. Caregivers who know or suspect that a staff member has abused or neglected a child should inform a supervisor and make sure that the appropriate agency is notified immediately.

Injury

If a child arrives with an injury requiring immediate medical attention, arrange for her to go to a doctor or to an emergency room for treatment. If you notice bruises, cuts, burns, or other injuries on a child, ask the parent how the injury occurred, what treatment was provided, and what care or precautions must be taken. As a routine practice, the program should keep careful records about every child, noting all injuries received in the program and any other injuries that come to attention that occurred elsewhere. Include a description of the injury, date, time, place it happened, and how it occurred, statements by parent or child, and treatment the child received. Always notify parents immediately if any injury or illness occurs. See Injury Report Form on page 44.

Sudden Infant Death Syndrome

The death of a child is always a tragedy, and one of the most frightening types of death is Sudden Infant Death Syndrome (SIDS), when a sleeping, apparently healthy infant dies with no apparent cause. Until the role of sleep positioning was discovered, SIDS, also known as crib death, was the major cause of death in infants after the first month of life (up to 2 deaths per 1,000 live births). Researchers do not yet fully understand the causes of Sudden Infant Death Syndrome, but a 40 percent reduction in SIDS deaths has been associated with putting babies down on their backs to sleep (other cases of presumed SIDS have been found to involve child abuse, and some have no known cause).

Studies show that babies are more likely to be positioned on their sides or stomachs by child care workers than by parents as a group. Also, data suggest that hour-for-hour of time spent, babies are more likely to die of SIDS in child care settings than in their own homes. Always put babies down to sleep on their backs, unless there are specific medical problems. (For example, certain types of breathing problems in premature infants call for prone sleep, but the reason should be prescribed and documented by the doctors.) If children subsequently roll over, there is no need to force the child to use back-sleeping. Back sleeping is the safest position for all but a very few infants. It could be argued that failing to put an infant down to sleep supine is neglectful.

Studies by the Consumer Product Safety Commission associate soft bedding with infant deaths. Families and caregivers should put babies on a firm, flat sleeping surface and never on top of soft, fluffy products such as pillows, comforters, or sheepskins. If bumpers are used, they should be firm pads attached securely to the sides of the crib where the bumper meets the mattress to prevent a child from becoming wedged under the bumper pad. Blankets, if used, should be tucked under the mattress with the infant's feet near the tucked-in portion and the other edge of the blanket reaching no higher than the neck.

Be aware that if an apparent SIDS death occurs in a child care program, an autopsy can verify that there was no identifiable cause of death (for example, disease, suffocation). Contact your state public health department and state chapter of the national SIDS program for help for the family, staff, and other families in the program who will understandably be very upset by knowing about a SIDS death in the program.

Administration of the Health Component

Competent administration is required to implement all aspects of the health component.

Role of the governing body and the administrator

The governing body of a child care center should appoint an administrator whose duties related to health and safety include

- ensuring compliance with all applicable health and safety rules
- developing and implementing health and safety policies in the facility
- hiring, supervising, evaluating, and firing or excusing adults who work in the facility, especially as the performance of these adults relates to health and safety (physical health, mental health, oral health, and nutrition)
- providing or ensuring that adults and children receive appropriate education about health and safety issues
- arranging or providing repair and maintenance to keep the facility safe and healthy for all who use it
- managing finances to support the operation of the facility in a safe and healthy way
- maintaining facility records to ensure confidentiality, appropriately using the data for prevention of injury and infection as well as planning for appropriate care of children and regulatory oversight
- reporting to the governing body on a regular basis about all facets of the operation of the program.

Of course, family child care providers wear "multiple hats" and do all administrative duties that the administrator of a center would handle.

Facility health policies

The facility should have written policies that cover the following:

- admission and enrollment procedures, information to be provided to parents and gathered from families before enrollment
- supervision
- discipline
- care of acutely ill children
- child health services
- use of child care health consultants
- health education for children, staff, and families
- medications
- emergency plan
- evacuation plan, drills, and closings
- authorized caregivers
- safety surveillance
- transportation and field trips
- sanitation and hygiene
- food handling, feeding, and nutrition
- evening and night plan
- smoking, prohibited substances, and guns
- staff health, training, benefits, and evaluation
- maintenance of the facility and equipment
- review and revision of the health policies.

Chapter 8 of *Caring for Our Children* specifies what must be in written polices and gives references to other standards that define practices covered by the policies. Administrators should use the standards to set objectives for the program. While the scope of what could be done is vast, getting started and working to improve over time will make a big difference in the quality of care. Health polices should be a living document used to orient new staff and families, evaluate the performance of seasoned staff, and annually reassess the intention expressed in the policies. In addition to using health policies as a tool for improvement, the administrator should ensure that there is a comprehensive written plan of daily activities. This plan should be based on developmentally appropriate practice that integrates health and safety practices.

Keeping health records up-to-date is important, but the value lies in the use of the data to ensure children are receiving the services they need both within the program and from their sources of medical and oral health professional care. Health records should be confidential, but families need to understand that their consent should be given for access by those who can use the information to help their children. The administrator must establish three-way communications about health issues; the family, the caregivers, and child's health professionals should share information to effectively coordinate supportive care.

Every child care program, large or small, needs a health consultant who is more than a name and phone number. The health consultant should visit the facility and be guided administratively to provide the most meaningful services. For a small family child care home, this might be answering the provider's concerns and pointing out some ways to improve health practices in the home. For a large child care center, observations need to be more extensive, and formal training and follow-up is necessary to see if training is effective. Communication requires willingness on the part of the consultant and the child care staff to learn each other's approaches and support working toward common goals together.

Administration is not an end; it is a process that leads to outcomes—and is most successful when those outcomes are defined at the beginning. With clearly defined common objectives, child care administrators can harness the efforts of families, staff, consultants, and community resources to make child care a truly safe and healthy place that supports the well-being of children and families.

Suggested Activities

- Contact the local school district and ask who is eligible for IDEA services in the community they serve. How long is the waiting time for an assessment of a child suspected to be developmentally delayed? What services are offered to children with complex medical problems in addition to a developmental delay?

- Inquire of the child welfare agency serving your area how child abuse and neglect reports are handled. How does your state define abuse and neglect? What type of professional help is available to stressed families who are at risk of abuse or have already abused their children?

- Contact a long-established child care center to ask about experience with child abuse and neglect. Has the program ever made a report? Have they ever had a staff person accused of abuse? How were these situations handled?

- Ask several child care providers to share a copy of their written health policies. Which of the items listed in this chapter are covered; which are not? If you were a new staff person at these facilities, would you know from what you read what you were expected to do about health and safety practice in each setting?

Appendices

Appendix 1. National Resources for Health and Safety Information

Academy of Breastfeeding Medicine
191 Clarksville Road
Princeton Junction, NJ 08550
Phone: 609-799-4900 or 877-836-9947
Fax: 609-799-7032
Online: www.bfmed.org

American Academy of Allergy,
Asthma, and Immunology (AAAAI)
611 East Wells Street
Milwaukee, WI 53202
Phone: 414-272-6071
Fax: 414-272-6070
E-mail: info@aaaai.org
Online: www.aaaai.org

American Academy of Family Physi-
cians (AAFP)
11400 Tomahawk Creek Parkway
Leawood, KS 66211-2672
Phone: 913-906-6000
E-mail: fp@aafp.org
Online: www.aafp.org

American Academy of Pediatrics
(AAP)
141 Northwest Point Boulevard
Elk Grove Village, IL 60007-1098
Phone: 847-434-4000
Fax: 847-434-8000
Online: www.aap.org

American Academy of Pediatric
Dentistry
211 East Chicago Avenue, #700
Chicago, IL 60611-2663
Phone: 312-337-2169
Fax: 312-337-6329
E-mail: info@aapd.org
Online: www.aapd.org

American Alliance for Health, Physi-
cal Education, Recreation, & Dance
1900 Association Drive
Reston, VA 20192-1598
Phone: 800-213-7193
Fax: 703-476-9527
Online: www.aahperd.org

American Association of Family and
Consumer Sciences
1555 King Street
Alexandria, VA 22314
Phone: 703-706-4600
Fax: 703-706-4663
E-mail: info@aafcs.org
Online: www.aafcs.org

American Association for Health
Education (AAHE)
1900 Association Drive
Reston, VA 20191-1599
Phone: 703-476-3437 or 800-213-7193
Fax: 703-476-6638
E-mail: aahe@ahhperd.org
Online: www.aahperd.org/aahe

American Automobile Association
(AAA)
1000 AAA Drive
Heathrow, FL 32746
Phone: 407-444-7000
Fax: 407-444-7956
Online: www.aaa.com

American Cancer Society
1599 Clifton Road, NE
Atlanta, GA 30329-4251
Phone: 404-320-3333 or 800-227-2345
Online: www.cancer.org

American College of Emergency
Physicians
1125 Executive Circle
Irving, TX 75038-2522
Phone: 972-550-0911 or 800-798-1822
Fax: 972-580-2816
Online: www.acep.org

American Dental Association
211 E. Chicago Avenue
Chicago, IL 60611
Phone: 312-440-2500
Fax: 312-440-2800
Online: www.ada.org

American Diabetes Association
1701 North Beauregard Street
Alexandria, VA 22311
Phone: 800-342-2383
Fax: 703-549-6995
E-mail: customerservice@diabetes.org
Online: www.diabetes.org

American Dietetic Association (ADA)
216 West Jackson Boulevard
Chicago, IL 60606-6995
Phone: 312-899-0040
Fax: 312-899-1979
Online: www.eatright.org

Americans with Disabilities Act
Accessibility Guidelines (ADAAG)
U.S. Department of Justice
950 Pennsylvania Avenue, NW
Civil Rights Division, Disability Rights
Section–NYAVE
Washington, DC 20530
Phone: 800-514-0301 or 800-514-0383
(TDD)
Fax: 202-307-1198
Online: www.usdoj.gov/crt/ada/
adahom1.htm

American Furniture Manufacturers
Association (AFMA)
P.O. Box HP-7
High Point, NC 27261
Phone: 336-884-5000
Fax: 336-884-5303
Online: www.afma4u.org

American Gas Association
400 N. Capitol Street, NW
Washington, DC 20001
Phone: 202-824-7000
Fax: 202-824-7115
Online: www.aga.org

American Heart Association (AHA)
7272 Greenville Avenue
Dallas, TX 75231
Phone: 800-242-8721
Online: www.americanheart.org

American Lifeguard Association
8150 Leesburg Pike #600
Vienna, VA 22182
Phone: 703-748-4803 or 888-4Life-
guard
Fax: 888-432-9252
E-mail: alalifeguard@aol.com
Online: www.americanlifeguard.com

American Lung Association
1740 Broadway
New York, NY 10019
Phone: 212-315-8700
Online: www.lungusa.org

American National Standards Institute
(ANSI)
1819 L Street, NW, 6th Floor
Washington, DC 20036
Phone: 202-293-8020
Fax: 202-293-9287
Online: www.ansi.org

American Nurses Association (ANA)
600 Maryland Avenue, SW, Suite 100
  West
Washington, DC 20024
Phone: 202-651-7000 or 800-274-4262
Fax: 202-651-7001
Online: www.ana.org

American Public Health Association
  (APHA)
800 I Street, NW
Washington, DC 20001
Phone: 202-777-2742 or 202-777-2500
  (TTY)
FAX: 202-777-2534
Online: www.apha.org

American Red Cross (ARC)
8111 Gatehouse Road
Falls Church, VA 22042
Phone: 703-206-6000
Online: www.redcross.org

American School Food Service
  Association
700 South Washington Street, Suite
  300
Alexandria, VA 22314
Phone: 703-739-3900
Fax: 703-739-3915
E-mail: servicecenter@asfsa.org
Online: www.asfsa.org

American Society for Testing and
  Materials (ASTM)
100 Barr Harbor Drive
West Conshohocken, PA 19428-2959
Phone: 610-832-9585
Fax: 610-832-9555
Online: www.astm.org

American Society of Heating,
  Refrigerating, and Air Conditioning
  Engineers (ASHRAE)
1791 Tullie Circle, NE
Atlanta, GA 30329
Phone: 404-636-8400 or 800-527-4723
Fax: 404-321-5478
Online: www.ashrae.org

Art and Creative Materials Institute
  (ACMI)
P.O. Box 479
Hanson, MA 02341-0479
Phone: 781-293-4100
Fax: 781-294-0808
Online: www.acminet.org

Association of Home Appliance
  Manufacturers
1111 19th Street, NW, Suite 402
Washington, DC 20036
Phone: 202-872-5955
Fax: 202-872-9354
Online: www.aham.org

Asthma and Allergy Foundation of
  America
1233 20th Street, NW, Suite 402
Washington, DC 20036
Phone: 202-466-7643
Fax: 202-466-8940
Online: www.aafa.org

Building Officials and Code Adminis-
  trators International
4051 West Flossmoor Road
Country Club Hills, IL 60478
Phone: 708-799-2300
Fax: 708-799-4981
E-mail: info@bocai.org
Online: www.bocai.org

California Drowning Prevention
  Network
27700 Medical Center Road
Fifth Floor Administration
Mission Viejo, CA 92691

Centers for Disease Control and
  Prevention (CDC)
1600 Clifton Road
Atlanta, GA 30333
Phone: 800-311-3534
Online: www.cdc.gov

Child Care Bureau
Administration for Children and
  Families
U.S. Department of Health and Human
  Services
330 C Street, SW
Washington, DC 20447
Phone: 202-690-6782
Fax: 202-690-5600
E-mail: ccb@acf.dhhs.gov
Online: www.acf.dhhs.gov/programs/
  ccb

Child Care Law Center
221 Pine Street, 3rd Floor
San Francisco, CA 94104
Phone: 415-394-7144
Fax: 415-394-7140
E-mail: info@childcarelaw.org
Online: www.childcarelaw.org

Children's Safety Network
National Injury and Violence Preven-
  tion Resource Center
  Education Development Center
55 Chapel Street
Newton, MA 02458-1060
Phone: 617-969-7100, ext. 2207
Fax: 617-969-9186
Online: www.edc.org/HHD/csn

Consumer Product Safety Commis-
  sion (CPSC)
Washington, DC 20207-0001
Phone: 800-638-2772 or 1-800-638-8270
  (TTY)
Online: www.cpsc.gov

Cooperative State Research, Educa-
  tion, and Extension Service
U.S. Department of Agriculture
1400 Independence Avenue, SW
Mail Stop 2207
Washington, DC 20250
Phone: 202-720-4651
Fax: 202-690-0289
E-mail: csrees@reeusda.gov
Online: www.reeusda.gov

Drowning Prevention Foundation
  (DPF)
P.O. Box 202
Alamo, CA 94507
Phone: 925-820-SAVE
Fax: 925-820-7152
Email: dpf@pair.com
Online: http://drownprevention.com

Early Childhood Education Linkage
  System (ECELS)
Healthy Child Care America Pennsyl-
  vania
Pennsylvania Chapter, American
  Academy of Pediatrics
Rosemont Business Campus
919 Conestoga Road
Building 2, Suite 307
Rosemont, PA 19010
Phone: 610-520-3662
e-mail: ecels@paaap.org
Online: www.paaap.org

Emergency Medical Services for
  Children National Resource Center
111 Michigan Avenue, NW
Washington, DC 20010
Phone: 202-884-4927
Fax: 301-650-8045
E-mail: info@emscnrc.com
Online: www.ems-c.org

Environmental Protection Agency
Ariel Rios Building
1200 Pennsylvania Avenue, NW
Washington, DC 20460
Phone: 202-260-2090
Online: www.epa.gov

Food and Nutrition Information
  Center
Agricultural Research Service, USDA
National Agricultural Library, Room
  105
10301 Baltimore Avenue
Beltsville, MD 20705-2351
Phone: 301-504-5719 or 301-504-6856
  (TTY)
Fax: 301-504-6409
E-mail: fnic@nal.usda.gov
Online: www.nal.usda.gov/fnic

Food Research Action Center
1875 Connecticut Avenue., NW, Suite
  540
Washington, DC 20009
Phone: 202-986-2200
Fax: 202-986-2525
E-mail: webmaster@frac.org
Online: www.frac.org

Healthy Child Care America Campaign
American Academy of Pediatrics
141 Northwest Point Boulevard
Elk Grove Village, IL 60007-1098
Phone: 847-434-4000
Fax: 847-434-8000
Online: www.aap.org/advocacy/hcca/
  materials.htm

Institute of Electrical and Electronic
  Engineers (IEEE)
445 Hoes Lane
Piscataway, NJ 08854-1331
Phone: 732-981-0060
Fax: 732-981-1721
Online: www.ieee.org

Juvenile Products Manufacturers
  Association (JPMA)
17000 Commerce Parkway, Suite C
Mt. Laurel, NJ 08054
Phone: 856-638-0420
Fax: 856-439-0525
E-mail: jpma@ahint.com
Online: www.jpma.org

La Leche League International
1400 N. Meacham Road
Schaumburg, IL 60173-4808
Phone: 847-519-7730
Online: www.lalecheleague.org
Maternal and Child Health Bureau
Health Resources and Services
  Administration
Parklawn Building Room 18-05
5600 Fishers Lane
Rockville, Maryland 20857
Phone: 301-443-2170
Online: http://mchb.hrsa.gov

National Association for Family Child
  Care
5202 Pinemont Drive
Salt Lake City, UT 84123
Phone: 801-269-9338
Fax: 801-268-9507
E-mail: nafcc@nafcc.org
Online: www.nafcc.org

National Association of Child Care
  Resource and Referral Agencies
  (NACCRRA)
1319 F Street, NW, Suite 500
Washington, DC 20004-1106
Phone: 202-393-5501
Fax: 202-393-1109
E-mail: info@naccrra.org
Online: www.naccrra.net

National Association of Diaper
  Services
994 Old Eagle School Road, #1019
Philadelphia, PA 19087
Phone: 610-971-4850
Fax: 610-971-4859
E-mail: jashiffert@multiservicemgmt.
  com
Online: www.diapernet.com

National Association of Pediatric
  Nurse Practitioners (NAPNAP)
20 Brace Road, Suite 200
Cherry Hill, NJ 08034-2633
Phone: 856-857-9700
Fax: 856-857-1600
E-mail: info@napnap.org
Online: www.napnap.org

National Association for Regulatory
  Administration
26 East Exchange Street, 5th Floor
St. Paul, MN 55101-2264
Phone: 651-290-6280
Fax: 651-290-2266
Online: www.nara-licensing.org

National Association for Sick Child
  Daycare (NASCD)
1716 5th Avenue North
Birmingham, AL 35203
Phone: 205-324-8447
Fax: 205-324-8050
Online: www.nascd.com

National Association of WIC Directors
2001 S Street, NW, Suite 580
Washington, DC 20009
Phone: 202-232-5492
Fax: 202-387-5281
Online: www.nwica.org

National Black Child Development
  Institute (NBCDI)
1101 15th Street, NW, Suite 900
Washington, DC 20005
Phone: 202-833-2220
Fax: 202-833-2222
E-mail: moreinfo@nbcdi.org
Online: www.nbcdi.org

National Center for Education in
  Maternal and Child Health
  (NCEMCH)
2000 15th Street, North, Suite 701
Arlington, VA 22201-2617
Phone: 703-524-7802
Fax: 703-524-9335
E-mail: info@ncemch.org
Online: www.ncemch.org

National Child Care Information
  Center
243 Church Street, NW, 2nd Floor
Vienna, VA 22180
Phone: 800-616-2242 or 800-516-2242
  (TTY)
Fax: 800-716-2242
Online: http://nccic.org

National Clearinghouse on Child
  Abuse and Neglect Information
330 C Street, SW
Washington, DC 20447
Phone: 703-385-7565 or 800-394-3366
Fax: 703- 385-3206
Online: www.calib.com/nccanch

National Commission for Health
  Education Credentialing (NCHEC)
944 Marcon Boulevard, Suite 310
Allentown, PA 18109
Phone: 610-264-8200 or 888-624-3248
Fax: 800-813-0727
E-mail: nchec@fast.net
Online: www.nchec.org

National Dairy Council
10255 W. Higgins Road, Suite 900
Rosemont, IL 60018
Phone: 847-803-2000
Online: www.nationaldairycouncil.org

National Early Childhood Technical
  Assistance System (NECTAS)
137 East Franklin Street, Suite 500
Chapel Hill, NC 27514-3628
Phone: 919-962-2001 or 877-574-3194
  (TDD)
Fax: 919-966-7463
E-mail: nectas@unc.edu
Online: www.nectas.unc.edu

National Fire Protection Association
  (NFPA)
1 Batterymarch Park
P.O. Box 9101
Quincy, MA 02269-9101
Phone: 617-770-3000
Fax: 617-770-0700
Online: www.nfpa.org

National Food Service Management
  Institute
University of Mississippi
P.O. Drawer 188
University, MS 38677-0188
Phone: 662-915-7658 or 800-321-3054
Fax: 800-321-3061
E-mail: nfsmi@olemiss.edu

National Heart, Lung, and Blood
  Institute
Health Information Center
P.O. Box 30105
Bethesda, MD 20824-0105
E-mail: NHLBInfo@rover.nhlbi.nih.gov
Online: www.nhlbi.nih.gov

National Healthy Mothers, Healthy
  Babies Coalition
121 North Washington Street, Suite
  300
Alexandria, VA 22314
Phone: 703-836-6110
Fax: 703-836-3470
E-mail: info@hmhb.org
Online: www.hmhb.org

National Highway and Transportation
  Safety Administration (NHTSA)
400 7th Street, SW
Washington, DC 20590
Phone: 800-424-9393
Online: www.nhtsa.dot.gov

National Information Center for
  Children and Youth with Disabilities
  (NICHCY)
P.O. Box 1492
Washington, DC 20013-1492
Phone: 800-695-0285
Fax: 202-884-8441
E-mail: nichcy@aed.org
Online: www.nichcy.org

National Institute of Health, National
  Institute of Child Health and Human
  Development
Building 31, Room 2A32, MSC 2425
31 Center Drive
Bethesda, MD 20892-2425
Phone: 800-370-2943
E-mail: NICHDClearinghouse@
  mail.nih.gov
Online: www.nichd.nih.gov

National On-Site Wastewater Recy-
  cling Association, Inc.
632 Main Street
Laurel, MD 20707
Phone: 301-776-7468
Fax: 301-776-7409
Online: www.nowra.org

National Program for Playground
  Safety
School of Health, Physical Education
  and Leisure Services
WRC 205, University of Northern Iowa
Cedar Falls, IA 50614-0618
Phone: 800-554-PLAY
Fax: 319-273-7308
E-mail: playground-safety@uni.edu
Online: www.uni.edu/playground

National Recreation and Park Associa-
  tion
22377 Belmont Ridge Road
Ashburn, VA 20148-4501
Phone: 703-858-0784
Fax: 703-858-0794
E-mail: info@nrpa.org
Online: www.nrpa.org

National Resource Center for Health
  and Safety in Child Care
UCHSC at Fitzsimons
Campus Mail Stop F541
P.O. Box 6508
Aurora, CO 80045-0508
Phone: 800-598-KIDS
Fax: 303-724-0960
Online: http://nrc.uchsc.edu

National Safety Council
1121 Spring Lake Drive
Itasca, IL 60143-3201
Phone: 630-285-1121
Fax: 630-285-1315
Online: www.nsc.org

National Sanitation Foundation (NSF)
P.O. Box 130140
789 N. Dixboro Road
Ann Arbor, MI 48113-0140
Phone: 734-769-8010 or 800-NSF-MARK
Fax: 734-769-0109
E-mail: info@nsf.org
Online: www.nsf.org

National School-Age Care Alliance
1137 Washington Street
Boston, MA 02124
Phone: 617-298-5012
Fax: 617-298-5022
Online: www.nsaca.org

National SIDS Resource Center
2070 Chain Bridge Road, Suite 450
Vienna, VA 22182
Phone: 703-821-8955
Fax: 703-821-2098
E-mail: sids@circlesolutions.com
Online: www.sidscenter.org

National Technical Information
  Service (NTIS)
5285 Port Royal Road
Springfield, VA 22161
Phone: 703-605-6000
Fax: 703-605-6900
E-mail: info@ntis.gov
Online: www.ntis.gov

National Training Institute for Child
  Care Health Consultants
Department of Maternal and Child
  Health
116-A Merritt Mill Road
Campus Box #8126
University of North Carolina at Chapel
  Hill
Chapel Hill, NC 27599-8126
Phone: 919-966-3780
Fax: 919-843-4752
E-mail: nticchc@sph.unc.edu
Online: www.sph.unc.edu/courses/
  childcare

National Weather Service
1325 East West Highway
Silver Spring, MD 20910
Online: www.nws.noaa.gov

Neurosciences Institute
10640 John Jay Hopkins Drive
San Diego, CA 92121
Phone: 858-626-2000
Fax: 858-626-2099
E-mail: info@nsi.edu
Online: www.nsi.edu

Occupational Health and Safety
Administration (OSHA)
U.S. Department of Labor
200 Constitution Avenue, NW
Washington, DC 20210
Phone: 800-321-6742
Online: www.osha.gov

Office of Special Education & Rehabili-
tative Services
Office of Special Education Programs
U.S. Department of Education
400 Maryland Avenue, SW
Washington, DC 20202
Phone: 202-205-5507
Online: www.ed.gov/offices/OSERS/
OSEP

Playground Safety Institute
National Recreation and Park Associa-
tion
Phone: 703-858-0784
E-mail: info@nrpa.org
Online: www.opraonline.org/
playgrnd/institut.htm

President's Council on Physical
Fitness & Sports
Department W
200 Independence Avenue, SW, Room
738-H
Washington, DC 20201-0004
Phone: 202-690-9000
Fax: 202-690-5211
Online: www.fitness.gov

Prevent Child Abuse America
200 S. Michigan Avenue, 17th Floor
Chicago, IL 60604-2404
Phone: 312-663-3520
Fax: 312-939-8962
E-mail: mailbox@preventchildabuse.
org
Online: www.preventchildabuse.org

Safe Kids Campaign
1301 Pennsylvania Avenue, NW, Suite
1000
Washington, DC 20004
Phone: 202-662-0600
Fax: 202-393-2072
Online: www.safekids.org

Sierra's Light Foundation
PMB 481
1048 Irvine Avenue
Newport Beach, CA 92660

Snell Memorial Foundation
3628 Madison Avenue, Suite 11
North Highlands, CA 95660
Phone: 916-331-5073 or 888-SNELL99
Fax: 916-331-0359
E-mail: info@smf.org
Online: www.smf.org

Society for Nutrition Education
9202 N. Meridian Street, Suite 200
Indianapolis, IN 46260
Phone: 317-571-5618 or 800-235-6690
Fax: 317-571-5603
E-mail: info@sne.org

State and Territorial Injury Prevention
Directors Association
2141 Kingston Court, Suite 110-B
Marietta, GA 30067
Phone: 770-690-9000
Fax: 770-690-8996
Online: www.stipda.org

Superintendent of Documents
U.S. Government Printing Office
Washington, DC 20402
Phone: 202-512-2000
Online: www.access.gpo.gov/su_docs

Tribal Child Care Technical Assis-
tance Center (TriTAC)
(Funded by the Child Care Bureau)
Phone: 800-388-7670
Online: nccic.org/tribal

Underwriters Laboratories (UL)
333 Pfingsten Road
Northbrook, IL 60062-2096
Phone: 847-272-8800
Fax: 847-272-8129
E-mail: northbrook@us.ul.com
Online: www.ul.com

U.S. Consumer Product Safety
Commission, see Consumer Product
Safety Commission

U.S. Food and Drug Administration
(FDA)
5600 Fishers Lane
Rockville MD 20857-0001
Phone: 888-463-6332
Online: www.fda.gov

USDA Food and Nutrition Service
3101 Park Center Drive
Alexandria, VA 22302
Phone: 703-305-2060
Online: www.fns.usda.gov/fns

USDA Food Safety and Inspection
Service
U.S. Department of Agriculture
Washington, DC 20250-3700
Phone: 800-535-4555
Online: www.fsis.usda.gov

Visiting Nurse Associations of
America
11 Beacon Street, Suite 910
Boston, MA 02108
Phone: 617-523-4042
Fax: 617-227-4843
Online: www.vnaa.org

Video Active Productions
4900 Washington Street Extension
Wilmington, DE 19809
Phone: 302-762-9520
E-mail: videodan@aol.com

Appendix 2. Fact Sheets Available from ECELS on Child Health Issues

Available online from the Pennsylvania Chapter of the American Academy of Pediatrics at ECELS (Early Childhood Education Linkage System) at **www.paaap.org.** Click on ECELS.

INFECTIOUS DISEASE

Bronchiolitis
Candidiasis (Thrush)
Chickenpox
Chickenpox (Center for Disease Control [CDC] Fact Sheet)
CMV (Cytomegalovirus)
Cold Sores (Herpes Simplex)
Common Cold
Conjunctivitis (*see* Pink Eye)
Coxsackievirus A16 (Hand, Foot, and Mouth Disease)
Diarrhea (infectious type)
Ear Infection (Otitis Media)
Fever
Fifth Disease (Human Parvovirus B19)
German Measles (Rubella)
Haemophilus Influenzae
Hepatitis A
Hepatitis B
Herpes Simplex (*see* Cold Sores)
HIV/AIDS
Impetigo
Influenza
Lice (Pediculosis)
Lyme Disease
Measles (Rubeola)
Meningococcal Disease
Mononucleosis
Mumps

Otitis Media (*see* Ear Infection)
Pediculosis (*see* Lice)
Pertussis (Whooping Cough)
Pink Eye (Conjunctivitis)
Pinworms
Poison Ivy/Oak/Sumac
Preventing Spread of Infectious Disease
RSV (Respiratory Syncytial Virus)
Ringworm
Rubella (*see* German Measles)
Rubeola (*see* Measles)
Scabies
Strep Throat
Universal and Standard Precautions

MENTAL/BEHAVIORAL HEALTH

ADHD (Attention Deficit Hyperactivity Disorder)
Behavior Problems—Overview
Biting
Discipline: Changing a Young Child's Behavior
Repetitive Behavior

SPECIAL HEALTH NEEDS

Asthma
Asthma and Tobacco Smoke
Children with Diabetes
Children with Seizures

Appendix 3. Health and Safety Checklist

Use this checklist to find hazards. Whenever a hazard is found, fix it if you can. If you cannot fix it, make a note of it and plan to get it fixed.

Safety checks should be done at least once a month. Having different people do the safety checks helps find more hazards. The more people who are involved in watching for hazards, the more they will help fix hazards whenever they see them. Safety is everyone's business!

The PA Chapter of the American Academy of Pediatrics does not accept any liability associated with the assessment of a child care facility using this checklist.

General Indoor Areas

Yes	No	
❑	❑	Guns, projectile toys, darts, and cap pistols are not kept in the child care setting.
❑	❑	Floors are smooth and have nonskid surfaces. Rugs are skid-proof.
❑	❑	Doors to places that children can enter, such as bathrooms, can be easily opened from the outside by a child or by an adult.
❑	❑	Doors in children's areas have see-through panes so children are visible to anyone opening the door.
❑	❑	Doors have slow closing devices and/or rubber gaskets on the edges to prevent finger pinching.
❑	❑	Glass doors and full-length windows have decals on them that are at the eye levels of both children and adults.
❑	❑	Windows cannot be opened more than 6 inches from the bottom.
❑	❑	All windows have closed, permanent screens.
❑	❑	Bottom windows are lockable.
❑	❑	Walls and ceilings have no peeling paint and no cracked or falling plaster.
❑	❑	The child care setting is free of toxic or lead paint and of crumbly asbestos.
❑	❑	Safety covers are on all electrical outlets.
❑	❑	Electrical cords are out of children's reach. Electrical cords are placed away from doorways and traffic paths.
❑	❑	Covers or guards for fans have openings small enough to keep children's fingers out.
❑	❑	Free-standing space heaters are not used.
❑	❑	Pipes, radiators, fireplaces, wood burning stoves, and other hot surfaces cannot be reached by children or are covered to prevent burns.
❑	❑	Nobody smokes or has lighted cigarettes, matches, or lighters around children.
❑	❑	Tap water temperature is 120° Fahrenheit or lower.
❑	❑	Trash is covered at all times and is stored away from heaters or other heat sources.
❑	❑	Drawers are closed to prevent tripping or bumps.
❑	❑	Sharp furniture edges are cushioned with cotton and masking tape or with commercial corner guards.
❑	❑	Emergency lighting equipment works.
❑	❑	Regular lighting is bright enough for good visibility in each room.
❑	❑	Enough staff members are always present to exit with children safely and quickly in an emergency.
❑	❑	All adults can easily view all areas used by children.

Yes	No	
❏	❏	Pets are free from disease, are immunized as appropriate, and are maintained in a sanitary manner.
❏	❏	Poisonous plants are not present either indoors or outdoors in the child care areas.
❏	❏	All adult handbags are stored out of children's reach.
❏	❏	All poisons and other dangerous items are stored in locked cabinets out of children's reach. This includes medicines, paints, cleansers, mothballs, etc.
❏	❏	Pesticides are applied only to surfaces that children cannot reach and surfaces not in direct contact with food.
❏	❏	A certified pest control operator applies pesticides while observed by a caregiver.
❏	❏	Cots are placed in such a way that walkways are clear for emergencies.
❏	❏	Children are never left alone in infant seats on tables or other high surfaces.
❏	❏	Teaching aids such as projectors are put away when not in use.
❏	❏	A well-stocked first aid kit is accessible to all caregivers.
❏	❏	Non-porous gloves are readily available for caregivers in all areas where child care is provided.
❏	❏	Heavy equipment or furniture that may tip over is anchored.

Toys and Equipment

Yes	No	
❏	❏	Toys and play equipment have no sharp edges or points, small parts, pinch points, chipped paint, splinters, or loose nuts or bolts.
❏	❏	All painted toys are free of lead.
❏	❏	Toys are put away when not in use.
❏	❏	Toys that are mouthed are washed after each use.
❏	❏	Children are not permitted to play with any type of plastic bag, balloon or latex/vinyl gloves.
❏	❏	Toys are too large to fit completely into a child's mouth and have no small, detachable parts to cause choking. No coins, safety pins, or marbles for children under 4 years of age.
❏	❏	Infants and toddlers are not permitted to eat small objects and foods that may easily cause choking, such as hot dogs, hard candy, seeds, nuts, popcorn, and uncut round foods such as whole grapes and olives.
❏	❏	Toy chests have air holes and a lid support or have no lid. A lid that slams shut can cause pinching, head injuries or suffocation.
❏	❏	Shooting or projectile toys are not present.
❏	❏	Commercial art materials are stored in their original containers out of children's reach. The manufacturer's label includes a reference to meeting ASTM Standards.
❏	❏	Rugs, curtains, pillows, blankets, and cloth toys are flame-resistant.
❏	❏	Sleeping surfaces are firm. Waterbeds and soft bedding materials such as sheepskin, quilts, comforters, pillows, stuffed toys, and granular materials (plastic foam beads or pellets) used in bean bags are not accessible to infants where they sleep.
❏	❏	Babies are always put down to sleep on their backs.
❏	❏	Hinges and joints are covered to prevent small fingers from being pinched or caught.
❏	❏	Cribs, playpens, and highchairs are away from drapery cords and electrical cords.
❏	❏	Cribs, playpens, and highchairs are used properly and according to the manufacturer's recommendations for age and weight. Cribs have no corner posts.

☐ ☐ Cribs have slats placed 2-3/8 inches apart or less and have snug-fitting mattresses. Mattresses are set at their lowest settings and sides are locked at their highest settings.

☐ ☐ Toys are not hung across the cribs of infants who can sit up.

☐ ☐ Rattles, pacifiers, or other objects are never hung around an infant's neck.

☐ ☐ Infant walkers are not used.

☐ ☐ Five gallon buckets are not accessible to infants and toddlers.

Hallways and Stairs

Yes   No

☐ ☐ Handrails are securely mounted at child height.

☐ ☐ Handrails are attached to walls for right-hand descent, but preferably are attached to the walls on both right and left sides.

☐ ☐ Stairway gates are locked in place when infants or toddlers are nearby. Gates should have openings small enough to prevent a child's head from fitting through. No accordion-type gates are used.

☐ ☐ Doorways to unsupervised or unsafe areas are closed and locked unless the doors are used for emergency exits.

☐ ☐ Emergency exit doors have easy-open latches.

☐ ☐ Safety glass is used in all areas of potential impact.

☐ ☐ Caregivers can easily monitor all entrances and exits to keep out strangers.

☐ ☐ Stairways and hallways are clear of objects that can cause a fall.

Kitchen and Food Preparation and Storage Areas

Yes   No

☐ ☐ Caregivers always wash hands before handling food.

☐ ☐ Caregivers always wash children's hands before mealtimes.

☐ ☐ Trash is always stored away from food preparation and storage areas.

☐ ☐ Refrigerator temperature is monitored by thermometer and is kept at or below 40° Fahrenheit.

☐ ☐ All perishable foods are stored in covered containers at 40° Fahrenheit or lower.

☐ ☐ Hot foods are kept at 140° Fahrenheit or higher until ready to be eaten.

☐ ☐ Pest strips are not used.

☐ ☐ Cleansers and other poisonous products are stored in their original containers, away from food, and out of children's reach.

☐ ☐ Nonperishable food is stored in labelled, insect-resistant metal or plastic containers with tight lids.

☐ ☐ Five gallon buckets are not accessible to children.

☐ ☐ Refrigerated medicines are kept in closed containers to prevent spills that would contaminate food.

☐ ☐ Food preparation surfaces are clean and are free of cracks and chips.

☐ ☐ Eating utensils and dishes are clean, free of cracks, chips and lead.

☐ ☐ Appliances and sharp or hazardous cooking utensils are stored out of children's reach.

☐ ☐ Pot handles are always turned towards the back of the stove.

Yes	No	
❐	❐	An ABC-type fire extinguisher is securely mounted on the wall near the stove.
❐	❐	All caregivers know how to use the fire extinguisher correctly and have seen a demonstration by members of the fire department.
❐	❐	There is a "danger zone" in front of the stove where the children are not allowed to go.
❐	❐	A sanitarian has inspected food preparation and service equipment and procedures within the past year.
❐	❐	Children are taught the meaning of "hot."
❐	❐	Trash is stored away from the furnace, stove, and hot water heater.
❐	❐	Kitchen area is not accessible to children without constant adult supervision.
❐	❐	Caregivers do not cook while holding a child.
❐	❐	Hot foods and liquids are kept out of children's reach.
❐	❐	Stable step stools are used to reach high places.

Bathrooms

Yes	No	
❐	❐	Stable step stools are available where needed.
❐	❐	Electrical outlets have safety covers or are modified to prevent shock.
❐	❐	Electrical equipment is stored away from water.
❐	❐	Cleaning products and disinfectants are locked in a cabinet out of children's reach.
❐	❐	Toilet paper is located where children can reach it without having to get up from the toilet.
❐	❐	If potty chairs are used, they are easy to clean with a bleach solution in a utility sink used only for that purpose, if possible.
❐	❐	Potty chairs are not used in the food preparation or dining areas, and potty chairs cannot be reached by children when they are not in use.
❐	❐	There are enough toilets so children do not have to stand in line.
❐	❐	Caregivers and children always wash hands after toileting and diaper changing.
❐	❐	The changing of diapers or soiled underwear is done in a special, separate area away from food and play.
❐	❐	The diapering or changing table has rails to keep the child from rolling off.
❐	❐	Trash cans for diapers, tissues, and other materials that come in contact with body fluids can be opened with a step pedal and are lined with a plastic bag, emptied daily, and kept clean.
❐	❐	Paper towels and liquid soap are readily available at the sink.
❐	❐	Thermometers are used to check that water temperatures are between 120° and 130° Fahrenheit or lower. The lower the water temperature, the safer it is for young children.
❐	❐	Cosmetics are stored out of children's reach.
❐	❐	Bathtubs have skid-proof mats or stickers.
❐	❐	Children take baths only when adults can supervise.
❐	❐	Children are never left alone on a changing table, bed, or any other elevated surface.
❐	❐	Children are never left unsupervised in or near water.

Active Play Areas (Indoor Areas and Playgrounds)

Yes	No	
☐	☐	The active play area offers a wide range of parallel and interactive activities.
☐	☐	Water for drinking and first aid is available near the play area.
☐	☐	A well-stocked first aid kit is accessible to all caregivers during outdoor play.
☐	☐	A file is available containing the name and address of the manufacturer of each piece of equipment.
☐	☐	The file also contains records of equipment purchase, installation, inspection, maintenance and CPSC/ASTM approval.
☐	☐	For old equipment, the file contains documentation of safety provided by an inspector who is certified by the National Playground Safety Institute (703) 858-2148.

Surfacing

Yes	No	
☐	☐	Measure the highest point that a child can climb to (critical height). For swings, the critical height is measured from the pivot point where the swing is suspended down to the ground. For elevated structures with guard rails, the critical height is measured from the top of the guard rail down to the ground. The highest accessible part for platforms with protective barriers is the deck. For all other structures, the critical height is measured from the highest point of the structure down to the ground.
☐	☐	Surfaces underneath indoor and outdoor play equipment that children can climb are covered with impact-absorbing material according to the CPSC recommendations for critical height.
☐	☐	The following surfacing materials are not in use underneath indoor and outdoor play equipment that children can climb: asphalt, concrete, soil or hard-packed dirt, grass, turf, linoleum, or carpeting.
☐	☐	The dirt in the play area has been tested and found free of toxic materials, including lead.
☐	☐	There are no toys or objects (including surfacing material) with a diameter small enough to completely fit in a child's mouth accessible to children who are still placing objects in their mouths.

Fall Zones

Yes	No	
☐	☐	Fall zones (the areas onto which a child falling from or exiting from a piece of play equipment would be expected to land) do not overlap.
☐	☐	Impact-absorbing surfacing material extends at least 6 feet beyond all sides of the equipment.
☐	☐	For to-fro swings: the impact-absorbing surfacing material extends in front and in back of the swings a distance that measures twice the height of the swing beam.
☐	☐	For slides: the impact-absorbing surfacing material extends at least 6 feet from the end of the slide chute—or—a distance that equals the height of the slide platform + 4 feet, whichever is greater. (It is not necessary for surfacing material to exceed 14 feet).

Depth Required for Tested Shock-Absorbing Materials for Use under Play Equipment

These data report tested drop heights for specific materials. All materials were not tested at all drop heights. Choose a surfacing material that tested well for drop heights that are equal to or greater than the drop height of your equipment.

Height of Playground Equipment (feet)	Shock-absorbing Substance	Minimum Depth Required Uncompressed (inches)	Minimum Depth Required Compressed (inches)
4	Coarse Sand	--	9
5	Fine Sand	6	9
	Coarse Sand	6	--
	Medium Gravel	6	9
6	Double Shredded Bark Mulch	6	--
	Engineered Wood Fibers	6	9
	Coarse Sand	12	--
	Fine Gravel	6	9
	Medium Gravel	12	--
7	Wood Chips	6	--
	Double Shredded Bark Mulch	--	9
	Engineered Wood Fibers	9	--
	Fine Gravel	9	--
9	Fine Sand	12	--
10	Wood Chips	9	9
	Double Shredded Bark Mulch	9	--
	Fine Gravel	12	--
10-12	Shredded Tires (see note 4 below)	6	--
11	Wood Chips--Double Shredded	12	--
	Double Shredded Bark Mulch	12	--
>12	Engineered Wood Fibers	12	--

Notes:
1. The testing of loose-fill materials was done by the CPSC in accordance with the voluntary standard for playground surfacing systems, ASTM F1292. CPSC reported these data as critical heights for varying depths of material. Since most users of the standard want to know what surfacing is required for a given piece of equipment that has a known fall height, the authors of *Caring for Our Children* converted the CPSC table to start from the known drop height, rather than a specific depth and type of surfacing material. Where CPSC offers no data, the table shows a dash (--). These playground surfacing requirements apply to play equipment whether it is located indoors or outdoors.
2. Fall height is the maximum height of the structure or any part of the structure for all stationary and mobile equipment except swings. For swings, the fall height is the height above the surface of the pivot point where the swing's suspending elements connect to the supporting structure.
3. Protective surfacing recommendations do not apply to equipment that the child uses standing or sitting at ground level like sand boxes or play houses that children do not use as a climber.
4. For shredded tires, the CPSC recommends that users request test data from the supplier showing the critical height of the material when it was tested in accordance with ASTM F1292.
5. Surfacing materials are available as two types, unitary or loose-fill. These recommendations for depth of materials apply to the loose-fill type. For unitary surfacing materials, the manufacturer should provide the test data that show a match between the critical height shock-absorbing characteristics and the fall height of the equipment where the surfacing is used.
6. Since the depth of any loose-fill material could be reduced during use, provide a margin of safety when selecting a type and depth of material for a specific use. Also provide a means of containment around the perimeter of the use zone to keep the material from moving out into surrounding areas, thereby decreasing the depth in the fall zone. Depending on location, weather conditions, and frequency of use, provide maintenance to insure needed depth and loosening of material that has become packed. By placing markers on the support posts of equipment that indicate the correct level of loose-fill surfacing material, users can identify the need for maintenance work.

Reference: United States Consumer Product Safety Commission. *Handbook for Public Playground Safety.* Washington, D.C.: U.S. Consumer Product Safety Commission: 1997. Publications 325.

Reprinted from *Caring for Our Children, National Health and Safety Performance Standards,* 2d ed. (Washington, DC: AAP & APHA, 2002), 435.

Protrusion & Entanglement

Yes	No	
❑	❑	All metal edges are rolled.
❑	❑	There are no equipment pieces that could catch clothing. There are no strings or loose items on children's clothing or around children's necks that could get caught on play equipment.
❑	❑	Any exposed bolts do not protrude more than two threads beyond the face of the nut; exposed bolts have no burrs or sharp edges.
❑	❑	There are no open "S" hooks.

Entrapment

Yes	No	
❑	❑	There are no openings in any pieces of active play equipment between 3½ and 9 inches that could cause head entrapment.

Equipment Spacing

Yes	No	
❑	❑	There are at least 6 feet of use space on all sides of each piece of equipment.
❑	❑	Play equipment pieces are spaced at least 12 feet apart from each other (each has its own 6 foot use space).
❑	❑	Traffic patterns are designed to prevent children from bumping into each other.

Trip Hazards

Yes	No	
❑	❑	All anchoring devices, such as footings and bars at the bottom of climbers, are below the playing surface.
❑	❑	There are no exposed tree/plant roots.
❑	❑	Changes in elevation are made obvious by the use of brightly colored visual or other barriers.

Appropriate Activities & Equipment

Yes	No	
❑	❑	Age-specific play areas are separated by distance or a physical barrier.
❑	❑	Equipment is warranted by the manufacturer as suitable for the age of the users (2–5 years and 5–12 years) according to ASTM Standard F1487-95.

Pinch, Crush, & Shearing Points

Yes	No	
❑	❑	All spaces are too big or too small to entrap a child's finger.
❑	❑	All wooden parts are smooth and without splinters.
❑	❑	All corners are rounded, especially at exit ends and sides along a slide bed.
❑	❑	Exposed ends of tubing have caps that cannot be removed without tools.

Guardrails, Handrails, and Safety Barriers

Yes	No	
❏	❏	Guardrails or protective barriers are used to prevent inadvertent or unintentional falls off elevated platforms.
❏	❏	For preschool children: elevated surfaces more than 20 inches high have a guardrail or protective barrier; those more than 30 inches high have a protective barrier (an enclosing device that is intended to prevent both inadvertent and deliberate attempts to pass through the barrier).
❏	❏	For school age children: elevated surfaces more than 30 inches high have a guardrail or protective barrier; those more than 48 inches high have a protective barrier.
❏	❏	Handrails are child hand-hold size, and are at waist to shoulder height of the child users (22"–38").
❏	❏	Boundaries such as painted lines or dividers separate play equipment from walking areas.
❏	❏	Bike or trike riding areas are separate from other areas.
❏	❏	Playgrounds are fenced in.

Unsafe Equipment

Yes	No	
❏	❏	There are no heavy swings or swings made out of wood, metal, or other rigid materials.
❏	❏	There are no animal figure swings.
❏	❏	There are no multiple-use occupancy swings (swings used by more than one child at a time) other than tire swings.
❏	❏	There are no swing sets with more than 2 swings per bay.
❏	❏	There are no rope swings; all ropes are anchored at both ends.
❏	❏	There are no trapeze bars.
❏	❏	Any see-saws present have a spring centering device for children 2-5 years of age. If see-saws are used, there must be a shock absorbing material required to cushion seat impact on surface and the maximum height of the seat above the protective surfacing must not exceed 5 feet.
❏	❏	There are no trampolines.

Maintenance

Yes	No	
❏	❏	Daily checks include: broken glass, animal waste, trash, toxic plants or plant debris, damage by vandals, displaced surfacing, broken equipment, chipping paint, puddles of water, insect hazards, need for lubrication of moving parts.
❏	❏	All hardware fasteners, permanent coverings, or connecting devices are tight and cannot be removed without tools.
❏	❏	All surfaces are intact.
❏	❏	All structures are sturdy enough that they will not move or tip over when the weight of an adult is put against them.
❏	❏	There is no peeling paint. (Lead in peeling paint on play equipment is a common hazard.)
❏	❏	All ropes are tight and strands cannot be pulled apart.

Supervision

Yes	No	
☐	☐	All areas where children can play are in view of an adult at all times.
☐	☐	Every child is accounted for at all times by a supervising adult. Some method of assuring that no child is hidden or missing from the group must be used.
☐	☐	When children must leave the play area to use the toilet, to get first aid, or for any other reason, supervision of the child who leaves and the children who remain in the play area is secure and consistent.
☐	☐	Children are prevented from playing in a way that challenges them beyond their abilities or that puts others at risk of significant injury.

Slides

Yes	No	
☐	☐	The impact-absorbing surfacing material extends at least 6 feet from the end of the slide chute -or- a distance that equals the height of the slide platform + 4 feet, whichever is greater. (It is not necessary for surfacing material to exceed 14 feet).
☐	☐	Slides are no taller than 6½ feet and have side rims at least 4 inches high.
☐	☐	Slides have an enclosed platform at the top for children to get into position to slide.
☐	☐	Slide ladders have flat steps and a handrail on each side. For users 2-12 years of age, steps are $\leq$ 9 inches apart. Rungs are $\leq$ 12 inches apart. (If steps are $\leq$ 9 inches apart, check for entrapment.)
☐	☐	Slide beds have a flat surface at the bottom to slow children down and are sloped at no greater than a 30 degree angle overall.
☐	☐	Slides with metal beds are shaded to prevent overheating.

Sand

Yes	No	
☐	☐	Sand digging areas are in the shade.
☐	☐	Sand digging areas are contained by smooth frames.
☐	☐	Sand is covered when not in use to prevent infectious disease and injury risk when animals and insects get into it.

Swings

Yes	No	
☐	☐	Swings are located away from other equipment and activities.
☐	☐	Swing footings are stable and buried below the ground or covered by protective surfacing.
☐	☐	There is no corrosion evident on hooks or chains.
☐	☐	There are no "A" frames with horizontal cross bars present.
☐	☐	Tot swings are in a separate bay from the other swings.
☐	☐	Swing hangers are spaced wider than the seats, not less than 20 inches.
☐	☐	There is a minimum space of 24 inches between seats and 30 inches between the swing and supporting structure.
☐	☐	The distance between the bottom of the seat and the protective surface is at least 12 inches.

Multi-Axis Tire Swings

Yes	No	
☐	☐	Tire swings do not share a bay with any other type of swing or are mounted on any structure with other play components.
☐	☐	There are no exposed steel belts in steel-belted radial tire swings.
☐	☐	There are drain holes in tire swing tires.
☐	☐	The minimum clearance between tire and support structure is 30 inches.
☐	☐	The tire swing itself weighs less than 35 pounds.

Climbers

Yes	No	
☐	☐	Climbers have a safe way off for children who cannot complete the activity.
☐	☐	No places exist where children can fall more than 18 inches onto any component of the climber.
☐	☐	Connections between ropes, cables, or chains are securely fixed.
☐	☐	There are no arch climbers or sliding poles accessible to preschoolers.
☐	☐	Horizontal ladders and overhead rings are used only by children who are over 5 years of age. Chinning bars may be used by 4 year olds.

Merry-Go-Rounds

Yes	No	
☐	☐	The platform is continuous, approximately circular.
☐	☐	There are no components, including handgrips, that extend beyond the perimeter of the platform.
☐	☐	Unless the merry-go-round is tub shaped, there are 1–1½ inch handgrips available.
☐	☐	There are no accessible shearing or crush points.
☐	☐	Peripheral speed of rotation is limited to 13 feet per second.

Spring Rocking Equipment

Yes	No	
☐	☐	The seat accommodates only the intended number of users at one time.
☐	☐	There are hand grips and foot rests for each seating position.
☐	☐	Handgrips are between 1–1½ inches in diameter; minimum length 3 inches for one hand, and 6 inches for two hands.
☐	☐	Foot rests are a minimum width of 3½ inches.
☐	☐	Seats are not less than 14 inches nor more than 28 inches above platform surface.

Other Hazards

Yes	No	
☐	☐	There is no litter or animal feces in the play area that may attract insects, hide hazards, and harbor infectious disease agents.
☐	☐	There are no attractive climbing hazards (such a trees) that are accessible from an object placed underneath them.

☐   ☐   There are no toxic or thorny plants present.

☐   ☐   There is a fence that encloses the play area.

Please explain your plan to fix or take out of play any items checked "No."

_____

_____

_____

Swimming Pools

Yes   No

☐   ☐   All pools and ponds are enclosed with four-sided fencing that is resistant to climbing, is at least five feet high, comes within 3½ inches of the ground, and has openings no greater than 3½ inches.

☐   ☐   Fence openings have self-closing latching gates with the latch at least 55 inches from the ground.

☐   ☐   Walk areas around the pool have a nonskid surface.

☐   ☐   The pool and pool maintenance have been inspected and approved by the local health department within the past year.

☐   ☐   Small, portable wading pools are not used for group water play.

☐   ☐   Equipment is available and used every two hours while children are in the water to test and maintain the pH of the water between 7.2 and 8.2.

☐   ☐   Water temperatures are maintained between 82° F and 93° F while the pool is in use.

Emergency Preparedness

Yes   No

☐   ☐   All caregivers have roles and responsibilities in case of fires, injury, or other disasters.

☐   ☐   One or more caregivers certified in infant and child first aid and where children swim or children with disabilities are in care, one or more caregivers certified in infant and child CPR are always present.

☐   ☐   All first aid kits have the required supplies. The kits are stored where caregivers can easily reach them in an emergency.

☐   ☐   Caregivers always take a first aid kit on trips.

☐   ☐   Smoke detectors and other alarms are tested monthly.

☐   ☐   Each room and hallway has a fire escape route clearly posted.

☐   ☐   Emergency procedures and telephone numbers are clearly posted near each phone.

☐   ☐   Children's emergency phone numbers are posted near the phone and can be easily taken along in case of an emergency evacuation.

- How to phone emergency medical services (EMS) system
- Transportation to an emergency facility
- Notification of parents
- Where to meet if the child care setting is evacuated

- Plans for an adult to care for the children while a caregiver stays with injured children. This includes escorting children to emergency medical care.
- Alternate location for care is known to staff and parents, and is stocked with essential supplies (formula, diapers, toys, first aid supplies).

Yes	No	
❏	❏	All exits are clearly marked and free of clutter.
❏	❏	Doors and gates all open out for easy exit.
❏	❏	Children are taught to report if they or anyone else is hurt.
❏	❏	Children are taught the words stop and no. Caregivers avoid using those words unless there is danger.
❏	❏	Children are taught their own telephone number, address, and parent's work numbers.
❏	❏	Children are taught how to phone EMS (911).
❏	❏	Children are taught how to Stop, Drop, Roll, Cool in case their clothes catch fire.
❏	❏	Children are taught to point out any matches they find to an adult.

Vehicles

Yes	No	
❏	❏	All vehicles are licensed according to state law and insured for the type of transport being provided.
❏	❏	All drivers are licensed and instructed in child passenger safety.
❏	❏	Everyone, during every ride, uses age-appropriate safety restraints.
❏	❏	Staff encourage correct use of age-appropriate seat restraints by parents.
❏	❏	Drivers use child-resistant door locks when the vehicle is in motion.
❏	❏	All vehicles are locked when not in use.
❏	❏	A well-stocked first aid kit is in the vehicle for every ride.
❏	❏	The caregiver has on hand current emergency contact information when driving children.
❏	❏	Trip plans include how to manage emergencies.
❏	❏	Children wear identification when transported.
❏	❏	Pickup and drop-off points are safe from traffic.
❏	❏	Infant seats are installed correctly, with seats facing the rear of the car until the child reaches 12 months of age. Infants must ride in the back seat.
❏	❏	Driver knows where children are before putting vehicle in reverse.
❏	❏	Bicycles and other riding toys are stable, well-balanced, and of the appropriate size. They do not have broken parts.
❏	❏	Children use helmets approved by ANSI (American National Standards Institute) or Snell Memorial Foundation when riding bikes, and other riding toys that have a wheel base of 20 inches.
❏	❏	Young bikers know traffic rules.
❏	❏	Children do not horse around while riding bikes and do not ride in the street.
❏	❏	Young children never cross the street without an adult. Children should know rules for crossing the street.
❏	❏	No child should ride in the front seat of a vehicle unless the child meets the criteria for front seat occupancy of the National Highway Traffic Safety Administration (800) 424-9393.

Appendix 4. Children's Literature about Health, Nutrition, and Safety

Melissa Ann Renck and Mary Renck Jalongo, Compilers

CHILD CARE AND HEALTH

Fiction Picture Books

Brown, M. 1983. *Arthur's eyes.* (Book and cassette.) Boston: Little, Brown

Carle, E. 1997. *From head to toe.* New York: HarperCollins.

Mayer, G. 1998. *This is my body.* New York: Golden.

Newcome, Z. 1999. *Toddlerobics.* Cambridge, MA: Candlewick.

Nonfiction Picture Books

Aliki. 1989. *My five senses.* New York: Crowell.

Aliki. 1992. *My feet.* New York: HarperCollins.

Balestrino, P. 1999. *The skeleton inside you.* New York: Crowell.

Civardi, A. 1994. *Going to the hospital.* Tulsa, OK: EDC .

Cole, J. 1998. *Your insides.*(Rev. ed.) New York: Morrow.

Cole, J. 1993. *How you were born.* New York: Morrow.

Feeney, K. 2001. *Get moving: Tips on exercise.* Mankato, MN: Bridgestone.

Frost, H. 1999. *Your senses.* (Series.) Mankato, MN: Pebble.

Hatkoff, J. 2001. *Good-bye tonsils!* New York: Viking.

Oxenbury, H. 1995. *I hear; I see; I touch.* (3-book set.) Cambridge, MA: Candlewick.

Perols, S. 1996. *The human body: A first discovery book.* New York: Cartwheel.

Priddy, R. 2001. *Baby's book of the body.* New York: Dorling Kindersley.

Rice, C., & M. Rice. 2001. *My first body book.* New York: Dorling Kindersley.

Rosoff, I., S. Awan, & H. Melville. 2000. *My first body board book.* New York: Dorling Kindersley.

Showers, P. 2001. *Hear your heart.* New York: HarperCollins.

Showers, P. 1997. *Sleep is for everyone.* New York: HarperCollins.

Simon, S. 1999. *The brain: Our nervous system.* New York: Mulberry.

Simon, S. 1999. *The heart: Our circulatory system.* New York: Mulberry.

Simon, S. 1998. *Bones: Our skeletal system.* New York: Morrow Junior.

Swain, G. 2002. *Get dressed.* Minneapolis: First Avenue.

Sweeney, J. 2000. *Me and my amazing body.* Sparks, OK: Dragonfly.

Thomas, P. 2002. *Don't call me special: A first look at disability.* New York: Barron's.

Thomas, P. 2002. *My amazing body: A first look at health and fitness.* New York: Barron's.

Thematic Bookpacks

Bedtime routines. *Bedtime Preschool Discovery Pack.* Madison, WI: Demco.

Physical activity. *Kids on the Go Preschool Discovery Pack.* Madison, WI: Demco.

Hearing impairments. *Sign Language Primary Discovery Pack.* Madison, WI: Demco.

Book and Audiocassette

Marshall, R., & S. Jordan. 2001. *Healthy habits for early learners.* (Song collection.) Niagara Falls, NY: Sara Jordan.

INFECTIOUS DISEASE, SANITATION, AND HYGIENE

Fiction Picture Books

Brandenberg, F. 1976. *I wish I was sick too!* New York: Greenwillow.

Brown, A. 1994. *Arthur's chickenpox.* Boston: Little, Brown.

Cole, B. 1994. *Dr. Dog.* New York: Knopf.

Cousins, L. 2000. *Maisy takes a bath.* Cambridge, MA: Candlewick Press.

Garelli, C. 2000. *Farm friends clean up.* New York: Crown.

Ross, T. 2000. *Wash your hands!* Brooklyn, NY: Kane/Miller.

Slate, J. 2000. *Miss Bindergarten stays home from kindergarten.* New York: Dutton.

Smith, D. 2000. *Dear Daisy, get well soon.* New York: Crown.

Swain, G. 2002. *Wash up.* Minneapolis: First Avenue.

Ziefert, H. 1993. *Harry takes a bath.* (Rev. ed.) New York: Puffin.

Nonfiction Picture Books

Berger, M. 1995. *Germs make me sick!* New York: HarperCollins.

Berger, M. 2000. *Why I sneeze, shiver, hiccup, & yawn.* New York: HarperCollins.

Caffey, D. 2002. *Yikes—Lice!* Morton Grove, IL: Albert Whitman.

Katz, B. 1996. *Germs! Germs! Germs!* New York: Scholastic.

Rice, J.A. 1999. *Those mean nasty dirty downright disgusting but invisible germs.* Minneapolis: Carolrhoda.

PREVENTING INJURIES AND SAFETY ISSUES

Fiction Picture Books

Beck, A. 1998. *Elliot's emergency.* Toronto, CAN: Kids Can Press.

Bond, M. & K. Jankel. 2001. *Paddington Bear goes to the hospital.* New York: HarperCollins.

Cuyler, M. 2001. *Stop drop and roll.* New York: Simon & Schuster.

Fink, C., & M. Marxer. 1998. *Help yourself! Safety and self-esteem songs for young children.* (Audio CD.) Boston: Rounder Select.

Gutman, A. 2001. *Gaspard in the hospital.* New York: Knopf.

Joyce, I. 2000. *Never talk to strangers: A book about personal safety.* New York: Golden.

Moore, E. 2000. *Franklin's bicycle helmet.* New York: Scholastic.

Pendziwol, J. 1999. *No dragons for tea: Fire safety for kids.* Toronto, CAN: Kids Can Press.

Rathmann, P. 1995. *Officer Buckle and Gloria.* New York: Putnam.

Zonta, P. 2002. *Jessica's X-ray.* New York: Firefly.

Nonfiction Picture Books

Brown, M. 1984. *Dinosaurs, beware! A safety guide.* Glenview, IL: Scott Foresman.

Cole, J. 1985. *Cuts, breaks, bruises, and burns: How your body heals.* New York: Crowell.

Cole, J. 1990. *The magic school bus: Inside the human body.* New York: Scholastic.

Gibbons, G. 1987. *Fire! Fire!* New York: HarperCollins.

Girard, L. 1992. *My body is private.* Morton Grove, IL: Albert Whitman.

McGinty, A. 1999. *Staying healthy: personal safety.* New York: Franklin Watts.

Mattern, J. 2000. *Safety first.* (Series.) Edina, MN: ABDO.

Loewen, N. 1996. *Safety sense.* (Series.) New York: Child's World.

NUTRITION

Fiction Picture Books

Carle, E. 1969. *The very hungry caterpillar.* New York: Putnam.

Child, L. 2000. *I will never not ever eat a tomato.* Cambridge, MA: Candlewick.

Degen, B. 1985. *Jamberry.* New York: HarperTrophy.

Dooley, N. 1992. *Everybody cooks rice.* Glenview, IL: Scott Foresman.

Dooley, N. 1996. *Everybody bakes bread.* Minneapolis, MN: Carolrhoda.

Ehlert, L. 1987. *Growing vegetable soup.* New York: Harcourt.

Gray, K. 2000. *Eat your peas.* New York: Dorling Kindersley.

Hayes, S. 1994. *Eat up, Gemma!* New York: Mulberry.

Landy, S. 2000. *Blue's snack party.* New York: Simon Spotlight.

Sharmat, M. 1980. *Gregory, the terrible eater.* New York: Simon & Schuster.

Nonfiction Picture Books

Aliki. 1987. *Corn is maize: The gift of the Indians.* New York: Crowell.

Bagley, K. 2001. *Tips for good nutrition.* Mankato, MN: Bridgestone.

Braman, A.N. 2000. *Kids around the world cook! The best foods and recipes from many lands.* New York: Wiley.

Dalton, C. 2000. *Avoid fatty foods.* Vero Beach, FL: Rourke.

Dalton, C. 2000. *Drink more water.* Vero Beach, FL: Rourke.

Dalton, C. 2000. *Eat carbohydrates that grow.* Vero Beach, FL: Rourke.

Dalton, C. 2000. *Eat power proteins.* Vero Beach, FL: Rourke.

Dalton, C. 2000. *Keep cholesterol low.* Vero Beach, FL: Rourke.

Dalton, C. 2000. *Love my vitamins.* Vero Beach, FL: Rourke.

D'Amico, J. 1999. *The healthy body cookbook: Over 50 fun activities and delicious recipes for kids.* New York: John Wiley & Sons.

De Paola, T. 1988. *The popcorn book.* New York: Holiday House.

Frost, H. 2000. *The food guide pyramid.* (Series.) Mankato, MN: Pebble.

Gibbons, G. 1985. *The milk makers.* New York: Macmillan.

Klingel, C. 2002. *Let's read about food.* (Series.) Milwaukee: Gareth Stevens.

Landau, E. 2001. *Tasty treats.* (Series.) Vero Beach, FL: Rourke.

Leedy, L. 1994. *The edible pyramid.* New York: Holiday House.

Morris, A. 1993. *Bread, bread, bread.* New York: Lothrop, Lee, & Shepard.

Pickering, R. 2000. *Good food.* (Series.) New York: Children's Press.

Richard, D. 1997. *My whole food ABC's.* Bloomingdale, IL: Vital Health.

Rockwell, L. 1999. *Good enough to eat: A kid's guide to food and nutrition.* New York: HarperCollins.

Showers, P. 2001. *What happens to a hamburger?* New York: HarperCollins.

Swain, G. 1999. *Eating.* (Small World Series.) Minneapolis, MN: Carolrhoda.

Thematic Bookpack

Foods and food preparation. *Cooking Primary Discovery Pack.* Madison, WI: Demco.

ORAL HEALTH

Fiction Picture Books

Brown, M. 1985. *Arthur's tooth.* Boston: Atlantic Monthly.

Langreuter, V. 1997. *Little Bear brushes his teeth.* Brookfield, CT: Millbrook.

MacCarone, G. 1995. *My tooth is about to fall out.* New York: Scholastic.

McPhail, D.M. 1988. *The bear's toothache.* Boston: Little, Brown.

Middleton, C. 2001. *Tabitha's terrifically tough tooth.* New York: Phyllis Fogelman.

Munsch, R. 1999. *Andrew's loose tooth.* New York: Scholastic.

Rice, J.A. 1997. *Those icky stick smelly cavity causing but invisible germs.* Mt. Rainier, MD: Gryphon House.

Sage, A. 2001. *Molly at the dentist.* Atlanta, GA: Peachtree.

Nonfiction Picture Books

Frost, H. 1999. *Dental health.* (Series.) Mankato, MN: Pebble.

Keller, L. 2000. *Tooth school inside.* New York: Henry Holt .

Thematic Bookpack

Dental care. *Teeth Primary Discovery Pack.* Madison, WI: Demco.

MENTAL HEALTH

Fiction Picture Books

Aliki. 1984. *Feelings.* New York: Greenwillow.

Carlson, N. 1997. *ABC I like me!* New York: Puffin.

Carlson, N. 1988. *I like me!* New York: Viking.

Curtis, J. 1998. *Today I feel silly and other moods that make my day.* New York: HarperCollins.

Modesitt, J. 1992. *Sometimes I feel like a mouse: A book about feelings.* New York: Scholastic.

Murphy, M. 2000. *I feel happy and sad and angry and glad.* New York: Dorling Kindersley.

Nonfiction Picture Books

Avery, C. 1992. *Everybody has feelings: Todos tenemos sentimientos.* Seattle, WA: Open Hand.

Cain, J. 2000. *The way I feel.* Seattle, WA: Parenting.

Hausman, B. 1999. *A to Z do you ever feel like me?* New York: Dutton.

Swain, G. 1999. *Smiling.* (Small World Series.) Minneapolis: Carolrhoda.

Thematic Bookpacks

Sharing. *The Rainbow Fish Preschool Discovery Pack.* Madison, WI: Demco.

Adaptability. *Stellaluna Preschool Discovery Pack.* Madison, WI: Demco.

Powerful emotions. *Feelings Preschool Discovery Pack.* Madison, WI: Demco.

Index

abdominal pain, 8, 58, 159
activities, suggested, 2, 21, 36, 46, 71, 86, 103, 117, 133, 159, 180
activity, physical. *See* exercise
ADA (Americans with Disabilities Act), 108, 110, 135–136, 143, 154, 162, 166–67
administration of health component, 179–180. *See also* policies and procedures
AIDS/HIV. *See* HIV/AIDS
air. *See* ventilation
allergies, 20, 129, 135, 137, 141. *See also* food allergies
anemia
    causes of, 97–98
    iron deficient, 56–57, 97
    screening for, 97–98
American Academy of Pediatrics (AAP), 4, 33, 40, 88, 95, 98, 110, 122, 138, 145, 157
art supplies, 27
asthma, 99, 135–142, 145

backs, protecting, 109, 121
bacteria, 4, 10, 11
batteries, 28
bedding, 13, 25, 178. *See also* SIDS
behavior problems, 77–82. *See also* mental health
blood. *See* fluids, bodily
body fluids. *See* fluids, body
bottles, 16, 25, 50, 69, 74, 77
building. *See* facility

car pools. *See* transportation
Centers for Disease Control (CDC), 4, 98
check-ups. *See* health care, preventive; screenings
chickenpox, 8, 14, 113, 146, 156, 159
child abuse, 58, 172–178
    in child care settings, 176–78
    HOTLINE, 177
    reporting, 175–77
    risk factors for, 174–75
    signs of, 172–74
    types of, 172
Child and Adult Care Food Program.
    See community and national resources
Child Health Assessment form, 5, 9, 98
CHILDHELP USA NATIONAL CHILD ABUSE HOTLINE, 177
chronic illness. *See* illness, chronic
cleaning, 127–33
    carpets, 20
    diapers and changing areas, 4, 19, 151, 156
    food service areas/equipment, 70–71
    kitchen, 130–32
    schedule, 127–28
    surfaces, 4, 6, 10, 14, 16, 19
    thermometer, 150
    toys, 4, 13–14, 16, 20, 131, 157
clothes. *See* laundry
CMV (Cytomegalovirus), 8, 13, 113

colds, 141, 149
communication, 82, 99–103, 171, 179
    with doctors, 95, 99–102, 143, 145, 148, 171, 179
    with families. (*see* families)
community and national resources, 182–86
    mental health, 83
    nutrition, 61–65
    for special needs children, 168–69
confidentiality. *See* health care, confidentiality
conjunctivitis. *See* eyes
consultant, health, 8, 114–117, 157–59, 179
contagious diseases. *See* diseases
cooking, 25, 28, 50, 54. *See also* eating, food service, meals, utensils
CPR, 38
cribs. *See* bedding; SIDS

dental health, 73–77. *See also* teeth
    brushing, 73–75
    education, 75
    fluoride, 73–74
    mouth sores, 8
    preventive care, 75–76
    referral criteria, 76
    toothbrushes, 73–75
Department of Health and Human Services (DHHS), 61, 95
development
    milestones of, 91–94
    problems in, 78
diapers, 10, 19, 132
    changing areas, 16, 19, 28, 34, 120, 151, 156
    rash, 151–53
diarrhea, 7–8, 11, 14, 58, 151, 156, 158
diets. *See also* eating; food
    special, 56–57
    vegetarian (*see* vegetarians)
diphtheria, 4, 114, 159
disabilities. *See* ADA; special needs
discipline, 82, 178
diseases
    control spread of, 4–10
    definition of, 3
    direct contact, 13–14
    immunizations for (*see* immunization)
    intestinal tract, 10–11, 13
    methods of spreading, 3, 4
    noncontagious, 15–16
    preparation for outbreak of, 8, 10
    respiratory tract, 7, 10
    spread through blood, 14
disinfection. *See* cleaning
doctors
    communicating with, 95, 99, 102, 143, 145, 148, 171
    notes from, 7
documentation. *See* records
doors, 24, 120
driving. *See* transportation; restraints, car seat
drowning, 33

safe areas. *See* security

safety
 checks, 23
 education, 35–36, 127
 food, 54–55
 pedestrian, 32, 127
 playground, 29, 120
 summer, 20, 33
 transportation, 32–33, 122–27
 water rules, 33
 winter, 33–34

sanitization. *See* cleaning

scabies, 8, 13, 158

screenings, 88, 90–96, 99

seat belts. *See* restraints, car seat

security. *See also* safety
 fences/gates, 45
 lighting, 45
 parents/guardians access, 46
 planning, 43
 safe area, 45, 120

seizures, 136–37, 144

separation of children by ages, 11, 21, 34–35, 112, 114, 155.
See also exclusion

sexually transmitted diseases (STDs), 7, 13

SIDS (Sudden Infant Death Syndrome), 25, 35, 178

Sierra's Light Foundation, 45–46

sinks, 18, 120, 122, 156

skin, diseases of. *See* diseases

snacks, 52–53, 65

snow. *See* safety, winter

space, 4, 24, 34, 119–20, 155

special needs, children with
 adaptations for, 116, 165, 169
 emergencies and, 143–45
 feeding, 58, 60
 inclusion of, 161–72
 overprotection of, 165, 171
 resources for, 168–69
 transportation of, 125

staff
 breaks for, 114
 disabled, 108, 110
 equipment for, 121
 hazards for, 112–113
 health assessment of, 107–08, 110, 112
 health promotion for, 113–14
 hiring and retaining, 106–08, 176
 immunizations for, 8, 14, 108, 113
 job descriptions, 106–07
 observations by, 91, 95, 99, 142, 147
 responsibilities of, 105–06
 and special needs children, 163–65
 as role models (*see* role modeling)
 training of, 110, 112, 153, 157
 turnover of, 20-21, 112

standard precautions, 19

STDs. *See* sexually transmitted diseases

stress. *See* mental health

Sudden Infant Death Syndrome. *See* SIDS

summer. *See* safety, summer

sunburn, 151–53

supervision, 35, 124, 156

supplies, 71, 129

teeth
 decay of, 50, 55, 73–74, 77
 injuries to, 76
 teething, 151, 153

toys
 chests, 26, 126
 mouthed, 10, 20, 131
 riding, 26, 30–31, 127
 safety, 25–26, 34
 sanitization of, 13–14, 16, 20, 131

transportation, 32–33, 106–07, 122–27

tuberculosis, 8, 159

USDA (United States Department of Agriculture), 61–62, 65

utensils, 10, 24, 28, 130–32

vaccinations. *See* immunizations

vegan diet. *See* vegetarian diet

vegetarian diet, 55–56

ventilation, 4, 8, 10, 20, 120–21

viruses, 4, 8, 10, 11

vision. *See* screenings

vomiting, 8, 58, 149, 153, 158, 159

water, 18, 121–22

weight, 56, 97. *See also* obesity; failure-to-thrive

whooping cough (pertussis), 8, 14, 159

WIC (Women, Infants, and Children). *See* community and national
 resources

windows, 45, 120–21, 176

winter. *See* safety, winter

wiring, 24–25, 121

Early years are learning years

Become a member of NAEYC, and help make them count!

Just as you help young children learn and grow, the National Association for the Education of Young Children—your professional organization—supports you in the work you love. NAEYC is the world's largest early childhood education organization, with a national network of local, state, and regional Affiliates. We are more than 100,000 members working together to bring high-quality early learning opportunities to all children from birth through age eight.

Since 1926, NAEYC has provided educational services and resources for people working with children, including:

• *Young Children*, the award-winning journal (six issues a year) for early childhood educators

• **Books, posters, brochures, and videos** to support your work with young children and families

• **The NAEYC Annual Conference**, which brings tens of thousands of people together from across the country and around the world to share their expertise and ideas on the education of young children

• **Insurance plans** for members and programs

• **A voluntary accreditation system** to help programs reach national standards for high-quality early childhood education

• **Young Children International** to promote global communication and information exchanges

• **www.naeyc.org**—a dynamic Website with up-to-date information on all of our services and resources

To join NAEYC

To find a complete list of membership benefits and options or to join NAEYC online, visit **www.naeyc.org/ membership.** Or you can mail this form to us.

(Membership must be for an individual, not a center or school.)

Name _____

Address_____

City_____ State_____ ZIP_____

E-mail _____

Phone (H)_____(W) _____

❒ New member ❒ Renewal ID # _____

Affiliate name/number _____

To determine your dues, you must visit **www.naeyc.org/membership** or call 800-424-2460, ext. 2002.

Indicate your payment option

❒ VISA   ❒ MasterCard

Card # _____

Exp. date _____

Cardholder's name _____

Signature _____

Note: By joining NAEYC you also become a member of your state and local Affiliates.

Send this form and payment to

NAEYC
PO Box 97156
Washington, DC 20090-7156